THE STORY OF FOWEY

Introduction to Fowey
(Photo by Graham Gullick, Fowey)

THE

STORY OF FOWEY

(Cornwall)

Awarded the Sir Edward Nicholl Silver Medal by the Royal Cornwall Polytechnic Society, 1949.

By

JOHN KEAST M.Ph., B.A (Hons.),
Bard Gorhelwas

DYLLANSOW TRURAN

First published 1950
This edition reproduced by photo-litho and republished
with the permission of the copyright holder.
By Dyllansow Truran
Trewolsta, Trewirgie, Redruth, Cornwall

Printed in Great Britain
by St. George Printing Works Ltd.
Redruth, Cornwall
ISBN 1 85022 035 2

TO

LINDA, PAUL and ESTELLA FOY

"All the greatest sea traditions of
Cornwall are locked up in Fowey."

A. H. NORWAY.

CONTENTS.

LIST OF ILLUSTRATIONS

PRINCIPAL ABBREVIATIONS USED.

Henderson: Essays	Charles Henderson: *Essays in Cornish History:* Clarendon Press, 1935.
Henderson MSS.	Henderson Collection of MSS. at the Royal Institution of Cornwall, Truro.
B.P.R.	Black Prince's Register: British Museum.
J.R.I.C.	Journals of the Royal Institution of Cornwall.
V.C.H.	Victoria County Histories: Cornwall.
Close Rolls	Calendars of the Close Rolls: British Museum.
Patent Rolls	Calendars of the Patent Rolls: British Museum.
Kingsford: Westcountry Piracy	C. L. Kingsford: *Prejudice and Promise in Fifteenth Century England:* Clarendon Press, 1925.
Rowse: *Tudor Cornwall* ..	*Tudor Cornwall:* A. L. Rowse: Jonathan Cape, 1941.
A.P.C.	Acts of the Privy Council: British Museum.
Cal. S.P. Dom.	Calendars of State Papers—Domestic Series: British Museum.
Cal. S.P. Venetian	Calendars of State Papers—Venetian: British Museum.

NOTE:

Where the year is self-evident from the text, this has not been repeated in the reference.

Detailed pedigrees and armorial bearings of the older families mentioned may be found in Sir John Maclean's *History of Trigg* and in Vivian's *Visitation of Cornwall.*

PREFACE

IN "THE STORY OF FOWEY", my aim has been to accomplish the task which A. H. Norway, after recalling that the greatest sea traditions of Cornwall are locked up in this port, suggested should be undertaken. His recipe was that the history of Fowey should be told in full,

> "humanising dusty documents, making good with a restrained imagination the missing pages of the tale, and building not only with a knowledge of what Channel seamen wrought elsewhere, but even more upon a full acquaintance with the people who dwell there today and a sympathy with their natures and a familiarity with their lives".

It may seem strange that a full account of Fowey has not appeared before, since the histories of most Cornish towns have already been published, and I think to some extent, this may be set down to the small amount of documentary evidence which is to be found locally. The old Corporation records were destroyed during the early part of the nineteenth century, parish records (other than the church registers) have not survived and most of the early Customs papers were burnt some years ago.

Fortunately the national records, both printed and manuscript, are available and from such sources as the Public Record Office and the British Museum, I have derived the bulk of my material. This has been supplemented by information drawn from that treasure house of Cornish local history—the Henderson Collection at Truro—and by a careful search for whatever is obtainable in the Fowey district.

Here, also, it is fitting to acknowledge the labours of Mr. Evelyn Rashleigh, who wrote a short history of Fowey, published in booklet form in 1887, and Dr. R. T. Cann, whose "Church of St. Fimbarrus" (revised and brought up to date by the present Vicar, the Rev. W. R. Guest) is a carefully written account: and to mention Dr. H. H. Drake's "St. Fimbarrus Church and its Founders", printed in 1876, and Commander the Hon. H. N. Shore's "Old Foye Days", with its interesting accounts of local smuggling.

The present book does not exhaust the subject and there is still a wealth of material for research—particularly in connection with the mediaeval port.

In preparing the text for publication I am grateful to Dr. A.L. Rowse and Mr. C.K. Croft Andrew for reading the typescript and for their valuable criticism and suggestions: also to Professor Charles Singer, the Rev. Canon W.R. Guest and Mr. W.S. Rashleigh for reading the sections dealing with Castle Dore, St. Fimbarrus Church and the Rashleigh family respectively. Any subsequent alterations and additions are, of course, my own responsibility.

The Fowey Borough Council have been very helpful in allowing me access to the old charters, the modern records and the papers left by the late Dr. R. T. Cann and Mr. T. H. Hony: from the Town Clerk, Mr. W. C. P. Gatley, I have always received a great deal of interest and encouragement.

I have also had much assistance from the Royal Cornwall Polytechnic Society, from Mrs. Varley, the late Secretary, who suggested that the work should be submitted to the annual competition where it was awarded the "Sir Edward Nicholl" Silver Medal in 1949, and from Mr. Winn, who holds the post at present. To the Royal Institution of Cornwall at Truro, and to Mr. Penrose in particular, I am indebted for permission to study papers in the Henderson Collection.

I would like to thank officials and staff at the Public Record Office and the Custom House Library in London for their courtesy: also the staffs of the Custom House at Plymouth and Fowey.

Mrs. Treffry has allowed me to reproduce the portrait of Hugh Peters at Place: Dr. John Rashleigh has permitted reproduction of the painting of his ancestors, which formerly hung at Menabilly: Miss Foy Quiller Couch has given me access to old newspaper cuttings concerning Fowey and Mr. W. H. Graham various papers on shipping.

With regard to illustrations, I must thank Mr. Graham Gullick for kindly supplying most of the photographs and material for the line drawings; Mr. George Kitto for allowing me to use his etching of "The Noah's Ark"; Mr. Henry Lamb the artist, and the Cambridge University Press for permission to reproduce the former's portrait of "Q" which appeared in Dr. F. Brittain's biography of Sir Arthur Quiller Couch; the Home Publishing Co. Ltd., Croydon, for the loan of a block depicting the interior of the "Ship" and the Harvard University Press for authority to reproduce a sketch map from "The Founding of Harvard" by S. E. Morison (1936).

During the course of some twenty years—for I have had this book in mind since leaving school at Fowey—I have approached many individuals not mentioned above, and I would here like to acknowledge my indebtedness to them all.

Finally, I can never adequately express what I owe to my wife, who has designed the jacket, checked the typescript with me and, in general, encouraged and speeded my efforts.

71, Runnymede Crescent, JOHN KEAST.
Streatham, London, S.W. 16. *June*, 1950.

PREFACE TO SECOND EDITION

The original edition of this book was already out of print by 1955 and a reprint is therefore long overdue. I would have liked a new revised edition but this would have been a lengthy matter and must wait for perhaps another decade. In the meantime I would be glad to answer any queries or discuss any matters on which new evidence has become available.

JOHN KEAST
1st October, 1983

CHAPTER 1

THE river Fowey, from which the town takes its name, springs from between the boulders on Brown Willy high up on that part of the granite backbone of Cornwall known as the Bodmin Moors. Little frequented by man even in the height of the summer when blue skies, yellow gorse and purple ling add colour to the ancient grey rocks, in winter the hazards of fog and patches of treacherous marsh make this neighbourhood a sanctuary for wild life.

Yet different prehistoric races throve there and traces of their huts can still be found. Centuries later, the tin workers scratched over the moorlands, washing and sifting their finds in the running water, for this was part of their stannary of Foweymoor.

During the first few miles of its course, the river gathers several small tributaries and then drops down into a richer, more fertile countryside, which the Norman settlers found to their liking and acquired as the important Manor of Fawiton. Through the beautiful wooded valley of Glyn it runs, and then by pleasant pastureland and small copses until it reaches Lostwithiel and hurries under the mediaeval bridge. Leaning over the angled parapet of the bridge it seems very reasonable to accept the suggestion of one authority, that most Westcountry rivers owe their names to the sounds which they conveyed to early man. Until the end of the sixteenth century the usual spelling of the name was "Fawi" or "Fauwy"—a very good sound picture of water running over shallows.[1]

Leaving the town of Lostwithiel the river begins to widen and banks topped with rank grass and bushes line its winding course—reminders of the great days of tin-streaming when the Black Prince's steward protested at the damage to his master's water mills and fisheries, caused by the great quantities of silt washed down from the tin works up on Foweymoor.[2] Soon these come to an end and the water course spreads out in a wide rippling stretch with St. Winnow church and a few houses nestling low between the trees on the far side and Penquite (Cornish, Pencoed—headland of the wood) high up on the near bank. Meanwhile in another valley, the Lerryn river has also been making its way down by many a twisting turn, each clothed with trees which reach down to the very water's edge, so that the boughs gather festoons of seaweed at each turn of the tide. Below Penquite it joins in and becomes part of the Fowey which now sweeps down past Golant

[1] Henderson: Essays, 28.
The Oxford Dictionary of English Place Names (1936) suggests—"Fowey may mean 'beech river', a derivative of the Old Cornish equivalent of Old Breton fau, fou, Welsh ffawydd—'beeches' (from Latin fagus). Faou occurs as the name of a brook in Brittany".
For a detailed and interesting description of the river see *The River Fowey* by Wilson Macarthur: Cassell (1948).

[2] B.P.R., 26–7.

village, lying almost hidden in a fold between two hills, takes in a small stream from Penpoll on the left and then swings abruptly around Wiseman's Stone. Once again the river makes a sharp bend, this time in the opposite direction, and there ahead lies the Passage, across which a ferry boat has been plying for the last six hundred years—perhaps longer. Around Pottery corner the waters swirl by quayside ladders and between the moorings of numerous small boats. Above the green-fringed quay walls, grey roofs straggle in a long uneven line from Passage Slip to the Town Quay and then climb up the steep hillside around the towers of the Church and Place. This is the old borough and port of Fowey. To seaward rise the neat terraces and prim gardens of the later, residential town, whilst high on the skyline the sun's after-glow reveals the small modern suburb which may be the nucleus for the town of the future.

When and where the first people inhabited this locality is a matter for conjecture. Although a bucket-shaped urn estimated to date from the late Bronze Age (some 3,000 to 2,500 years ago) has been discovered at Place, near the present centre of the town, together with a great midden of shell fish remains and animal bones,[1] it seems likely that the first permanent settlements were made on high ground and not along the wooded slopes which must then have covered the whole of the Fowey valley, where wild animals and creeping intruders could deny even that modicum of peace and safety which man has desired from earliest times.

Carn or Cairn (Cornish—Caer—a fortified place) just beyond Passage Slip may well have been the site of such an encampment. It is a height rising steeply from the river on the one hand and from the old Caffa stream (now dammed up to form Fowey Pill) on the other. A spring of clear water is close at hand and the place is comparatively easy to defend. Early habitations were probably at Cairn and on the hillside of Langurthow (where Fowey Hall now stands) rather than in the lower region which became the mediaeval town. Actual traces of such encampments may be seen at Coombe overlooking the Pridmouth valley and farther inland near Trenython.

But for more substantial evidence it is necessary to go to the great earthwork of Castle Dore, two miles or so to the north of the town, where excavations have laid bare at least part of the story.[2] Situated near the southern end of the ancient highway which ran across Cornwall from Harlyn Bay in the north, Castle Dore has a circular rampart nearly seven feet in height, surrounded by a deep trench and with an entrance on the sloping ground to the east. This entrance is guarded by a second semi-circular rampart and ditch, divided by an outer gateway. The position of the earthwork is ideal as it crowns the very highest land in the district—some four hundred feet above sea-level.

[1] J.R.I.C. 1840 for description of the urn which is now in the R.I.C. Museum at Truro.
Worth: *Dev. Transactions III* describes the results of the excavations at Place.

[2] Ralegh Radford: Interim Report on Excavations at Castle Dore, 1936.

CASTLE DORE—A SETTLEMENT TWO THOUSAND YEARS AGO
(*Air Photograph H.M.S.O. Crown Copyright reserved*)

From the top of the walls, the watcher could command a view of the blue sea and the landing place at Tywardreath (Cornish for the house on the strand or shore) on the one hand, and the valley leading up from the river Fowey—a pool of deep green lying between the hills—on the other. During the summer days the earthen walls are ablaze with the yellow Cornish gorse and the fanciful rendering of the name as Castle D'Or—the "Golden Castle"—tempts the imagination.

What sort of people were they who laboured to build themselves this great camp over two thousand years ago? Recent excavations point to an open village having existed here perhaps two hundred years before Julius Cæsar brought his legionaries ashore in Britain. The inhabitants of the village, numbering about one hundred and fifty, lived in rectangular huts of wood and wattle and made themselves pottery which was surprisingly well designed and ornamented. Fragments of the pottery have been found here and one can almost hear the grunt of annoyance from the craftsman as he accidentally breaks the bowl which has cost him so much labour and hurls the pieces into a corner. And these remnants of coloured glass bracelets and yellow beads—did their loss bring tears to the eyes of some maiden who lived here so long ago?

The spot was evidently congenial, for a later generation decided to add to their comfort and security by digging a ditch around the camp and throwing the earth up into the walls which exist today. Styles in housing had changed, the new folk preferring a round structure about thirty-five feet in diameter, with an inner colonnade of wooden posts supporting the roof and probably leaving a little space open to the sky in the middle. Rough cobbled paving formed the floors of the houses, which seem to have been erected against the inner side of the ramparts. Standing within this beautifully round, almost level enclosure, it is easy to imagine the animated scenes as the men toiled up the hill to the gateway with their burdens of fish and flesh, the elders and children standing expectantly around whilst the women throw more branches on the fire in anticipation of the coming feast.

Yet this generation passed away in the fullness of time and Castle Dore became deserted and remained so for more than three centuries. Then in those dimly known years which followed the Roman withdrawal from Britain—possibly about the year 500 A.D.—a new community chanced upon the old camp and set to work to strengthen and improve it. They brought up stones and heightened the inner rampart and in time commenced to build a large wooden structure over eighty feet long and thirty-six wide, not far from the main entrance. The holes in the ground for the three or four rows of wooden pillars which framed this building have been discovered and also the hearth stones, burnt and reddened by fire. A paved road ran alongside this important building which was, no doubt, the dwelling of the local chieftain or prince.

In the absence of documentary records, the Longstone now at Four Turnings may furnish some clue to the identity of this personage or one of his successors. It is a shaft of granite bearing on one side a "T"-shaped or "Tau" cross and on the other an inscription which probably dates from the sixth century commemorating Tristan, son of Cunomorus. The stone formerly stood nearer to Castle Dore and an old Breton manuscript describes how two Christian priests travelled along the old highway across Cornwall on their way from Wales to Brittany. At one place they encountered the local king whose name they give as Marcus Cunomorus. One of these travellers was Sampson and his name is remembered in the church of St. Sampson[1] at Golant, a little more than a mile from Castle Dore.

Even more remarkable is the link which exists between this district and the old Cornish folk story, also popular with other races, which tells of Tristan and Iseult. The Cornish tale is woven around the lands of a certain King Mark and relates how the young Tristan is sent by the king to bring home to Cornwall his prospective bride and queen, the beautiful Iseult. Somewhat naturally, Tristan and the lady fall in love but the latter goes through with her arranged marriage and later visits a church of St. Sampsons.[2] King Mark's court in the story is called "Lancien"—strikingly similar to Lantyne, the actual name of the old manor close to Castle Dore and a place of considerable importance right down to the fifteenth century. A nearby field bears the name Mark's Gate and also within the Fowey peninsula is Kilmarth (i.e. Mark's Grove). Possibly the old Cornish storyteller found it convenient to use this locality for his romance, yet it is odd that the old names should have persisted. As cliffs and headlands are momentarily revealed through a drifting sea-fog and quickly enveloped again, so these human figures reach out to a new generation and are then lost in the mists of age. An odd stone monument, great walls of earth and a few pathetic broken beads and utensils are the only tangible links with these active men and women who lived and loved, dreamed and died here in this Fowey peninsula so long ago.

As late as the time of Queen Elizabeth treasure seekers evidently believed the Longstone marked the grave of some great prince,[3] for Carew records how they started to dig for gold beneath the stone until a great storm and superstitious fear drove them away. The chief source of gold in early times was Ireland—two very fine gold collars or lunettes have been discovered at Harlyn Bay on the north coast near where an ancient track runs southward across the county. There seems to have been a constant flow of traders and Christian missionaries along that highway and among the latter, no doubt, came the holy "Finn Barr"—"He of the Shining Hair". The Irish relate that he made the journey to Rome and it is feasible that using this route across the country he was made welcome by the king at his fortified palace at Castle Dore. Before embarking—perhaps whilst waiting for a

1 O'Neil Hencken: *Archæology of Cornwall and Scilly.*
2 Henderson: Essays, 28.
3 Carew: *Survey of Cornwall* (1602).

THE LONGSTONE, NOW AT FOUR TURNINGS

Sketch-diagram to show position of inscription

(Inset—The Tau Cross)

favourable wind—he may have taught the local inhabitants—including the settlers at Carn and Langurthow. Certain it is that the church at Fowey is dedicated to this Irish saint. Finn Barr returned to Cork after his trip to Rome and, after becoming its first Bishop, died there in the year 604.[1]

The next three or four centuries are once more submerged in darkness. Whilst the Saxon settlers in England drove the people they displaced steadily westward into Wales and Cornwall, Norsemen ravaged the coastal towns and valleys, sacking and burning and carrying off their plunder. Few records survived and yet it is evident that this part of Cornwall was far from a barren wasted region when Edward the Confessor died. Both Penventinue and Trenant were in existence and were manors of some considerable size, extending beyond the boundaries of the farms now bearing those names. In the time of King Edward, Ailsi held Penventinue and Brismer the neighbouring lands of Trenant.

[1] O'Brien: *Life of St. Finn Barr* (Cork, 1902).

CHAPTER 2

THE Norman Conquest brought new blood into the Fowey district and the landholders with Anglo-Saxon names disappeared. A considerable English rising against King William centred around Exeter and was ruthlessly put down, whilst in 1068 the sons of Harold raided the Cornish coast. But the real Cornish people—descendants of Celts—had little in common with the rest of England: they were much more akin to those of the invaders who came from Brittany, speaking almost the same language and honouring the same local saints. Cornishmen saw only a change of master—the Anglo-Saxon with his gutteral tongue making way for the Norman. Cornwall seems to have attracted a large proportion of settlers from Brittany and with these fighting men there undoubtedly came a number of artificers and clerks, household and farm servants of Breton stock who would use words which the native Cornish would understand.

Nearly twenty years later the Doomsday Survey was completed. At least two entries relate to places in the Fowey district and it is strikingly apparent how their different characteristics have survived to the present day:[1]

> "The Count (i.e. of Mortain) has one manor which is called Penfontenio which Ailsi held during the time of King Edward (the Confessor), wherein is one hide, and it rendered geld for one virgate. 4 teams can plough this. Hamelin holds this of the Count and he has thereof in demesne, one ferling and one plough, and the villeins the remaining land and one plough. There Hamelin has 6 bordars and 2 serfs and 5 acres of wood (land) and 10 acres of pasture. And it was worth 10 shillings (i.e. during the time of King Edward) and when the Count received it, 20 shillings."

> "The Count has one manor which is called Trenant which Brismer held during the time of King Edward, wherein is one hide and it rendered geld for one virgate. 5 teams can plough this. Hamelin holds this of the Count and he has thereof in demesne, 2 ferlings and 3 ploughs and the villeins the remaining land. There Hamelin has 6 bordars and 3 serfs and 6 beasts and 30 sheep and 10 acres of pasture. This is worth 15 shillings and when the Count received it 20 shillings."

Taking into account the fact that these manors then covered a greater area than the present farms, it will be seen that Penventinue contained more woodland whilst Trenant was richer in arable and pasture land. A glance at the map or a visit to the district will show that after nearly a thousand years, this description has hardly changed. Hamelin held 22 manors in Cornwall and it is interesting to note that the few houses named Hambland lie within two miles of Trenant farm.

[1] V.C.H.: *Domesday Survey of Cornwall* (1924).

Of the settlements at the mouth of Fowey river the King's surveyors are silent. The village of Langurthow on the hill-side, the settlement at Carn and the little church lying between them, are not mentioned. Possibly, since Doomsday was essentially a land survey, these habitations of free men, making a scanty living out of fishing and seafaring, were not yet worth exploitation. There were other lands, more accessible and fertile, such as the manor of "Tiwardrai", some three miles distant. In early times this place also stood near an inlet so that a long ship could be run straight in from the sea. Moreover the landing place could be approached from inland without the perilous descent down precipitous paths.

So the Conqueror's men took note of Tywardreath as being one of the possessions of William, Earl of Mortain, half brother of the King himself. Now the Earl was a great landowner elsewhere in England and he presumably left the management of his Westcountry estates to his underling, Richard, son of Turold, who thereby figures as the holder of many parcels of land in Devon and Cornwall. Old Turold had been a companion of King William and has been identified in the Bayeux tapestry—a short stocky man, holding the heads of two horses.

Richard fitz Turold's descendants, William and Robert, founded and generously endowed a religious house at Tywardreath. The prior and monks were Benedictines and came under the protection and guidance of the rich Abbey of Saints Sergius and Bacchus at Angers in Brittany. Turold's family were connected with the town of Dinan, also in Brittany, and it seems that their new home in Cornwall—far up the Fowey river—took its name, perhaps for sentimental reasons, as "Caer-dinan"—the castle of Dinan. At any rate they took Cardinham as their family name and as such, Robert fitz (i.e. son of) William de Cardinham witnessed a charter about 1170, confirming the gifts of his ancestors to Tywardreath Priory and also mentioning the "church of St. Barrianus with its lands, tithes and other appurtenances".[1] Barrianus was, of course, one of the variations of Finn Barr. One link with this old Norman church at Fowey still remains—the font which stands at the west end of the present building. It is decorated with a simple tracery of honeysuckle pattern and is one of several similarly carved—probably by the same mason—which are only found in this part of Cornwall.[2]

The Cardinhams were by now well established in the district and had interests along the whole length of the lands bordering on the river Fowey. In 1194 Andrew de Cardinham witnessed a charter of liberties granted to the town of Lostwithiel whilst Robert de Cardinham granted Geoffrey of Lanwoer (Lawhire) the stream which runs down to Pridmouth.[3] (The manor of Penventinue was also in their hands in the time of Henry III). Their line ended in a daughter who, in 1245, was possessed of the castle at Restormel.

[1] Oliver: *Monasticon Dioc. Exon.* (1846). [2] Cann: *St. Fimbarrus Church* (1907).
[3] Henderson MSS.

One extremely interesting document has come down from these years. It is a charter granted by the Prior of Tywardreath to the leading inhabitants of Fowey, and was drawn up probably during the first quarter of the thirteenth century—perhaps just before or after the date on which the greatest of all national charters—Magna Carta—was signed at Runnymede.[1]

A broad translation is as follows:

"Be it known to all, present and future, that I, Theobald, Prior of Tywardreath and the Convent there, have confirmed to all our Burgesses of Fowey all the honours, dignities, liberties and quittances which a free borough ought to have, that is to say:—

1. Every burgess shall hold his land by inheritance, paying whatever he has been accustomed to pay at the date on which this charter was confirmed, and when he dies his heir shall, after paying a duty of 30 pence, hold his inheritance peacefully.
2. The burgesses shall be exempt from the customary land and sea dues (i.e. those local dues which were normally payable to the lord).
3. If anyone be summoned by law he shall answer the charge either before us or before our bailiffs in Fowey, and at no other place.
4. The maximum fine shall be six pence and for conviction of bodily harm he (the accused) can have bail after depositing 30 pence as security, either with us or our bailiffs.
5. And if we wish to make a Praepositus (that is a Provost or Mayor) the burgesses shall elect him from the residents.
6. Burgesses may marry off their sons, daughters, nieces and kinswomen without having to seek permission, and to whomsoever they will.
7. But no stranger shall set up a shop (or business) without obtaining permission of the Praepositus and burgesses (this does not apply to the merchants of a ship who carry on business aboard their vessel whilst in the port).
8. Any burgess may sell his rights without seeking previous authority to do so, provided the purchaser pays us or our bailiff the sum of twelve pence.
9. If any burgess has a tenant in Fowey he can, if necessary, bring him to jurisdiction in his own court.

And to ratify this for the future we have placed our signature and seal to this charter.

Witnesses: Richard of Sirsiau
Richard of Keilgat
Baldwin of Trened
Onger of Tregverioc
Walter of Saint Winnow
Thomas of Collen
Thomas of Polgru and many others."

[1] For Latin text see Appendix A.

THE NORMAN FONT—ST. FIMBARRUS CHURCH
(Photo by Graham Gullick, Fowey)

Now this is no mere benevolent grant to some insignificant village of fishermen. It is a legal document by which the Prior who, next to the Cardinhams, is now the greatest landholder in the district, agrees to see that certain customs and rights are continued to a select and responsible council of free men. The Praepositus, who was to be elected by these free men was to some extent the precursor of the Portreeve and Mayor of later times. Thomas Taillour, "Praepositus of the town of Fowey" is mentioned in 1403 and mediaeval customs and subsidy proclamations are frequently addressed to the "mayor" of the town.[1] Possibly the "Praepositus" is also identical with the "bailiff" who was instructed to forbid Fowey ships to sail to France in 1226, for it is hardly likely that the Priory bailiff would be concerned in shipping matters.[2] On the other hand the Prior no doubt found it very useful to be on good terms with local merchants and shipowners whose vessels could be hired when occasion required.

For this part of Cornwall was undergoing a great economic change. Inland, on Foweymoor and Blackmoor, tin streaming was becoming increasingly productive. There was a ready market for the tin, a great deal of which was used in the making of pewter, and after smelting locally the slabs of metal were shipped to London and foreign parts by ships which returned with wine and salt.

Of the towns on the Fowey river, Lostwithiel was the first to profit. About 1194 the burgesses had obtained a Charter from the Cardinhams, whose castle of Restormel overlooked the town and river. It was soon established as a Coinage town (one of the centres where the corner, or coin, of each slab of tin was marked with the official stamp) and here the trade was regulated and the tinners had their own court of justice and gaol. By 1304 Lostwithiel was sending members to Parliament.

For some time vessels made their way from the sea right up to Lostwithiel and there discharged and loaded their cargoes, but as ships became larger and the river silted up, Fowey at the harbour mouth gradually superseded its rival as a port and quays were built to accommodate large vessels. Only small craft and barges continued to use the numerous inlets and landing places up to Lostwithiel, but it was not until the eighteenth century that river traffic became negligible.

In 1230 Fowey was of sufficient importance to receive a royal order[3] impressing all local ships capable of carrying 16 or more horses for the intended invasion of Brittany, and by 1301 it ranked with the two manors as one of the three "tithings" into which the district was divided for judicial purposes.[4]

[1] Henderson MSS.
[2] Close Rolls, m. 27 (1833–4 ed.).
[3] Close Rolls, 483.
[4] Henderson: Essays.

CHAPTER 3

Now although Cornwall must have seemed to the thirteenth-century London merchant a very remote corner of the kingdom, being several days' riding distance from the capital, he was well aware that a considerable amount of trade was carried on from its harbours and creeks. He may even have seen a vessel or "cog" unloading great slabs of tin alongside the wharves of London river and remarked her swarthy crew conversing in some strange tongue. A Breton business acquaintance of the merchant, had he been standing near, could have confirmed that these were indeed Cornishmen and that they understood but little of the English tongue. Then, for a jest, he might offer to take his companion aboard and translate for him into good English or French the remarks of these outlandish strangers.

For in this age Cornwall's relations with the duchies of Brittany and Normandy were as close as with the neighbouring county of Devon. Cornishmen and Bretons spoke practically the same language and for many years after the Conquest the old traffic between the ports of Cornwall and those on the opposite shore persisted. Thus, in religious matters Tywardreath Priory for long paid allegiance to the rich Abbey at Angers. Did the Prior require a new brother for his establishment or masons for the building of a new church, he naturally sent across to the Abbey; along the same route came church furniture, vestments and books. Even holy relics were brought across the water to Cornwall and taken on tour through the towns and villages, inviting alms for some good cause in Brittany.

In consequence shipping was always in demand. Moreover, the long ship of earlier days—so well featured in the Bayeux Tapestry—which could be quickly run up on any sloping beach and as easily hauled off again, was now giving place to a different type, broader in the beam, slower but capable of carrying a greater cargo. Such vessels needed more depth of water and could only be berthed alongside quays. Loading and discharging their cargoes took more time and merchant ships increasingly needed shelter from the sudden storm. So the harbour of Fowey gradually replaced the old landing place at Tywardreath and the quays which are so frequently mentioned from this time onwards were constructed; in time each merchant had his own particular "kaia", usually with storehouse and dwelling house attached.

John Leland, the traveller, who visited Cornwall in the time of Henry VIII, had another explanation to account for the rapid rise of Fowey as a port. He wrote "The glorie of Fowey rose by the warres in King Edward the first and thirde"('s time). It must be remembered that in Leland's day the monasteries and priories were generally unpopular and it is hardly likely that he would ascribe the town's growth to its religious patrons. Even so, there is a great deal of truth in his statement.

Just as the lord held his land primarily by the service he could provide, so the shipowner enjoyed his freedom and the king's protection which he could call upon if in trouble in foreign waters, by virtue of his willingness to furnish ships upon such occasions as the king or realm required. Only a small permanent force of fighting ships was ever maintained and that was of variable strength.

It was upon the impressed trading vessel that the country really relied for defence by sea in time of peril or for transporting men and material overseas when expeditions to other realms were contemplated. Such ships were now being measured by the number of "tuns", or casks of wine which they could carry—(as late as 1401 the king's commissioners were being advised to hold in the ports of "Loo, Porpirr (Polperro) and Fawy" any ships of the portage of 30 tuns of wine and more) and could readily be converted into ships of war.[1] In build they had some likeness to a wine cask cut in half lengthwise—being very broad in the beam. They were open-decked but carried raised platforms fore and aft, which in time of battle housed the complement of archers and men-at-arms. A single short mast, which could easily be lowered, carried a great square sail slung from a yard-arm. Navigation was by dead reckoning, aided at night by the stars, for although the compass had been invented, it was not in general use, and steering was by means of a great oar fixed in a socket over the starboard quarter.

Although the Cinque Ports—guardians of the Channel—provided the majority of the actual fighting ships, the Western seamen were never at a loss when it came to fighting, as will be seen later. In general, however, ports such as Fowey were usually summoned to furnish transports and it was no doubt a vessel of this type which was ordered to report at Dublin in 1301.[2] The following year, Fowey and Polruan were joined with Lostwithiel and Bodmin[3] in a proclamation calling for one ship and on this occasion security was taken to ensure that she duly appeared. It was the war with Scotland which necessitated these levies, but a little later two of the king's clerks were sent to all the ports between Southampton and Falmouth to take up ships, at the expenses of the burgesses, for the guard of the Channel.[4] In 1317 Looe and Fowey were instructed to provide a ship to serve for one month at their own expense.[5]

In 1323[6] Fowey had sent one ship to help transport an army intended for Gascony[7] and three years later the port was ordered to provide two vessels and forty-six men, one of the ships to be above fifty tons in burden. Apparently these continued demands were causing murmurs, for in 1336 officials were sent around to explain matters and to see that the service was forthcoming. Then new tactics were tried and with

[1] Patent Rolls, 487.
[2] Patent Rolls, 584.
[3] Patent Rolls, 75.
[4] Patent Rolls, 447.
[5] Rot. Scot: pt. 2, m. 7.
[6] Close Rolls, 187.
[7] Close Rolls, 610.

other ports, Fowey was invited to send representatives to London to discuss maritime affairs in council. John Hurston attended before the Great Council at Westminster on behalf of both Fowey and Looe men in 1341, and three years later the community of mariners in Fowey chose John Trevenor[1] to go to London for the purpose of informing the king and his council upon the state of the shipping in the realm of England. He was away for nearly a month up country and received two shillings a day for his expenses.

The port of Fowey seems to have been kept pretty busy during these years. In 1342 three ships had been sent out to help carry Sir Walter Manny[2]—the famous knight whose exploits are set out in the Chronicles of Froissart—to Brittany and later in the year six ships and a barge, all from Fowey, joined the transports which took the king himself across to France.[3]

The difficulties of keeping an impressed fleet together are shown very clearly in the following year when a great number of Fowey vessels,[4] including the "Trinity", "Fakaundieu", "Michael", "Katherine" and "La Jouette", together with two unnamed ships belonging to John att Yate and Laurence William, went with the king to Brittany. Either through a misunderstanding or possibly a desire to earn a little freight money whilst the army was busy ashore, all these vessels calmly left the port of Brest and sailed away. No doubt they fully intended to return by the time King Edward had won the victory and required transport back to England! Unfortunately the king took a different view of the matter and gave orders for the masters and mariners involved to be detained in Newgate gaol. Polruaners were also concerned, their contingent being the "Savoie", "Peter", "Katherine", "Alissote" and a ship of Thomas Adams's. As, however, a great part of the English fleet had behaved in a similar manner, it seems likely that an amnesty closed the affair.

Good fortune was with the king in these early years and Crecy in 1346 was followed ten years later by the victory of Poictiers, where John Treffry of Treffry near Lostwithiel is said to have won his knighthood on the field. It was in the year of Crecy that Calais was besieged and eventually captured. A document of later times[5] purporting to show the sources of the English fleet which moved in to the siege of Calais shows 47 vessels and 770 men as having come from Fowey. Whilst it is difficult to believe that such a large squadron was provided by the town itself, there is no reason why Fowey should not have been the gathering place for this force. According to the same document, Polruan sent one ship and sixty men and no doubt there were several vessels actually belonging to Fowey in the great contingent which departed from the port.

A curious episode which illustrates the unpopularity of forced service was the attempt in 1339 to induce the men of Bodmin, an

[1] Close Rolls, 360.
[2] Patent Rolls, pt. 1, m. 17.
[3] Patent Rolls, pt. 1, m. 17.
[4] Close Rolls, 130–1.
[5] Cott. MSS., Brit. Museum. V.C.H.

inland town, to provide vessels for the king's service.[1] As a matter of fact the merchants of Bodmin were an enterprising body who, although removed from the sea, participated in the trade out of Fowey river—chiefly in the export of tin. In this year several of them, namely William Sever, William Scarlet, Roger Blake and Thomas le Goldesmyth, were partners, together with Thomas Queynt of Lostwithiel, in a ship which sailed from Fowey. The king's commissioners were at the time scouring the ports for ships and hearing of the maritime activities of the Bodmin men, they thereupon rated the town to provide no less than four vessels ! This was too much for the Bodmin inhabitants and they refused the demand, whereupon the commissioners promptly seized the Mayor of Bodmin, John Dreu, together with several of the burgesses, and lodged them in the gaol at Lostwithiel. The townsmen put up a good case, showing that Bodmin was six leagues from the nearest port, that the inhabitants possessed no ships or mariners of their own and that in time past they had not been wont to provide ships for the royal service. So, in due course the aggrieved Mayor and his companions were released and returned home but on condition that the vessel in question should be employed with the king's fleet.

Now although no merchant relished the idea of having to set out ships at his own expense, even for the service of the realm, it was quite a different proposition when his vessels were duly hired and the hiring paid for in gold. As early as the time of Edward II a vessel belonging to the port was hired to carry provisions from Cornwall to the army preparing to march into Scotland. The story commences with Thomas Lercedekne being sent down to buy up within the county 40 tuns of wine,[2] 62 quarters 7 bushels of wheat and 300 quarters of oats. The wheat was ground into flour, brought around from Falmouth to Fowey in a small ship or lighter and then loaded aboard the "great ship"—the total cost of transport and stowage being 65/5¼d.; the oats were brought on horseback to Fowey at a cost of £7 and the wine came down, probably by barge, from the storehouses at Lostwithiel, whither it had been imported from France.

The "great ship" was the "Seynt Saviour", no doubt named after the chapel which made such a good landmark high on Polruan hill. When her cargo was stowed she lumbered out into the Channel until the westerly breeze filled her sail and then bore away up the coast. The master of the "Seynt Saviour" was paid 80 marks, the "lodisman" or head stevedore 26/8d. and the supercargo, John Rydale, an equal sum.

Another document of the same period gives some idea of the charges involved in re-exporting 40 jars of wine. Here again the wine is brought down by barge from Lostwithiel and loaded at Fowey:[3]

[1] Close Rolls, 196.

[2] Cal. Inq. Misc. No. 1088.

[3] Exchq. KR. 17/34. Article by Dr. N. J. G. Pounds in *D. & C. Notes and Queries,* July, 1947.

"In rolling the said 40 dolea of wine—from the cellar of the said merchants to the water — 10s.
And in towage of the same on the water for 4 leagues from Lostwithiel to the ship at Fowey — 13s. 4d.
And in lifting (gyndage) them into the ship — 5s.
And in stowage (rumagio) of the same 40 dolea in the ship — 21s. 8d."

The Black Prince also made it a practice to hire ships from Fowey and these were prosperous years for this Cornish port.[1] In 1351 John Teget, master of the ship "Godebiete" of Fowey received a letter of safe-conduct which he was to produce if molested in the Channel. It was addressed to all admirals and their lieutenants, keepers of ports, master mariners and others and recalled the fact that Teget and his followers had already well and faithfully completed one voyage in the Prince's service and that they were once more being employed to fetch from the ports of Cornwall to London, wheat, flour, oats and other victuals intended for the coming expedition to France. No harm was to be done to the ship, cargo and mariners. Eight years later Teget was still in the Prince's pay and then commanded the cog "Johan" of Fowey;[2] he received £60 "for his great labours and expenses in coming from Gascony to England in the Prince's service".

Richard de Michelstow, whose descendants were going to do very well for themselves in the port during the following century, also hired the cog "St. Saviour" to the Prince, and in 1357 was paid £20 for his trouble. Others so employed were Henry Skuryn, whose ship "Le Seinte Mari" of Fowey earned him 100 shillings for the carriage of victuals from Cornwall to Sandwich in 1359, and the master of the "Christopher" of Fowey, who received 59/6. as freight money some four years later.[3]

As Duke of Cornwall, the Prince also benefited from the customs dues of the Cornish ports and in 1348, as a special mark of favour,[4] the masters of the "St. Saviour" of Fowey and the "St. Mary" of Polruan, together with two ships of Dartmouth and Sidmouth, were required to give up only one tun of wine, instead of the five which they would normally have surrendered; evidently they were then trading on their own account and this concession the Prince had promised them when the fleet was at Plymouth on its return from Gascony.

As for outboard bound cargoes, they were plentiful enough. Here is what one ship loaded at Fowey in Easter week of the year 1344:

375 pieces of tin worth £240 of the stamp of Edward, prince of Wales and duke of Cornwall.
17 bundles of horse hides worth £8.10.0.
1,707 stones of cheese value £100.
54 bacon hogs price £10.12.0.
57 stones of butter price £3.6.8.
6 sacks of feathers price £6.

[1] B.P.R., 18. [2] B.P.R., 283. [3] B.P.R., 283. [4] B.P.R., 497.

together with cloth of divers colours, beds and armour to the value of £30.[1]

Tin was pre-eminently the greatest export and the tinners up on the moors were never so busy as in these years. Although a great part of the duchy revenues came from the coinage on tin, the Prince's council were alarmed at the damage being caused to both the water mills at Lostwithiel and to the harbour of Fowey[2] and the tin workers were ordered at their peril not to make any working which might lead to damage or destruction of the mills and haven. In 1401 John Nicol[3] of Bodmin loaded 254 pieces of tin in the "Jonet" bound for London and it is likely that Bodmin Pill (now Sawmills Creek) between Fowey and Golant, with its ancient sluice gates and quays, owes its name to the merchants of that town who were always very active in trade out of the Fowey river. Leland mentions it as the place "whence goods were carried overland to Bodmin".

Cornish cloth was also sent out from the port.[4] In 1364 William Michelstow of Fowey and two others received a licence to export 200 packs of cloth of white and russet colour, together with a hundred barrels of fish—no doubt the "fish called hakes" mentioned in another licence.

That it was a flourishing period for Fowey may also be judged from the multitude of proclamations which were sent out to the customs officials instructing them how to deal with the various taxes and subsidies. In addition the "bailiffs and keepers of the passage are exhorted to see that no men-at-arms, archers, horses, bows, arrows or armour pass out of the realm without the king's command or special licence and to watch for knights returning to England from the wars without the king's leave"—deserters, in fact. Even pilgrims were to be carefully watched—the officials were to make sure that they were loyal subjects of the king and that they carried no gold or silver out of the country. The shrine of St. James of Compostella in Spain was the favourite objective of many pilgrims, and no doubt such a band as Chaucer describes often rode into Fowey after spending the night at Tywardreath Priory. Perhaps as they made their way up the steep hill leading to Castle Dore, some cast a speculative glance out at the great expanse of startling blue stretching away on their right. If the weather turned bad the passage down Channel and across the Bay of Biscay could be a sore trial, even for the most devout. A mediaeval poet with a fine sense of humour has left a wonderfully vivid picture of the voyage: "Men may leave all games who intend to sail to the shrine of St. James", he says. "Before midnight the pilgrims will be coughing and groaning, lying across the ship's boat

[1] Close Rolls, 334.

[2] B.P.R., 21.

[3] Close Rolls, 355. Was this the Nicol who, according to the old song, slew John Dory in a sea-fight:

> "And Nichol was then a Cornishman
> A little beside Bohyde- a." ?

[4] Patent Rolls, 32.

and refusing all food. Warm malvesy wine is all they will cry for. Then the master will make a tour of the ship to see that all is well, whilst the passengers lie about in their clothes. Woe betide him who goes to bed near the ship's pump for a man were as good as dead 'as smell thereof the stynk' ".

Nevertheless many made the trip. The vicar of Fowey went in 1332,[1] and 35 years later John Colf, master of the "Nicholas of Fowey,"[2] received permission to go with his mariners on this pilgrimage. In 1394[3] the "George" barge, master Richard Robyn, carried no less than eighty tightly packed pilgrims out from Fowey and just twenty years later John Russell,[4] who was not averse to a little piracy, conveyed fifty pilgrims to Spain. Sailings from Fowey appear to have been particularly popular in 1433:[5] licences to carry pilgrims to the shrine of St. James being granted to Thomas Gerard in respect of the "Julien", John Nicholl for the "Cok John", Philip Mayowe for the "Barry" and Ralph Wythyall for the "Mary". The last-named vessel seems to have been engaged in the traffic some twenty years later, when Thomas Tregyn and John Blaunche obtained permission to convey pilgrims to Spain.

* * * *

From an entry in the register of Bishop Grandisson at Exeter, it appears that on the 1st July, 1336,[6]

> "He dedicated in honour of St. Nicholas, Bishop and Confessor the church of Fawy, newly constructed, with the Great Altar and two other altars in the same place."

The old dedication to St. Fimbarrus was discarded, one modern theory being that the popular shortened form of the Irish Saint's name—Barry or Barrianus—was confused with Bari—the birthplace of St. Nicholas. It is certainly an ingenious explanation.[7] On the other hand Bishop Grandisson was a learned man and hardly likely to make such a mistake. Probably he intended to replace the shadowy figure of an obscure Irish Saint with the more substantial and far better known personality of St. Nicholas, the patron of sailors. Whatever the intention, it did not succeed, and the church remains dedicated to St. Fimbarrus.

[1] Reg. of Bishop Grandison: quoted by Cann: *St. Fimbarrus Church.*
[2] Patent Rolls, 46.
[3] Patent Rolls, 362.
[4] Patent Rolls, 399.
[5] Cal. French Rolls, 295, 7.
The scallop shell was the emblem worn by those who had made the pilgrimage to St. James of Compostella. It is possible that the fine porch now part of the eighteenth-century house in Custom House Hill (see plate) with its scallop shell carving, came originally from a rest house for pilgrims established near by. It is close to the quays from which the pilgrims must have set sail.
"Cok", or cogge=ship, hence the derivation of "coxswain".
[6] Cann: *St. Fimbarrus Church.*
[7] Henderson: Essays, 32.

THE SCALLOP SHELL PORCH
(Photo by Graham Gullick, Fowey)

The builders made a clean sweep of what was probably a severe, rather heavy Norman building. Styles in architecture had broken away from the heavily buttressed walls, rounded arches and small deep-set windows of Norman times and the architects were more at liberty to use their imagination and skill. The results remain to be admired in the church at Fowey, and to an even greater measure, in that at Lostwithiel.

The situation of the great altar and the two smaller altars would probably be that occupied by the present altar and the two side chapels, although the whole of the east wall appears to have been taken down and the length of the church extended during the later re-building of 1460–1510. The graceful walls which flank the centre aisle, with their simple, pointed arches and rectangular "lights" or window spaces above, belong to the years about 1336 (the outer walls of the church are of a later date) and prove that it was a spacious, well-lit building, more akin to Flemish church architecture than to the usual English pattern. The stone-paved floor would have been more in evidence in that day when a few oak benches and stools were the only seating. Around the walls, lit by large flickering candles, would hang brightly-coloured paintings of the Virgin and Child, of St. Katherine or St. James. Kneeling before one of the shrines might be found a pilgrim embarking from Fowey on the morrow, a merchant giving thanks for the safe return of himself and his cargo, or a devout mariner praying for the welfare of his family in the town and for a speedy voyage.

Little is known concerning the early vicars of this church. Ralph, "vicar of the church of Fauwy," is mentioned in a list of clergy dated 1297 and his successor was probably John de Trevenor who in 1314 managed to secure from Bishop Stapledon,[1] a definite share in the tithes which it would seem the Priory had hitherto appropriated. John Brey, vicar in 1332, had three months' leave of absence to enable him to go on a pilgrimage to the shrine of St. James of Galicia. He seems to have returned safely and may have been officiating when the church was re-dedicated some four years later. In February, 1349, John Bagga, like Trevenor, a Fowey man, was appointed to the living. This was the illfated year in which the Black Death carried off so many. Whether Bagga survived is uncertain,[2] but one authority has traced the spread of the plague day by day from the time it first came to Fowey until it reached Bodmin, basing his estimate on the rapid succession in which the clergy of the riverside churches were stricken down and died. The living was then in the king's gift because of the war with France. A later incumbent, Hugh Thornham, does not seem to have been happy in Fowey since only six weeks after his appointment in 1380[3] he was attempting, but apparently without success, an exchange of livings with the parson of St. Katherine's

[1] Cann: *St. Fimbarrus Church.*
[2] Gasquet: *The Great Pestilence*, 89.
[3] Patent Rolls, 447.

within Aldgate, London. He then fell foul of the local authorities and was brought before the justice, who deprived him of "a saddle, a bow and a sheaf of arrows", together with some pieces of armour. It was not until the autumn of 1381 that this militant priest received back his accoutrements.

There were also a number of chapels in and around the town. One of the ambitions of a family of standing was to possess its own domestic chapel—a custom copied from the great households—and the newly rich Michelstows were not behindhand in this respect.[1] In 1390 they had one, dedicated to St. Katherine the Virgin and in 1436 John Michelstow, whose piratical exploits are dealt with in the next chapter, was granted a renewal of licence for the chapel in his mansion at Fowey. The fifteenth-century windows in the walls of the present Town Hall seem originally to have been part of such a private, or perhaps "guild", chapel, whilst just across the water at Bodinnick, exists one of the best preserved of its kind in Cornwall, complete with belfry—the family chapel of the Mohun family, whose mansion was formerly here. It is now in use as a cow byre.

Nor must the twin chapels of St. Saviour and St. Katherine which crowned the cliffs on either side of the harbour be forgotten. St. Saviour's, one buttress of which still braves the weather above Polruan, is mentioned as early as 1315 when, together with Lanteglos church,[2] it was held by the hospital of St. John at Bridgewater. St. Katherine's Chapel was licensed by the Prior of Tywardreath[3] in 1390 and the two buildings were for many long years welcome marks for seamen making a landfall.[4] In 1464 the Prior leased St. Katherine's on the headland to John Williams, vicar of Fowey, for life. The rent—33/4—was a high one but doubtless the Vicar had shrewdly estimated that the total offerings, together with the tithe of fish, would make it a worth-while investment.

It was a long walk from this chapel into the town by way of a path cut in the hillside with hardly a trace of habitation until the South Gate was reached. During the Middle Ages the town of Fowey comprised only that area which extended from the North Gate, situated just beyond the Passage to Bodinnick, to the South Gate at the bottom of Lostwithiel Street. On one hand it was bounded by the river and on the other it probably stretched up Lostwithiel Street, around to Cobb's Well and Place and thence, defended by a steep natural wall of rock, back to the North Gate. Yet within this narrow compass was contained an almost incredible number of dwellings, quays and storehouses. Several of the old cob-walled houses in North Street, built right into the rock, must date from the fifteenth century, and in some instances occupy plots of ground hardly more than 15 feet in length and 12 in breadth—that is the space occupied by a single room in a small house of today.

The principal streets were the "Passage Way" (now Passage Street

1 Henderson: Essays, 33.
2 Patent Rolls, 258.
3 Henderson: Essays, 33.
4 Henderson: Essays, 33.

MEDIAEVAL REMAINS—WINDOW AND MASONRY EMBODIED IN THE 18th CENTURY TOWN HALL.

and Captain's Row) mentioned in 1344, the "North Street" (1497), the "High Street" (now Fore Street) and the "Churchyard" (now Church Side)—1416. Others, more difficult to place, but probably leading to the Town Quay, were "South Street" (1368), "St. Katherine's Street" (1489) and the "Welsh Way". The last-named is interesting as being the likely quarter of the Welsh portion of the cosmopolitan population which then inhabited the port.[1] The name persisted long after these people had drifted away or intermixed with the native Cornish folk, although it had degenerated in Elizabethan times to the "Weyshewaye" or "Washewaye".

Imagine then, the mediaeval town of Fowey, as closed in and crowded as any walled city. The merchants' houses invariably stood on the river side and during the fourteenth century the Trevenors, Michelstows and Udys all had their "house, quay and garden" overlooking the water so that they could keep an eye on their business from the parlour window, as it were. At the western end rose the newly-built church and on the landward side of the thoroughfare the tenements of humbler folk with an occasional open booth or shop. Only a contemporary Flemish painting could do justice to the subject—the tall houses (here built of timber and cob), the small courtyards and tiny gardens, the cobbled streets and busy wharves. These crowded buildings—unhealthy in time of plague and sickness—undoubtedly inspired comfort and warmth when the storm raged and there was fear of enemy invasion.

Outside this compact town lay the villages of Langurthow and Carn. The former had evidently been an ancient manor or holding, part of which was absorbed in the growing town of Fowey during the thirteenth century. This would, no doubt, be the hilly portion adjoining the church and churchyard on the west. The remainder of the old manor, lying just outside the boundary of the new town, probably continued in the hands of the Langurthow family, for in 1296 Roger de Langurthow leased the windmill above to Roger le Carpenter. It may be fragments of the mill which remain in the grounds of Fowey Hall, and it was certainly one of the two "molendinorum ad ventum" which were mentioned in 1314 as being recently built. (Possibly the other was at Coombe where a field is still known as Windmill Field.) A visitor to Fowey in 1644 says "The church is Langode (Langurthow) in the parish of Foye; the old towne of Foye is on the river nearer Lestithiel",[2] and in 1597 the Town Lands included one tenement "in Langurthowe".

The other "suburb" of Carn lay outside the North Gate and remained a separate entity when Langurthow had become just a name. It consisted of a number of houses and gardens on either side of the Pill—the creek of the river Fowey into which the stream named Caffa then flowed (it has only been blocked up within the last eighty years). A few hundred yards up what then must have been a beautiful

[1] Henderson MSS.
[2] Diary of Richard Symonds, 69. Camden Soc. (1859).

little wooded valley was the busy wheel of Caffa watermill—undoubtedly one of the two "molendinorum ad aquam" also referred to in 1314 when their tithes went to support the vicar.

The remainder of the Fowey peninsula was devoted to agriculture, as it is today, with a certain amount of wood cutting along the banks of the river. Trenant and Penventinue still held their courts and collected "heriots"—the best beast or its value—when one of their tenants died. Unlike the townsmen who were invariably free, the farm workers were only slowly emerging from the state of "villeinage" which tied them to their masters and the soil. Thus, as late as 1389—some forty years after the Black Death[1] which is popularly supposed to have swept away the old system, Robert Mathew of Fowey, in order that he and his children might not be claimed as villeins of the manor of Tregrehan, obtained a bond binding Oto de Bodrugan, lord of Tregrehan, in a sum of £20 not to enforce such a claim.

A number of farms were now in existence, originating, no doubt, as offsprings of the older manors of Trenant and Penventinue. Lawhire is frequently mentioned and passed from the family of that name to the Tregodeks. Hillhay, Lescrow, Lanherriot, Tregaminion and Pinnick are all referred to in documents of this time. Much could be written about these holdings and their various owners and tenants—of John Lawhyer who represented Lostwithiel in the Parliament of 1420—of the sisters, Joan and Elizabeth Lawhyre who brought in Sir Hugh Courtenay and Sir William Bonville to arbitrate between them and their cousin Thomas Tregodek "touching a dispute about Lawhyer" in 1446, and of how Elizabeth, now aged and a widow, made over Lawhyre to John Tregodek nearly fifty years later, but on condition that he allowed her a pension of 5 marks, 6 shillings and 8 pence,[2] together with the right to cut wood from the hedges and other perquisites.

As early as 1316 the Prior of St. Andrew's[3] had obtained from the royal court permission to hold fairs in the town of Fowey on the feasts of St. Fimbarrus and St. Lucy. These were important events and perhaps the occasion for the brewing of church ales from produce contributed by local farmers, religious processions and even a Cornish miracle play, with visitors flocking in from the countryside to enjoy the respite from labour. In addition there was a weekly market, held on Mondays.

Some of the families prominent in the life of this mediaeval town have left descendants here to the present day. There are still Udys, Lewarnes and Robins in Fowey whose forbears were then masters, mariners and "victuallers" of the ships which helped to carry Henry V's army across to France before Agincourt or sailed with Mixstow to plunder Spanish galleys.

Other names have vanished from the locality in the course of time.

[1] Henderson MSS.
[2] Henderson MSS.
[3] Charter Rolls, III, 306.

The Trevenors, for instance, had a great deal of property in Fowey about 1350. One member of the family was vicar in 1311, whilst another represented the community of mariners at Westminster a few years later, and can probably be identified with the John de Trevenor who became the Black Prince's attorney in this part of Cornwall and held lands near the Passage, in the vill of Carn and adjacent to the Church. The last of the family seems to have been William de Trevenor, who flourished in the fifteenth century.

So with the Baggas. Richard Bagga had lands here in 1310[1] and twenty years later Mark Bagga is mentioned as having been one of the adherents of the late Earl of Cornwall. Carew, writing nearly three hundred years afterwards, tells also of Fisart Bagga as having been a great commander at sea and commemorated in the chancel window of Fowey Church.

The early members of the Langurthow family have already been mentioned. John Langurthow was among a party accused of assaulting the Black Prince's servants at Lostwithiel in 1371[2] and carrying off two hundred casks of wine, but this did not prevent his being appointed to search all boats on the waters of Fowey for uncustomed goods in 1383. In 1404 he was in debt and was dead before 1406, when his widow and son, also named John, are mentioned. With this son the name came to an end.

There there were the Michelstows. Their name was possibly Michell in the first instance and they were much to the fore as owners and masters of ships in the time of Edward II.[3] It seems likely that they used the small creek of Mixstow for loading and careening their ships. Richard Michelstow hired his vessel to the Black Prince on several occasions and in 1371 was one of the collectors of the subsidy in the ports of Lostwithiel and Fowey. He engaged in a little piracy at times, but in this was more than surpassed by his descendants—Mark and John Michelstow (or Mixstow as their name is frequently spelt).

Another Fowey man served at the royal court. John Davy held the post of yeoman of the King's chamber and valet to the King's crown and no doubt was in a good position to obtain the custody of the ferry between Bodinnick and Fowey.[4] This was in 1478, the ferry having previously been in the hands of Oliver de Bretaigne. In 1483 William Longe of Southwark in Surrey granted three tenements, a garden and a wharf in Fowey to Davy: the lands had been sold to Longe in 1468 by a Bristol vintner.[5] By 1492 John Davy was dead

[1] Hambley Rowe: *Cornwall Feet of Fines.*

[2] Patent Rolls, 170–2.

[3] Although on the far side of the river, Mixstow remained within the boundaries of Fowey for centuries. It was not included within the present borough when the Charter was renewed in 1913.

[4] Patent Rolls, 118.

[5] Henderson MSS.

"The King's yeomen . . . were sent hither and yon on special missions, now to receive or deliver money or gifts, now to carry special messages, now to act as attendants for their lord or his friends".

Sir G. Sitwell, quoted by Mildred Campbell, *The English Yeoman*, Yale (1942).

and his widow Gonetta married to Thomas Glover, another valet of the king's crown.

More permanent in their associations with Fowey were the Treffrys. They were already possessed of lands near Lanhydrock, when one of the family settled in Fowey, probably at the beginning of the fifteenth century. Two fortunate marriages with heiresses of the Bonefaces and Michelstows brought them additional lands and wealth. In 1434 Thomas Treffry was Customer of Devon and Cornwall and was occasionally deputed to investigate captures made at sea.[1] There were two if not three Thomas's in succession, but the Collector of Customs was most probably the husband of Elizabeth Treffry, who defended Place in 1457 and perhaps the father of John, William and Thomas, whose tomb is in Fowey church. It was also Thomas Treffry who is reputed to have given various lands to the town in the time of Henry VI.

All through these years and particularly when the power of the English government was weak, there was the fear of enemy landings. The possibility of the sudden appearance of hostile ships, with armed men landing and bursting into the town, hacking down doors, setting lighted torches to storehouses and carrying off gold and silver, must have worried merchant and king's official alike. Moreover the people of Fowey had reason to fear the visit of a vengeful enemy whose commerce had been harassed and spoiled.

In the unsettled reign of Richard II, son of the Black Prince, this alarm was considerable and in 1380 John de Kentwode was ordered to enquire into a complaint made by the men of Polruan and Fowey. These maintained that in former times 160 archers had been levied from the neighbouring parishes to watch upon the seacoast,[2] day and night from the beginning of May to the end of August each year. Since these archers had been allowed to drop their duties the Fowey and Polruan ships and boats "have been well nigh annihilated by galleys and the enemy landing there". It is more than likely that the twin blockhouses guarding the haven were built following this enquiry and not a hundred years later as is usually supposed.

The heaviest blow came one night in 1457. The French fitted out an expedition under the Sieur de Pomier to harass English shipping and also the ports along the south coast. Before returning home this force raided Fowey. Great destruction is said to have been caused and the story has been handed down that Elizabeth, wife of Thomas Treffry, defended her house in her husband's absence and ordered boiling lead to be flung upon the enemy advancing under the walls. An old statue at Place commemorates the lady's courage. The church must have suffered badly, since it is described as being in a ruinous condition a few years later.

[1] Patent Rolls, 219.

[2] Close Rolls, 388. cf. a verse of about 1437 quoted by Hakluyt:

"To fortifie anon he did devise
Of English Townes three, that is to say
Dertmouth, Plymouth, the third it is Fowey."

THE BLOCKHOUSE AT POLRUAN BUILT ABOUT 1380

The decline of Fowey as a principal sea-port must, however, be set down not so much to the results of this raid nor to the government's stern measure taken some thirty years later to suppress local piracy, but to the fact that other English ports were growing more rapidly. Fowey had little space for expansion and because of silting the landing places were unable to accommodate the larger ships. Southampton, Bristol and Plymouth were now leaving such places as Dartmouth, Poole and Fowey far behind in the commercial race.

CHAPTER 4

It may seem difficult to understand why the port of Fowey, the ships of which were busily engaged in peaceful trading right through the Middle Ages should, at the same time have acquired such a black name for piracy. It is true that the meaning of the term "piracy" has been enveloped with something sinister and romantic since the days of the Spanish main. Before then it was more prosaically viewed as a scourge to honest business but at least a practical form of redress when such was needed. On either side of the Channel it was too generally practised to be considered otherwise.

At the beginning of this period sea-borne trade had been chiefly in the hands of foreigners and even London relied to a great extent upon her colonies of alien merchants. At times, particularly when their contributions of wealth were badly needed by the king, they received many privileges and favours, but as English trade gradually came into its own, these merchants of the Hanse and of Flanders were increasingly threatened by the jealousy of their English rivals. This feeling may partly explain the alacrity with which Englishmen were always ready to seize a foreign ship and her cargo. Southampton, Plymouth, Bristol, Dartmouth and even the Cinque Ports were involved in this plundering but Fowey seems to have taken as large a share as any.

It is true that representations were often made to the sovereigns of the various states by the aggrieved parties but success was always problematical. Thus a Spanish merchant made numerous petitions to the English Council when his galley was seized in 1449 by ships of Fowey and Polruan. He was rich and influential but after twelve years' wrangling he received little satisfaction although his case seemed as plain as a pikestaff. English merchants met with similar treatment abroad. Here, for instance, are the experiences of two Cornish merchants who ventured to Paris to lay their complaints.[1] Their ship which had loaded at Fowey, had been attacked by certain Frenchmen and Normans who had killed the master and sixteen men and then carried the vessel to Leure, where they sold the cargo and divided the spoils. The owners said they

> "went to Philip de Valoys at Paris and his justices for a remedy, and they utterly refused and the said buyers of the goods (who had known them to be stolen), after the merchants had laid their petitions, pursued them and would have killed them if they could have taken them".

They did eventually receive some compensation in the form of certain French cargoes which had been confiscated and held by the English crown. Others were not so fortunate. A strong fleet would have maintained the freedom of the seas and put a stop to piracy but until the time of Henry VIII no such force existed. Henry V did

[1] Close Rolls, 381.

make an effort to build up a standing navy but the advisers of his successor, Henry VI, soon disposed of the ships, possibly because they feared such a fleet might be mis-employed by ambitious seekers after power.

Combined with the motives of jealousy and expediency there was the lust for excitement and plunder. To men with the mercurial temperament of Cornishmen, the humdrum ferrying of tin, wheat and wine may well have seemed tedious. In spirit they were fearless and regardless of consequence—witness the Lostwithiel, Fowey and Polruan men who in 1320 went aboard a ship belonging to the proud Cinque Ports and dragged off a wretch accused of murder.[1] In the scuffle which followed several of the Portsmen were killed and when the news reached their homes the cry went up to fit out ships to hunt down these meddlesome Cornishmen. Eventually the King's writ was necessary to restore peace.

In later years there is much evidence to show that the exploits were well planned and organised, less spontaneous in execution and on a much larger scale. Men of influence in Cornwall and elsewhere began to join with the local squires and merchants in fitting out ships with their stores and war-like equipment, in return for a share in the profits. One Fowey captain, John Mixstow,[2] had a crew of no less than two hundred men aboard his ship when he cruised off the Portuguese coast in 1433: the victualling of such a vessel must have been considerable. Cornwall was never rich agriculturally and the numerous small landholders were ever ready to take part in such profitable enterprises.

It is not surprising that 1346—the year of the great English victory at Crecy—was also notable for the many captures made at sea. Not content with French prizes, however, certain Fowey men boarded a Spanish merchantman off St. Mattieu in Brittany.[3] Her name was the "Seynt Bartelmeu" and she was laden with red and white wine. The Spaniards put up a stout but unavailing resistance and when all the crew were dead or dying the captain's son crept below and hid among the barrels; nor did he appear until the pirates and their prize reached Fowey. Now, fortunately for themselves, the Spanish master and supercargo had gone ashore at the town of St. Mattieu just before the English ships hove in sight. Having thus narrowly escaped, they made strong complaints regarding the outrage and in view of the recently concluded treaty with Spain, something had to be done. The English Council ordered the immediate release of the "Seynt Bartelmeu" and the poor lad who had survived the slaughter. The cargo of wine was also to be restored, but it was found that eighteen casks had already been disposed of.

Within a few months of this episode the boot was on the other foot and pinching badly. It seems that two Cornishmen, Thomas Lewyn and Richard Broun, had loaded their ship, the "James" of Fowey, with

[1] Patent Rolls, 557.
[2] Kingsford, *Westcountry Piracy*.
[3] Close Rolls, 20.

a valuable cargo estimated as being worth £2,000.[1] Broun sailed as master and they were on passage from Fowey to Bordeaux when off the island of Barspale two Spanish ships ran alongside and attacked the "James". Here also, blood was shed, several of the Cornishmen being killed before the ship was finally taken and carried off to the harbour of Portugalet in Castile.

In the same year the owners of another Fowey ship made the mistake of incurring the wrath of one whose interests around the town of Fowey were considerable—none other than the Black Prince, duke of Cornwall. This ship—the "Michel"—had captured a ship from the Baltic, part of the cargo of which consisted of wine intended for the Prince's household. Moreover the seizure was made in Fowey harbour over which the Prince had rights. Thus the seizing of a ship belonging to a nation allied with England in the war against France and within the Prince's own jurisdiction at that, doubly embarrassed him. Possibly the culprits feared the consequences, for they fled to Haverford in Wales. The authorities there were ordered to arrest the ship but it was too late, for the "Michel" had left Haverford and in May of the following year was still at large. Then it was reported that she had put back into Fowey, whereupon the Prince sent word that she was to be arrested and hauled up on dry land. Evidently he realised that these Cornishmen were as slippery as the eels in their own river and was taking no chances. Even now they were not in the net. No doubt with the aid of some friends in the town,[2] the "Michel" once more slipped out of Fowey and made for another Cornish port where the prince's authority was less powerful.

About this time a great storm blew a certain ship far out of her course and forced her to seek shelter in St. Ives Bay. She had a cargo of wine aboard which the owners now decided to sell in Cornwall, perhaps to defray the cost of victualling and repairs. So they went ashore at St. Ives and duly paid their duties to Thomas Botiller, the "Customer" of the port. Whilst this business was proceeding, a "crayer" slipped into the Bay and her crew steered her in alongside the weather-beaten ship. The merchants ashore then perceived armed men clambering aboard their vessel and immediately appealed to the "Customer". He seemed to know what was afoot and promised to regain the ship and her cargo—provided they handed over to him fifteen tuns of wine. But having done this (according to their story) they found the "Customer" had over-rated his powers with the intruders, for they next saw the great sail of their ship being hoisted, and in a very short time she and the "crayer" were standing out to sea. The Spaniards, stranded at St. Ives, protested strongly and after an investigation, an indictment was drawn up in which no less than sixty-four men from Fowey and the vicinity were named, among them being Richard Johan, master of the "Michel". There is no evidence that any were ever brought to justice.[3]

[1] Close Rolls, 79.
[2] B.P.R., 77–8.
[3] Patent Rolls, 115–6.

Such marauders did not always escape scot free; this is confirmed by the arrest and subsequent punishment of a number of Dartmouth men who had plundered a Spanish merchantman in 1365. They were tried before the admiral of the west and two were hanged. It was in connection with this trial that the activities of certain Fowey men were investigated. Mark Davy and Alan Roberd had bought part of the cargo alleged to have been stolen from this Spanish ship and had fetched it home to Fowey. Two others, John Richard and Matthew Clemowe, also had a share in the spoils, but all pleaded that they had acted in good faith. Their story was that they had crossed the seas in a ship called "La Pedrok" to the Garonne to take in a cargo of salt. They were returning to Cornwall when they were driven by a violent wind to a port in Brittany and long detained there. During this enforced stay they had sold their salt to merchants of the town in order to buy provisions. Subsequently they had bought the iron from some traders and when the wind changed had set sail for Fowey. A plausible tale, but if they were so hard up as to have to sell the salt, it is difficult to understand how they were able to purchase the iron.[1] Spanish iron was of considerable value—its quality being esteemed in the forging of swords and armour—and this particular cargo must have been worth about £2,000 in modern money.

If iron was expensive, wine from the vineyards of France was comparatively cheap and reckoned almost a necessity in the households of English nobles, religious orders and the richer merchants, ale being the usual drink for husbandmen, mariners and poorer folk. With so much wine being shipped across the Channel, it is hardly surprising that the cargoes of prizes were often sampled. In 1360 the "Savoie" of Fowey, master John Thomas, was involved with other ships in the capture of a vessel laden with wine at Southampton and in the orgies which ensued no less than thirty casks of wine were drunk or wasted.[2]

Unfortunately Edward III's successor, Richard II, possessed few of the qualities of his grandfather and by 1400 most of the English lands in France had been lost. English shipping suffered from the frequent attacks of French and Spanish vessels and the prestige of the country was low. Dartmouth and almost certainly Fowey were fearful of enemy landings and small castles or blockhouses were built to guard the entrances of both harbours. In 1382 Richard de Michelstow was in trouble over the seizure of a Portuguese barge, but in general the men of Fowey were lying low.

Twenty years later another spate of piratical activity broke out. Dartmouth and Fowey men were again to the fore, and of the latter, Mark Michelstow or Mixstow was the most prominent. On Ascension Day in the year 1402[3] he took a Spanish barge. It would seem that her lading was not up to expectations, for he took only some grease

[1] Inquisitions Misc. No. 583.
[2] Inquisitions Misc. No. 423.
[3] Close Rolls, 545.

and hides, but the merchant of Bruges, who owned the cargo, was naturally indignant and made the usual complaint to Westminster. About this time Mark Mixstow was also concerned in the seizure of another vessel named the "Seint Marie", and a barge, the "Seint Kateline". One of his partners in these affairs was William Russell, who appears on other occasions as the master of a vessel engaged in taking pilgrims to Spain.

So great was Mark's success and so numerous the complaints received that he and his fellows were duly ordered to appear before the king and council at Westminster so that matters might be investigated. But Mark was evasive and failed to put in an appearance. A further command instructed him to report at Calais, but it seems doubtful whether he attended even then,[1] for in June, 1403, he was warned

> "to leave all else and ceasing every excuse to be in person before the king and council at Westminster on the morrow of the Purification next, in order to answer touching what shall by the Flemings be laid against him".

Oddly enough, the very next thing recorded of Mixstow is that he is acting as "admiral" of a little squadron of three barges, armed with a commission to "search for the king's enemies at sea" ![2] In this capacity he sailed out of Falmouth but could not resist taking a ship laden with wine on her voyage to Prussia. The Hanseatic merchants were not slow to seek compensation and it would have been interesting to learn how far the royal commission protected him.

Mark's contemporaries at Fowey were John Hobbe,[3] whom the king's admiral in the west was ordered to arrest in 1401, Walter Gloucestre and John Gascoigne. Gloucestre was master of a balinger of Fowey which was concerned with men of Plymouth and Barnstaple in the seizure of the "Marie" of Danzig, whilst the last of the trio had gone to sea with John Mayhewe of Dartmouth in two balingers "with many persons arrayed in war-like manner" and had boarded a Portuguese ship which had just put out from the island of Jersey on a voyage to Middleburg. This vessel was laden with salt and other merchandise to the value of 500 marks and the captors took her to Shoreham, where they imprisoned the crew and sold the ship and cargo. Since England and Portugal were at peace, an order was made for the restitution of the Lisbon ship, the order being addressed to the *mayor* of Fowey and to Thomas Wadyngfeld, one of the king's serjeants-at-arms.

Certain Fowey mariners were also at this time implicated in the capture of the "Seint David" of Quimperlé. Her master was a Breton, his name being Cynon Pasceu—convincing proof of the link between Brittany and Cornwall, where Pascoes have always had a home.

It is a great pity that so little is known concerning the really

[1] Close Rolls, 27.
[2] Patent Rolls, 133.
[3] Patent Rolls, 67.

FIFTEENTH CENTURY BRASSES IN ST. FIMBARRUS CHURCH
(*Photo : British Museum*)

legitimate prizes of war which were taken by Westcountrymen. In 1413, for instance, three commissioners, Thomas de Carewe, John Hauley, the great shipping magnate of Dartmouth, and John Stonard,[1] were instructed to watch the fair division of merchandize captured by Dartmouth and Fowey men and brought into the latter port. This precaution was necessary since part of the haul had belonged to the King's enemies of France, and as fair prize of war was to be divided between the king's lieges who were present at the capture; the remaining part, being the property of merchants of Brittany, was to be restored to the rightful owners.

Two years later Parliament passed an Act which was designed to put an end to piracy.[2] In addition to making the breaking of truces and safe conducts a treasonable offence, it provided for officers at the ports to enquire into all such cases. It would have seemed an admirable cure but in practice it could not, at this stage, be enforced. Moreover, it was unpopular among English merchants, for it afforded them no protection against foreign marauders and yet prevented them from making reprisals. A few years later this Act was suspended.

During the reign of Henry VI piracy thrived to such an extent that it attracted the scum of other nations. Some of these, natives of "Ducheland", captured a Flemish vessel and brought her into Fowey. The owner of the cargo tried to obtain satisfaction from a merchant in Fowey named Smyth, who had bought the goods from the "Duchelanders".[3] Smyth not only refused but had the unfortunate Fleming seized and kept aboard ship in the harbour until in very fear of his life, he signed a document relinquishing his claim.

In 1434 a commission was addressed to the mayor and water bailiffs of Fowey for them "to enquire who were the malefactors of that town who lately being at sea in a carrack of Fowey, took Master James Ram, subject of the duke of Burgundy, while coming in a ship from Bordeaux, and robbed him of 600 crowns of gold, a pipe (i.e. a case) full of books valued at 1,000 crowns, a tun of wine worth 20 crowns and other goods,[4] plate and jewels to the value of 550 crowns; and in whose hands the goods now are". John Mixstow, the third of that family to engage in these activities, was in 1429 sailing with Henry Nanskaseke of Truro.[5] Now Nanskaseke was in possession of an authority granted to his father in 1410, from which it would seem that the father was the William Nanskaseke who was a contemporary of Mark Mixstow in many exploits some twenty-six years before.

John Mixstow and his brother-in-arms seized three Breton vessels in this year but found them a poor catch inasmuch as they had already been despoiled by men of Mousehole. Two years later his name appears in a list of pirates[6] and in 1433 he was really advanced in

[1] Patent Rolls, 36.
[2] Kingsford: *Westcountry Piracy*, 79 *et seq.*
[3] Kingsford: *Westcountry Piracy*, 79 *et seq.*
[4] Patent Rolls, 426.
[5] Patent Rolls, 276.
[6] Kingsford: *Westcountry Piracy.*

his profession, being in command of a fine great seaworthy ship named the "Edward" and cruising off Cape St. Vincent, with a balinger as consort, and two hundred armed men aboard. Here they fell in with a rich Genoese carrack. Mixstow's men were soon aboard and in possession. The Genoese crew made no resistance, so Mixstow bundled them into a boat and put them ashore on the bleak coast of Portugal. The "Edward" and the balinger then escorted the carrack to Fowey, where apparently the merchants offered to prove their ownership of the goods before the mayor, but were refused.

John Mixstow's daughter (and heiress) Amicia married Thomas Treffry, who appears with John Hody or Udy on a commission to enquire into piracy and the disposal of certain booty in 1432.[1]

The influx of foreigners has already been mentioned and is borne out by the number of aliens residing in Fowey in 1439. There were 9 Irishmen, 2 Bretons, 3 Normans, 1 Portuguese, 1 Gascon, 5 Dutchmen, 1 Fleming and 5 others in possession of houses in the town,[2] and a further 29 of various nationalities who were not householders.

The "Duchelanders" seem to have been particularly troublesome and much addicted to piracy. Between 1436 and 1456 they accounted for at least fourteen Flemish, Breton and Spanish merchant ships.[3] Their leaders appear to have been Hankyn and John Seelander (owing to the confusion in names it is just possible that they were one and the same person) and they were quite unscrupulous, threatening to murder John Salter, the constable of Fowey, when he attempted to take a Breton ship into custody and throwing overboard letters of safe conduct found in a captured vessel.

Another very rich prize fell into the hands of the ship "Edward" of Polruan and the barge "Makerell" of Fowey in the late November of 1449.[4] They were in Plymouth at the time when a great galley named the "Seynt Antonye and Seynt Francisse" was driven by storm to take shelter in the Sound. She had aboard a rich cargo valued at £12,000. Needless to say the opportunity was not neglected, despite the fact that the galley had a safe conduct, and she was very soon being escorted into Fowey harbour. What happened afterwards when the cargo was shared out can best be seen from the proceedings of the enquiry which was subsequently held. One witness, Robert Ferrour, confessed to receiving a bonnet and a pair of knives; Thomas Butside to receiving two yards of woollen cloth, 3 yards of linen cloth, 2,000 pins, 3 bonnets and 4 bundles of linen thread; John Mark agreed to a varied haul, namely a sword, six bonnets, a painted cloth and two barrels of red herrings, and Thomas Pennarth confessed to taking woollen and linen cloth bonnets and knives, but swore that the items had been delivered to his household whilst he was absent in London. A similar excuse was made by Nicholas Carmynow, who had victualled

[1] Patent Rolls, 201.
[2] Henderson: Essays, 34–5.
[3] Kingsford: *Westcountry Piracy*.
[4] Kingsford: *Westcountry Piracy*.

the "Makerell" and had received among other things a great pan of brass, a pair of spurs, 12 pairs of scissors, 6 pairs of pens and inkhorns (price 9 pence), 2 pairs of Flemish knives (worth 1d. the pair) and 1 quire of paper (worth 1d.). John Watte had the only really sound excuse—he pleaded that it was a case of mistaken identity and that it was John Wattes, sometime park-keeper at Restormel, who was the wanted man.

The owner, Francis Jungent, a merchant of Barcelona, used every endeavour to regain such a valuable cargo and for twelve years laboured to get a settlement. In the end it is doubtful whether he succeeded. For one thing there were some influential people among the owners and victuallers of the "Edward" and the "Makerell". Sir Hugh Courtenay was one of the victuallers of the Polruan ship and John Trevelyan of Penpoll the principal owner. It is true that both these gentlemen were committed to the Tower of London for breaking safe conducts, but they were soon released and the next thing is that Sir Hugh is one of the commissioners appointed to investigate the case! Furthermore, when the "Edward" was condemned and put up for sale, who should buy her but John Arundell of Talvern, who had received some of the stolen goods, and Thomas Bodulgate.

The latter was well known in the profession and in 1454 brought the Mary of Dublin into Fowey as a prize. Six years later he was present when the "Carvel of Tuke" and the "Mighell" of Fowey brought in the "Marie" of Biscay, with a cargo consigned to three Bristol merchants. Bodulgate's servant is alleged to have fetched 4 casks of wine and a pound of saffron from Fowey to his house whilst John Trevelyan's man—one Richard Hogan of Polruan—carried off a similar amount for his master.

It is interesting to note the names of the witnesses who testified to the disposal of the goods. They include Thomas Treffry, William Dawe, William Brewer, John Robyn, John Davy, William Cobbe, William Pole, Thomas Mayowe, Julyan Hykks and the "Zeelander" Hankyn Dort.

On the 27th March, 1471, a Breton ship called the "Margaret" was on a voyage to England when a carvel named the "Peter Courtenay" came alongside and forced her to make sail to Fowey harbour. Here the crew were put ashore as prisoners, whilst the "Margaret" and her cargo of wine were disposed of. Unfortunately the wine had been intended for the ransom of certain Bretons previously captured by an English knight and the Breton vessel carried a letter of protection granted by the English king. Complaints were duly made and orders given for the release of the ship with her crew and merchandise. This was easier said than done, for the owner of the Fowey ship was none other than Sir Hugh Courtenay of Boconnoc, a gentleman of some standing in the neighbourhood, and four years later the Bretons were still clamouring for their goods.

Sometimes luck was against the Fowey men, as in 1462, when

after lawfully capturing one of the King's enemies at sea,[1] they waited for the ransom which they could properly expect. Thirty tuns of wine were loaded in the port of Nantes as payment of this ransom and duly brought across to Plymouth, but here the wine was seized under pretext that it was wine of Aquitaine and not produce of Brittany. It took another commission to sort this matter out and meanwhile the poor prisoners were forced to enjoy the amenities of Fowey a little longer and perhaps marvel at the amount of plunder being brought into this nest of pirates.

For matters were now getting quite out of hand. In 1469 the Fowey men excelled themselves.[2] The "Barbara", John Wilcock, master, was about Whitsuntide sailing near Belle Isle when she fell among a whole fleet of Breton merchantmen. Like Mixstow's "Edward" the "Barbara" must have been a stout ship and well armed, for in a few days she captured the following:—

A ship of Roland Pinzin laden with 37 tuns of wine and other goods to the value of 1,000 crowns,
The "Katherine of Crauzon", with 8 packs of cloth,
The "Nostre Dame de Seynt Michel" laden with 23 tuns of wine,
The "Saint Julian de Benaudet" with 27 tuns of wine,
A ship of Morlaix with 4 packs of cloth of divers colours and 1 pack of linen cloth,
A carvel of Ivo Guiole, laden with 140 quintals of iron and other goods, coming from the ports of Spain,
A ship of Spain with 23 tuns of wine, fruit, iron and other merchandise,

together with nine other vessels burdened with iron, wine and cloth.

Next year Sir Hugh Courtenay, who certainly should have been in a position to know the intricacies of the business, was appointed to enquire into the seizure of a Spanish ship, the "St. John Baptiste," with her cargo of iron, wools and furs called "bevers", which had been taken by a Fowey ship.

A little later the "Anne" of Fowey, Edward Phelip,[3] master, and John Stephens, boatswain, took another Breton vessel. Phelip was one of those who had investigated the piracy of Thomas Bodulgate some years before. In 1486 John Gaye and William Bruer of Fowey molested two ships of the powerful Hanseatic merchants.[4] These were dangerous people to offend and the commissioners appointed to look into the matter were not merely local merchants or land-holders. The Bishop of Exeter, Edmund, Earl of Devon (a Courtenay), Sir John Halliwell and Sir John Treffry were to arrest the persons who seized and plundered the two ships, and their vessels, equipment and cargoes were to be arrested "no matter in whose hands the same shall be". The offenders were to be committed to prison until

[1] Patent Rolls, 492.
[2] Patent Rolls, 517–8.
[3] Patent Rolls, 105.
[4] Patent Rolls, 545.

compensation was made and the whole proceedings were then to be certified to the royal council.

By this time complaints were increasing and it was becoming necessary to compensate some of these foreign claimants with grants of money which were usually taken out of the income from the customs. In a sense this affected the king's purse and it is also unlikely that Edward IV would have any great regard for this part of Cornwall, where his late enemy, the Earl of Warwick (the Kingmaker), and his father-in-law had exercised much influence. In the winter of 1474 it was ordered that Thomas St. Leger, Sir Richard Willoughby, Alvred Corneburgh and the sheriff of Cornwall should:—

> "arrest all masters, mariners, pirates, possessors and victuallers of any ships and vessels of the towns and ports of Fowey, Bodinnick and Polruan as they have committed great depredations on goods and merchandise of merchants and others, contrary to the form of treaties and friendships with and safe conducts of the king, and do not heed the king's mandates, but daily do worse; and also all into whose hands such goods and merchandise have come, and to bring them before the king and council, and to seize their goods and merchandise and the said ships and vessels and the gear of the same and put them in safe custody."

What exactly did happen is uncertain. A later account tells of the Fowey men slitting the ears of the King's messenger, of Dartmouth men being sent down to remove the chain which stretched across the harbour and of one Harrington being hung in chains. There is reason to doubt this dramatic climax. For one thing the terms of the commission, apparently so severe, only employ the usual forthright language of the time. Richard Harrington is mentioned on several occasions after 1474 and within a very short time there were fresh cases of piracy reported.

It was probably the more settled government of the Tudors and their tighter control over the revenue which eventually discouraged Westcountry piracy.

CHAPTER 5

It seems likely that in common with other buildings in the town, the Church was damaged in the French raid of 1457. In 1486 it was prostrate and ruinous and the churchwardens, Thomas Hall, John Lyffe and John Bedcokk, found it necessary to borrow £30 from two citizens of London.[1] These good men lent the money on October 8th to help with the edifying and new building of the church, but it seems that the wardens found the project more expensive than they had anticipated, for they could not carry out their undertaking to repay the loan by the following Easter and the Londoners eventually had to seek the assistance of the law to retrieve their money.

Possibly the tower was commenced earlier—about 1465 when the Earl of Warwick, the Kingmaker, was in high favour. His associations with the neighbourhood have already been mentioned and it is likely that it is his emblem—"the ragged staff"—which appears at each corner. His downfall and that of his local adherents, as well as the punitive measures against the sea-faring inhabitants of Fowey in 1470 may account for the delay in completing the church.

Altogether the rebuilding would seem to have taken some forty years, for in 1500 the south aisle was not completed.

The builders must have been proud of their tower—the second highest in Cornwall—judging by the detailed carving they expended on the four stages into which it is divided, the parapet and battlements and the four elaborate pinnacles which crown the whole. The land slopes in this vicinity and the ground was obviously excavated to a depth of twenty feet to provide a level foundation for the west end of the church.

The porch, also constructed at this time, is a small building in itself with open archways facing east and west and a room over it which probably contained the books and reading desk of the priest. Over the doorway is the empty niche which once contained a small image, probably thrown down at the time of the Reformation.

Perhaps some of the thirty pounds went towards the cost of putting up the beautiful oak waggon roof which extends the whole length of the church and spans the fine arcaded walls which were so sensibly preserved from the earlier church of 1336. Carved angels bearing shields were fashioned to spring from the wall plates.

The end of the church facing the river seems to have been pulled down altogether and the walls extended. The great chancel window was then constructed and in the closing years of the fifteenth century the south aisle was altered to provide a chapel at the eastern end.

If the Kingmaker's influence can be traced during the early years of the rebuilding, the Treffrys were certainly most active in the later stages and this Chapel was destined for their particular use. The

[1] *Early Chancery Proceedings:* Vol. 141, No. 84.

members of this family had prospered since the accession of Henry VII and were also benefactors to the Priory.

John and William Treffry had thrown in their lot with the Lancastrian party and as early as 1483 they had been involved in the conspiracy which aimed at overthrowing Richard III.[1] The first attempt was a failure and after joining with Courtenay of Boconnoc, Trevelyan of Penpoll and others in proclaiming Henry Tudor as king, at Bodmin and Exeter, John Treffry fled to Brittany. Here the supporters of the red rose waited a more favourable opportunity to strike again. The chance came in August, 1485, when with a considerable force they left Harfleur and landed at Milford Haven. Treffry's services were valued sufficiently to earn him a knighthood as soon as the army was ashore.[2] This time there was no doubt as to the outcome—Richard was defeated and killed at Bosworth.

Sir John was something of a rover, and as much at home on the sea as on land.[3] In 1486, it is true he was with others appointed to investigate a local case of piracy, but as shown in the previous chapter this carried no real significance, and a little later he was himself in trouble over a ship of Croisic which he had seized at Fowey.[4] When Sir Richard Edgecumbe went on a mission to Ireland in 1488[5] he sailed in the "Anne" of Fowey and was accompanied by four other ships, including a "bark" of Sir John Treffry's. Two years later Sir John is described as captain of the "Christopher" of 200 tons which, in company with the "Gabriel" of like tonnage, the "Anthony" of 140 tons, the "George" and the "Anne" of 120 tons and the "Barbara" of 110 tons, all ships of Fowey, accompanied the English expedition to Brittany.

He died in September, 1500, after making, in accordance with the custom of the time, careful provision for the future.[6] His will provided that his name be placed with those of the founders at Tywardreath Priory, so that he might be prayed for daily and yearly, as the founders were, for which service the Prior and Convent were to receive a gown and two vestments of blue velvet, two silver cruets and other items. In addition "I will that there shall be an honest priest singing within the Church of St. Barry in Fowey in our Lady Chapel by the space of 3 years next after my decease, to pray for my soul and all the souls that I am bound to pray for, having for his wages for 3 years £15".

A quarter share in the vessel "Mary Hardford" was to go to his brother, Thomas, and a quarter share of the "George" to his nephew, John Trevanion. To his other brother, William, he left his best basin and ewer of silver, his best dozen of spoons, three silver candlesticks and a ring of gold with a sapphire loop.

William Treffry had many connections in London, where he was

[1] Rowse: *Tudor Cornwall*, 110.
[2] Rowse: *Tudor Cornwall*, 113.
[3] Rowse: *Tudor Cornwall*, 104.
[4] Rowse: *Tudor Cornwall*, 75.
[5] Rowse: *Tudor Cornwall*, 115.
[6] Drake: *St. Fimbarrus Church* (1876).

Surveyor of the Customs—a lucrative post. In the year of Henry VII's accession he became Controller of the Coinage of tin in Devon and Cornwall[1] and at court exercised the duties of Gentleman Usher of the Chamber. To crown this career he was chosen as Sheriff of Cornwall.

It was in London that William Treffry noted the fine tomb of a merchant[2] and was so impressed that he left directions for a similar slab of Purbeck stone to be brought to Cornwall and carved with

> "3 ymages, oone for my broder, another for me and another for my wife, after their discretion and lyke unto a tombe which lyeth on Th. Browne in the Crotched friers of London."

This is the great flat tomb-stone, still to be seen in the Treffry aisle of Fowey church, although the image of the wife has had to give place to that of the third brother, Thomas. Sir John appears in full armour, the others are in civilian dress. Here they lie together, although the altar of the Virgin Mary, near which Sir John wished to be buried, has disappeared and the singing priest has long ceased to chant intercessions for their souls.

Of Thomas Treffry, very little is known except that he married Janet, the daughter and heiress of William Dawe of Plymouth.

In these years the export of tin from Fowey probably reached a record.[3] 143,400 lbs. of tin were sent away from here in 1498—more than from any other Cornish port. Small craft were used, such as the "John" of Golant, which loaded five blocks weighing 1,300 lbs., and the "Magdalen" of Polruan[4] which took aboard ten blocks weighing 2,500 lbs. A few years ago five such blocks of tin were recovered from the bed of the river near Bodinnick[5]—probably the cargo of some unseaworthy vessel which had sunk at her moorings. As in the Black Prince's day, there was the usual complaint—that the tinners recklessly released sand and gravel into the river—and a petition of 1532, drawing attention to the state of affairs, affirms that the harbour had become so silted up that a ship of a hundred tons burden could hardly enter at half flood.[6] Of course, in addition the river Fowey did silt up rapidly from natural causes.

There was also a considerable trade with Brittany, Wales and Ireland. Cloth and hides (together with fish) still made up a great part of the exports, whilst wines from France and Spain were in constant demand.

At the same time there were always ships available for the royal service and the owners now seemed eager to place vessels at the King's disposal. Thus in 1514[7] Sir William Trevanion writes to the Earl of Surrey from Fowey offering his own balinger and hints that the

[1] Rowse: *Tudor Cornwall*, 118.
[2] Drake: *St. Fimbarrus Church*.
[3] Rowse: *Tudor Cornwall*, 73.
[4] Rowse: *Tudor Cornwall*, 73.
[5] J.R.I.C., 1898.
[6] Dredging sand for use in agriculture relieved the harbour entrance in the seventeenth and eighteenth centuries.
[7] Brewer: Letters and Papers of the Reign of Henry VIII.

PLACE—HOME OF THE TREFFRY FAMILY SINCE THE FIFTEENTH CENTURY
(Photo by late Fred. Kitto, Fowey)

"poor men of Fowey, John Power and others desire that their ships, the 'George' and the 'Peter' may be taken into the King's service". He further suggests that it were a good deed for Surrey to help the town of Fowey and proudly asserts that there are few better ships in England of her burden than the "George". Trevanion's advice seems to have been taken, for in the squadron of ships detailed to keep the seas between the islands of Jersey and Guernsey and the Tweed in 1522 appears the "George" of Fowey, 120 tons, Gilbert Malyvery, captain; Philip Tyce, master, and 90 men aboard. Next year she is at sea between Wales and Ireland under Sir Anthony Poyntz, vice-admiral, after being engaged in carrying ordnance and artillery to Portsmouth.

Great ships of a thousand tons and more were experimented with, the single short mast of early mediaeval days had given place to foremast and mainmast, each crossing at least two yards and a mizen mast carrying the triangular lateen sail imported from the Mediterranean. Variations and additions were tried out as the years went by until the "Revenge" took the water as the pride of her time. All these improvements meant that the fighting ship was becoming a specialized unit and that trading vessels were impressed only in exceptional circumstances or for special purposes. But the change was gradual and in 1514, Richard Gresham (some time Lord Mayor of London) and William Copeland were being charged £300 for freighting the King's ship, the "Anne" of Fowey on two voyages, one to "Estland" and the other to the river Garonne.

John Chapman, writing to a business acquaintance from "Foye" on the 29th March, 1532, mentions that three days before he had encountered three ships of war near Start Point and had been obliged to run into Fowey harbour.

Nor was this harbour the safe refuge that it might have been. There was discontent in the town and talk of neglect—fortifications falling into decay, whilst those who should be watching over such matters were indifferent.

The Priory at Tywardreath had lost much of its former prestige and the Bishop of Exeter had already complained to Prior Collins of the bad management and ill discipline of his establishment. Thomas Treffry was the son (or possibly the nephew) of Sir John Treffry but was less in sympathy with the inmates of the Priory than his forbears. He was possessed of one of the most modern and spacious houses in Cornwall and here he entertained John Leland, the traveller and antiquary. Treffry was well acquainted with London and no doubt the two men discussed events at Court—King Harry's latest marriage and whose head lay nearest the block. Being a Protestant and sensing the approaching disintegration of the Priory he apparently approached Thomas Cromwell, now the King's trusted adviser. Cromwell was at this moment well disposed to listen to any complaints about the religious houses and Treffry returned to Cornwall bearing the following letter for delivery to the unfortunate Prior:—

"Mr. Prior, ... I have me comended unto you, that whereas it is comen unto the Kings highnes knowledge that the Towne of Fowey is sore decayed and th' occasion thereof partlie is that in the said Towne is no order of justice because the liberties concerning the same . . . . . .[1] remayne in yor handes and kepinge, so that betwene you no maner good order, equitie nor justice is executed and used wtin the said Towne; wherefore I require you . . . . . . As ye shall agre therein to certifie me in writinge by Thomas Treffry berer hereof. For his Highnes thinketh that the saide Port of Fowey oweth to be his . . . . . . so that his Grace intendeth to have it as well provided for Wt good govern'nce and of defence . . . . . .
Wherefore his Highnes thinketh that ye be veray unworthy to have rule of any town that cannot well rule yorself. And that I may have answer . . . . . . by this berer what ye intend to do I require you . . . . . . And thus fare ye well. At London the xxjth daie of Maie (1536).

Your Freend,
Thomas Cromwell."

Collins seems to have been a scheming old man whose chief concerns were to hold on to his office for as long as possible and to push the interests of his relatives.[2] In 1518 he himself took over the vacant living of Fowey and held it for ten years. Even when he did relinquish it, another Collins was appointed as Vicar of Fowey. It is possible that the inhabitants of Fowey resented these changes and that this feeling was shared by the Treffrys, who had so recently laid out money and bequests for the improvement of the parish church. When the end came it was probably not unexpected, for not only St. Andrew's Priory but hundreds of similar establishments, great and small, were swept away and their inmates pensioned off.

Treffry's part in the dissolution of the Priory is clear and it is also evident that he hoped to obtain the Manor of Trenant—one of the Priory's most valuable possessions. Curiously enough, he was not successful in this. The lordship and manor of Trenant were granted to Philip Rashleigh "to be holden of the King".[3] Eventually, by deed dated 26th August, 1545, Rashleigh purchased the manor from the King, paying £209 into the Court of Augmentations.

The younger son of a family settled in Devon, Philip Rashleigh followed the custom of the time by going into trade and by this date had set up as a merchant in Fowey, where he acquired a good deal of property. In the same year as he bought Trenant he was named as one of the commissioners to enquire into prizes taken at sea by the fleet under Sir George Carew.

However, Treffry had no grounds for complaint, having just been appointed to superintend the building of the larger castles at Pendennis

[1] Cann: *St. Fimbarrus Church.*
[2] Cann: *St. Fimbarrus Church.*
[3] Henderson MSS.

and St. Mawes,[1] as well as that of Fowey. He was evidently still in close communication with Cromwell and in March, 1540, was writing to the latter on several matters.[2] Certain Truro merchants just returned from Morlaix in Brittany and passing through Fowey on the 25th of that month had reported that an Irish lord, believed to be the rebel Desmond, had landed on the Breton coast; he had recently been to Falmouth, where a Southampton ship, said to be laden with cloth, but in reality carrying a cargo of barley, had disobeyed his instructions to stay in the King's name and had departed by night to Spain and winding up with a gentle reminder that his request for "keeping the said fortlett" (St. Mawes) might be granted. If he obtained the command of St. Mawes he would willingly relinquish his office of the customs of Cornwall, the more willingly since he had lost 100 marks by that office and had suffered much from his journeys in consequence of a hurt from a horse. The matter seems to have been settled in his favour and the inscriptions in the keep of St. Mawes are said to have been placed there by Treffry, who had persuaded his visitor, John Leland, to compose them in honour of the King. It is just possible that he removed some of the guns at Place to St. Mawes,[3] for in 1545 it was reported that "Treffry's house has great miss of the ordnance which was taken away". There were setbacks of course: besides his apparent loss over the customs, he had lent money for the fitting out of the Lord Admiral's vessel, the "Falcon Lisle", most likely as a privateer against the French, but had difficulty in getting it back.[4] Moreover, his son had been captured by the French and he had to find the necessary ransom.

Fortunately a detailed map made about 1540 has survived, so that it is possible to view Fowey very much as it was in the days of Thomas Treffry and his guest.[5] The map may have been drawn up in connection with the surveys carried out for the proposed fortification of Cornwall and like many maps of the period it illustrates the main features—the rivers, creeks, bays and headlands—very graphically without being overmuch concerned with scale or comparative distances. Its great value lies in the thumbnail sketches of the towns and prominent buildings. From the architecture which has remained to the present time and which is usually accurately shown on the chart, it is safe to assume that the cartographer was acquainted with each place and that his sketches of buildings and features long since swept away, can be accepted without too much reserve.

Various great ships ply up and down off the entrance to the haven, and two are anchored under the guns of a small fort overlooking the cliffs to the west of Polkerris but marked "not built". Evidently

[1] Rowse: *Tudor Cornwall*, 247.
[2] Rowse: *Tudor Cornwall*, 247.
[3] Rowse: *Tudor Cornwall*, 247.
[4] Rowse: *Tudor Cornwall*, 247.
[5] B.M. Cotton, Aug. I, i, 38. The section of the chart from which the illustration facing p. 40 is reproduced is printed in Lysons' *Magna Britannia:* Cornwall. The Bodinnick ferry boat is shown in the original but not in Lysons' sketch.

this was contemplated but never commenced. The new castle at St. Catherine's point and guarding the approach to Fowey is also shown as "half made" but on the highest point behind the castle appears the chapel which fulfilled so important a duty over the centuries. It is a small building with a square tower at its western end, in which two small windows are set high up facing out to sea. The western gable bears a cross and this is evidently the St. Catherine's Chapel which gave its name to headland, cove and castle. On the other side of the harbour entrance, standing like a sentinel, rose the sister chapel of St. Saviour. Now with the Priory gone, St. Catherine's Chapel is doomed to decay.

A little further inland and built on the rocks just above highwater level at a point where the harbour entrance is narrowest, stand the blockhouses. The one on the Fowey side is marked "decay'd" but is represented in good outward appearance. It is connected with the mainland by a small drawbridge which gives access to the second floor. The building is square in shape and appears to have three or four floors as well as a parapeted/platform at the top, in which are cut two or three portholes for great guns. A further two ports appear on a lower floor facing Polruan and an additional pair in the seaward wall. Several slit-like windows let in the light above the ports. The blockhouse seems larger and more imposing than its companion on the Polruan shore, although it has since suffered more severely from storm and decay.

The town does not commence until the Town Quay is reached. To the seaward of the quay stands a massive building with battlemented parapet which has now entirely disappeared. It was evidently the residence of an important townsman and was only second to Place in size. Possibly this is the "Havenor's Hall", sometimes "Havenor's Place",[1] mentioned in mediaeval documents and may have been the residence and offices of the Black Prince's "Havenor" or Harbour Master.

Place presents a striking appearance and has been given prominence on the chart. It is protected by a high battlemented boundary wall which sweeps in a great curve from behind the church to as far as Passage Slip. Within the great space enclosed by this wall stands the house itself, built in the shape of a letter F, the upright part representing the main body of the mansion and the horizontal parts the projecting wings. Thus in plan the building has remained almost unchanged up to the present day. A sloping roof covers the whole of the house but the frontage has been embellished with so many battlements that the whole structure resembles a regular fortress, within which the inhabitants of Fowey could withstand a siege if necessary. That at least seemed to have been in the mind of the Treffry

[1] Henderson MSS.
Compare Leland's description: "In the Midle of the Toun, apon the Shore self, is a House buildid quadrantly in the Haven, which shadowith the Shippes in the Haven above it, from three Partes of the Haven Mouth, and defendith them from Stormes".

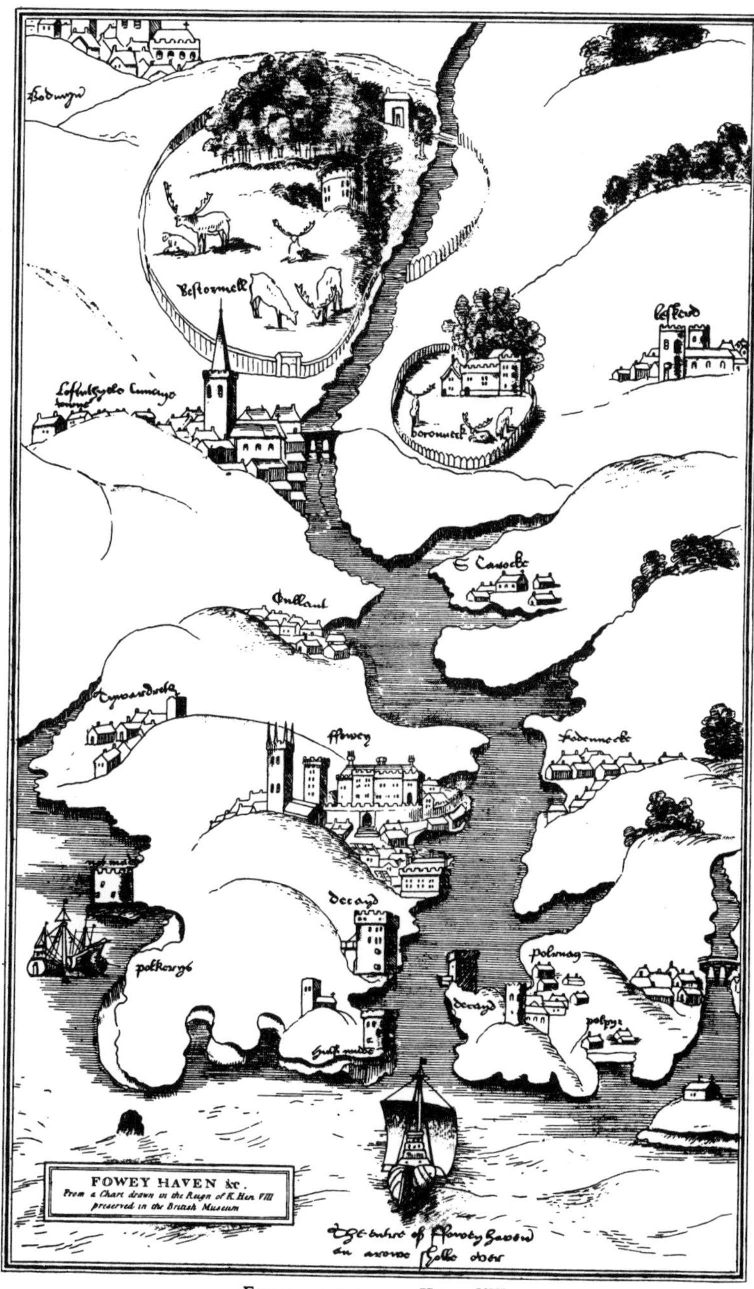

FOWEY IN THE TIME OF HENRY VIII

(Reproduced from Lysons' Magna Britannia, *based on a chart in the British Museum)*

ST. CATHERINE'S CASTLE, BUILT ABOUT 1540
(*Photo by Graham Gullick, Fowey*)

who built it some seventy or eighty years previously and who also raised the tall tower which stands a little aloof from the main building and of which Leland wrote: "Treury builded a right fair and stronge embattled towr in his house; and embattling al the waulles of the house, in a manner made it a castelle and onto this day it is the glorie of the town building in Foweye". The main entrance as shown on the chart is also very impressive, a great flight of wide steps leading from the open space—probably that part now built over by Union Place—up to a large arched gateway in the outer wall. A number of smaller buildings are enclosed by this wall but the town itself seems to be made up of three sections—a number of houses clustered against the hill at the back or westernmost part of the Church; a group of dwellings situated around what is now the lower end of Lostwithiel Street, Whitfords Yard and Trafalgar Square, including the buildings straggling along the shore from the Town Quay up as far as Bodinnick Ferry. Here there is a boat in mid-stream, whilst the village of Bodinnick is represented by a number of houses—none apparently of any importance. Since Hall and its chapel were definitely standing in 1540, the cartographer has evidently neglected to show these. Coming down to the harbour entrance again, Polruan appears on something like the same scale as Bodinnick but contains two buildings of note, the blockhouse, also marked "decay'd", and the Chapel (St. Saviour's) standing high above the village and consisting of a round, embattled tower and nave containing three large windows facing seawards. One massive buttressed corner stands today.

The country farther inland is illustrated with less detail. "Gullant" church is not shown, although "S. Carocke" in Penpoll creek appears. Lerryn is not marked by a single house but "Lostuthyel—a Cunage towne" is drawn in more detail with its steepled church tower and mediaeval bridge crossing the river Fowey. Both Restormel and Boconnoc are shown as palisaded enclosures with beautiful antlered deer browsing and lying in the pastures. "Polpyr" (Polperro) the cartographer calmly places within a stone's throw of Polruan whereas it is a good six miles off, as he would have known had he walked the up hill and down dale road which joins the two villages!

So the port and surrounding country appeared in the latter years of Henry VIII's reign. It is interesting to see that a castle or fort was evidently being considered to defend the entrance to Polkerris, but the truth of the matter was that much of the money and property taken from the dissolved monasteries, ostensibly to be used for the defence of the realm, found its way elsewhere. The castle, which was actually raised at St. Catherine's Point, turned out to be a very small fort and certainly called for little in the matter of expense or material, since it consisted only of a small round tower rising from a platform intended to mount a few great guns. Possibly the builder relied more on the strength of its natural position high up on the cliffs and difficult approach from the landward side.

Yet despite these precautions against a foreign enemy, the next excitement arose from rebellion at home. It was in the summer of 1549 that a great body of Cornishmen, incensed by the proposal to go a step further in Protestantism by adopting a new English prayer book in the churches, marched up to Exeter. This was primarily a Catholic rising and Treffry with his strong Protestant views probably lay low for a time.

The rebels were defeated with great slaughter and their leaders,[1] including Richard Bennet, vicar of St. Veep, were hanged.

By 1553 the government was extremely hard up for money and commissions were set up to enquire into the quantities of church furniture and plate held in each parish, with instructions to dispose of any surplus items and to send the proceeds to London. The recent rebellion showed how the Cornish had clung to the old religion and in the parishes of the county the commissioners found ample proof of the former devotion and piety with which they had furnished their churches. At Fowey were found two chalices and patens, a censor, a pax and a ship, all made of silver. The "ship of silver" may have been a model placed in the church in accordance with an old custom which existed in many seaport communities.[2] Such gifts were often replicas in miniature of the actual ships, and as the congregation knelt to pray their eyes might alight on the models, which were often suspended from the roof, and offer up a special prayer for the safety of those at sea. In Brittany the custom continued until recent times. To the prosaical new Protestants, such baubles savoured only of superstition and popery and the silver ship from St. Fimbarrus Church, together with the remainder of the plate, was sent down to St. Mawes Castle, where Thomas Treffry, its governor and one of the commissioners for Cornwall, was collecting a great haul from the churches in the county.[3]

Suddenly the Protestant boy king, Edward VI, died, leaving his half-sister, Mary, nearest to the throne. For a moment the whole country was in a desperate state of uncertainty. The duke of Northumberland hastily had his daughter-in-law, Lady Jane Grey, proclaimed queen. Many Cornish gentlemen, amongst them Treffry, happened to be in Launceston when the news came through, but although they duly proclaimed Lady Jane,[4] they were none too sure of themselves and rapidly dispersed when Mary's Catholic friends made it plain that they meant business. Lady Jane Grey and her young husband went quickly to the block.[5] The Protestants were in a quandary and Thomas Treffry must have had many misgivings when in 1554 he was ordered to take to London part of the silver which he and his fellow commissioners had collected. There is a story that he fled abroad to the Low Countries about this time. A few years later he had the satisfaction of seeing the restoration of the Protestant faith in England. Thomas Treffry died in the year 1563, and some-

[1] Rowse: *Tudor Cornwall*, 284.
[2] Alternatively, it may have been the boat-shaped receptacle for incense.
[3] Rowse: *Tudor Cornwall*, 298–9.
[4] Rowse: *Tudor Cornwall*, 300.
[5] Rowse: *Tudor Cornwall*, 299.

what appropriately his tombstone in Fowey church now stands not within the mellow peacefulness of the Treffry "chapel" with that of his more orthodox forbears, but in the open porch.

Six years later the town played a small part in one of the events which led to the actual outbreak of war with Spain.[1] It happened that certain Spanish ships had taken shelter at Saltash and Fowey after being chased by French privateers. They had good cause to be wary since they carried nearly half a million pounds worth of bullion and plate intended for the Spanish army in the Netherlands, and since England and Spain were ostensibly at peace, they dropped anchor in the English ports quite unsuspectingly. But the peace had already been broken—at San Juan de Ulloa their compatriots had fired upon the ship of John Hawkins—and orders were swiftly sent from London to ensure that the treasure ships were held.

At Fowey there were two pinnaces. Thirty-two cases, each containing 20,000 golden reals, were brought up from their holds and carried ashore by the Spaniards "to the house of Mr. John Treffry and there locked and sealed with their seal and ours, and four or six of the Spaniards with some of our men with watch guarding the same did so remain". Each case was opened, the contents checked in front of the Spaniards, the Queen's officers and merchants of the place and entered in a book before being put into safe keeping at Place. Thus was the legal atmosphere of the seizure preserved, whilst £50 was expended in feeding the crews during their enforced stay in Fowey.

On January 26th, 1569, a great armed cavalcade left Plymouth, to which place the treasure had been removed from Saltash and Fowey, and convoyed the precious gold to the Tower of London. From now onwards the war was in earnest and preparations were made for the defence of the westernmost counties against a Spanish invasion. Enquiries were made into the forces available in Cornwall, with the arms they had available, and amongst the information obtained it is interesting to notice the armoury with which John Treffry was equipped—2 pairs of corselets, 10 pairs of almain rivets, 20 pikes, 4 long bows and sheaves of arrows, 3 harquebuses and 3 halberds.[2] In 1574 a commission came down to survey Fowey and Falmouth defences.

Two years after the landing of the treasure a step was taken which was greatly to affect the corporate life of the town. Since the days of Edward III representatives from Fowey had occasionally been called to London, with those from other parts, to give their opinion on maritime matters. Other Cornish towns had sent members to the Parliaments of the times; Bodmin from as far back as 1295, Lostwithiel from 1304.[3] In 1571 the Queen's counsellors advised the creation of a number of new Parliamentary boroughs, and among other places Fowey and East Looe found themselves elevated to that position.

[1] Rowse: *Tudor Cornwall*, 380–1.
[2] Rowse: *Tudor Cornwall*, 382.
[3] Hist. MSS. Comm.: Hatfield Papers I, 542.

The first members elected were Robert Peter and Thomas Cromwell, although the official return for 1572 shows William Russell and Edward Harryngton as representing Fowey.[1] One theory is that the creation of these new electoral boroughs was purely a political move designed to give the Crown, already holding the Duchy and various manors in Cornwall, virtual power over a number of parliamentary seats. Of the members elected for Fowey in Elizabeth's reign, the majority had strong local interests.

Philip Rashleigh died in 1551, leaving two sons. Robert, the elder, married into a prosperous yeoman family—the Colquites of Lawhyre—and seems to have settled at Coombe. He was a merchant and ship-owner—his vessel, the "Anne", is mentioned in 1571—and at the time of his death in 1578 was in possession of eleven tenements in Fowey rented from the Queen's manor.[2]

It was the younger son, John, born in 1519, who was to become the more prominent. Unlike his contemporary, Thomas Treffry, he does not seem to have involved himself in either politics or religious disputes, and by 1567 he was able to buy the extensive buildings which had once been Bodmin Priory.[3] Six years later he purchased the lands of Menabilly, but like the merchants of mediaeval days, he preferred to live in Fowey with his parlour and well-stocked warehouse under the same roof. His town house is still standing, although the South Gate, which adjoined it at the lower end of Lostwithiel Street, has long since been pulled down and the exterior of the house itself has been altered. It was possibly built—but more likely renovated, as most Fowey houses have been at one time or another—about 1570 and much of the old carved oak and panelling remains. Over the fireplace is the inscription "John Rashly—Alce Rashly 1570".[4]

By the end of the century a great deal of property in and around the town had passed into the hands of the Rashleighs: there were now two local branches of the family—the one settled at Coombe and the other in Fowey, but within a few years to be established at the newly-built mansion of Menabilly. There was probably a decline in property values, for Plymouth was now fast outstripping Fowey as a port. In 1565 it was said of Fowey that her trade had been declining for some thirty years past[5] and if such was the case the Rashleighs

[1] Lawrance: *Parl. History of Cornwall*, 269. Gilbert shows Peter and Cromwell as the first members for Fowey.

[2] Henderson MSS.
There are the remains of a brass to Robert Rashleigh in Fowey Church. Dunkin—"Monumental Brasses of Cornwall" erroneously ascribes this to John Rashleigh, but a rubbing made in 1850 (now in the British Museum) shows a part of the original inscription which has since been lost.

[3] Henderson MSS.

[4] Some of the panelling in the "Ship" is reputed to have been removed from the Church: possibly it came from the Priory buildings when they were dismantled. The panelling was for long hidden by coats of paint but was restored under the direction of Mr. Isbell of Fowey some years ago. Two stone window mouldings were uncovered during the removal of an adjoining house in 1948.

[5] V.C.H., 492.

Elizabethan fireplace and panelling of "The Ship"

(Photo by the late Fred. Kitto, Fowey)

were able to buy cheaply. As early as 1555 John Rashleigh acquired the manor house of Thomas Hendly[1] in the Market Street of Fowey for the trifling sum of £6. 13s. 4d. in cash and a quantity of choice wines, namely, a butt of sack, a cask of claret wine, a pipe of white wine and eight gallons of aqua vitae. A curious bargain even allowing for present values. From William Elliot of Polruan he bought another house in the Market Place and in 1571, a house,[2] shed and market stall "standing next to the flesh market of Fowey". A quay in South Street and two gardens outside the South Gate, a house near Bull Hill—nothing was too small for this careful investor in land and property. As time goes by Rashleigh's shrewdness bore fruit, for the holders of these properties in the town had the power to vote at the parliamentary elections and so for the next two hundred and sixty years the family of Rashleigh had a sure and certain seat in the House of Commons. John Rashleigh the elder died in 1582 and is commemorated in Fowey church by an elaborate monument which depicts him lying at full length in cap, ruff and long robe.

Only four years previously his ship, the "Francis of Foy", had sailed down Channel with Martin Frobisher on his voyage to Meta Incognita[3]—that unknown land lying to the west of Greenland and reputed to contain much wealth. In the articles for the voyage it was laid down that the "Francis" was to be part of Frobisher's own squadron in battle array, should they encounter any enemy. By the 20th June, 1578, they were off Frizeland and observing "great Isles of ice lying on the seas like mountains" and were later in peril when, surrounded by ice, a great fog came down and the "Francis" was almost lost. Eventually after killing a great white bear and loading the ships with a quantity of ore mistakenly supposed to contain gold Frobisher sailed back to England.

Whilst the "Francis" was in English waters, another small English craft had the misfortune to be seized by Spaniards.[4] Her captain, Edward Rawes, a native of Fowey, carried about him papers which revealed that he was employed by the English to spy out the naval preparations being made in Spain. He and his companions were handed over to the dreaded power of the Inquisition and there, his end perhaps hastened by torture, Rawes died. As some recompense for her loss, his widow, being left with her children "in a very poor estate", was granted permission in 1580 to export a hundred quarters of corn from Cornwall and Devon, probably without having to pay duty. The merchant instinct was never stronger than in the Elizabethan age.

John Rashleigh the younger succeeded to his father's possessions at the age of thirty. He and his cousin, also named John, had married two sisters, Alice and Katherine, daughters of Richard Bonython of

[1] Henderson MSS.
[2] Henderson MSS.
[3] *Hakluyts' Voyages*, vii, 236–9, 322–4, 341.
[4] A.P.C. 36.

Carclew. Thus another Mistress Alice now ruled over the domestic household in Fowey. As for the "Francis", she was soon away with Drake on his great voyage to the West Indies. The fleet put out from Plymouth Sound on the 14th September, 1585, and arrived at the little island of St. Christopher in time to spend Christmas. Then they sailed on to Hispaniola[1] (the modern Cuba) where the Spanish town of St. Domingo was captured, Sir Francis watching the landing on the beaches from the deck of the Fowey ship.

The climax came when the rich city of Carthagena was taken, but the "Francis" lost her captain in an ambush. His name was Moon and it is possible that he was related to the Mohuns of Hall.

Three years later she was to the fore again, when rumours were reaching England of a great invasion force being prepared in the ports of Spain. Her owner was already busy in the spring of the year, seeing to the battery which he had erected near the Quay, where the guns would present their muzzles at any vessel having the temerity to venture far into the harbour entrance. A regular little garrison comprising twelve of Rashleigh's tenants manned this battery. Meanwhile, the "Francis" and her pinnace, the "Christopher", of 15 tons, were being prepared, and the former ship seems to have been in harbour, perhaps taking stores aboard, when on the 19th July, 1588, a small vessel scurried into Plymouth Sound with the news that the great Spanish fleet had been sighted off the Lizard. Slowly but steadily the vast concourse of over a hundred and fifty galleons and smaller craft pressed on up Channel and by about three o'clock on the Saturday afternoon, in driving showers of rain, were passing Fowey harbour.[2] Meanwhile the smaller English fleet under Drake and Howard, handicapped by a south-westerly wind, used every means, warping and towing by boats, to get their ships out of Plymouth. They succeeded at last and whilst the Armada was still off the Cornish coast, crossed the bows of the oncoming enemy, tacked around to westward and came up again in the rear of the Spaniards and, of course, to windward of them. Meanwhile a squadron of English ships had worked down along the Cornish coast and early on the Sunday morning, in weather which had now cleared to bright sunshine, this squadron and the main English fleet engaged the enemy. It is likely that the "Francis", putting out from Fowey, joined at this stage since she later received pay for victualling, etc., from Monday, 22nd July.

So commenced the Armada's progress in English waters. Of the fighting off Portland and the Isle of Wight, the havoc wreaked by the English fireships at Calais and the disastrous stormy journey up through the North Sea, around the Orkneys and Ireland, little need be said here. With sixty-four great galleons and transports lost, the majority by shipwreck and foundering, it was truly said "God blew with His wind and they were scattered".

[1] *Hakluyts' Voyages*, viii, 343–4; x, 98.

[2] Rythers' charts shew Drake's squadron hotly engaging de Valdez on the Spanish left wing when between Lansallos and Looe Island.

Rashleigh was awarded £600 to cover his expenses in fitting out the "Francis" and the pinnace,[1] but seems to have had some difficulty in collecting the money, which was raised by a tax on Fowey and Looe and districts adjoining. For some years after the Armada scare he continued to fortify his house at Fowey. In 1597 Sir Walter Raleigh thought sufficiently of these defences to agree to Rashleigh,[2] his servants and family, together with twelve of his tenants in the town, continuing to man them and they were absolved from all other military training.

One of the captains of the troops which embarked from the port for Ireland remarked in the same year,[3] "The gentlemen of the towne of Fowey have especially had a care for the provision of shipping and chiefly one, Mr. Rashleigh, whose care was wholly employed therein; giving great and most kind entertainment unto the captains; where we lay during the time of our abode in the towne at his own great cost".

During this reign, Fowey seems to have regained a good deal of her prosperity and was vigorously employed in the coastal trade, particularly with Wales. In 1567 the "Russel" of Fowey sailed into Milford with a cargo which included linen, canvas, iron, train oil, newlande (Newfoundland) fish, tar, pitch, and to add a touch of variety, prunes and a quantity of cheese.[4] A number of Fowey vessels loaded small quantities of coal at Swansea between 1580 and 1600, including the "Philip", "Angel", "Michael", "Saviour", "William and John", "Jonas Fortune", "Mondaie" and "Gifte". By the "Peter', a little vessel of 10 tons, Rashleigh sends to London a consignment of "Neweland" fish and a piece of brass ordnance.[5] In November, 1601, the "Dyamont" arrived at Tenby having come from Bordeaux with eight tons of Gascon wine, and a quantity of prunes and walnuts. She was owned by Peter Holmes of Fowey and under the command of James Goodall. At Beaumaris in North Wales, the "Hopewell" of Fowey arrived in May, 1598, with another mixed cargo—bay salt, hops, packing canvas, iron, pitch, pilchard train, figs and prunes. It is to be hoped that the Elizabethan seamen had adequate means of stowing such varied and oleaginous goods! The "Diana", owned by John Rashleigh, was at Beaumaris in February, 1599, unloading a cargo of Spanish iron and wool and train oil.

Large quantities of pilchards were brought into Fowey by the fishermen and it is likely that these were packed into casks in the warehouses and stores which extended from Passage Slip to the present Town Quay. The "train" or "pilchard train oil" so often mentioned was pressed out of the fish when they were packed and was useful in a number of ways, one of the most important being the making of soap. The fish were also pickled or cured and exported in casks to

[1] Cal. S.P. Dom., 502.
[2] Henderson MSS.
[3] Hist. MSS. Comm.: *Hatfield I*, 449.
[4] Welsh Port Books: E. A. Lewis.
[5] P.R.O. Customs Accts. E. 122/202/1.

Brittany and the French ports,[1] (in 1585, Leonard Dare, merchant, had licence to transport 54 casks of pilchards and conger to St. Malo), from whence the Fowey ships brought back wine and canvas. Despite the wars with Spain there were interludes of peace and it is remarkable that even when hostilities were commenced, a certain amount of trading continued. Spain, in particular, could contribute many items which were needed in this country—good quality iron, salt, figs and prunes. In a letter written to Lord Burghley in July, 1586,[2] there is a complaint that one of the officials had been ill-treated for seizing certain quantities of prunes and currants at Fowey.[3] On May 5th, 1580, Thomas Saunders, writing to his father from Spain, says he has helped the owners of a Fowey ship who were in trouble at a Spanish port and continues "come this summer and I will load your ship with oranges and pay your freight". Oranges were selling at 6s. 8d. per thousand in England at this time, figs at 1s. 8d. for twenty pounds.

The Westcountry ports were also increasingly engaged in the fetching from the Newfoundland fishing grounds cod or "stockfish", which found a ready market both in England and Wales and in Catholic countries.

For Customs purposes, Fowey continued to be linked with Plymouth, a port which had now greatly outstripped its Cornish partner.[4] As early as 1559 the Customer and the Controller had confirmed that at the "Towne and Port of Fowey, the Key there is appoynted for the only place of Loding and unloding, charging and discharging of all wares and merchandizes". Actually this "Key" consisted of a number of wharves and was 500 feet in length and 120 feet in width, being "bounded on the South side with a key commonly called Burlaces Key; And on the North side with a Key there commonly called Trevarrock's Key".

Nevertheless there were still many landing places on the river as far up as Lostwithiel. Rashleigh himself had trouble over the right to use one of these landings and years later was involved in a law suit in which one of the witnesses testified that his grandfather, Nicholas Kendall, "and the old Mr. Veal did keep their shipping in Fowey. Upon the return of their voyages they would land their wares at Blohan (Bloughan Moor) viz. wine, iron, salt, etc., and the old John Courtis never durst question them which he would have done had he any title to the landing place for he and my grandfather were bitter enemies".[5]

Like most of the Elizabethans, John Rashleigh, the younger, contrived to take an active interest in everything that went on around him. An account book which he kept during the latter years of this period provides a sketch of his domestic and business occupations. On one day he receives three chests of white sugar out of a captured

[1] Cal. S.P. Dom., 49.
[2] Cal. S.P. Dom., 31.
[3] Cal. S.P. Dom., 12.
[4] The King's Customs: Acton and Maitland.
[5] Henderson MSS.

vessel; on another he sells five tuns of Gascon wine to Thomas Penhillick of Helston. His ships are like those of Antonio in Shakespeare's recent play called the "Merchant of Venice", constantly coming and going. The "Trifle" sets out for Civita Vecchia, laden with pilchards and lead, the "Diana" is freighted for Rouen, brings back more Gascon wine and later makes the crossing to Newfoundland, whilst his "small barke", the "Jonathan", is provisioning for another voyage.[1] In 1601 the "Marygold" brings in a cargo of beer from London which is soon sold.

At home he sets out his great chamber with writing paper and playing cards and hangs his dining chamber with arras, a coarse kind of tapestry.

In the town he busies himself with the accounts of Mr. Basil, vicar of Fowey, and pays the masons for building the houses on his new quay, next to the salt store, besides seeing to the unloading of stone brought down from his son's and Sawle's quarry. When the hot days approach, the sheep out on the new lands of Menabilly are sheared and in winter five acres of woodland are cut down, the timber made into fagots and sold.

Nor is it all plain sailing. The miller who works his windmill over at Polruan is in arrears with rent and the Bonythons, his relatives, are constantly borrowing money to go to London and Oxford. Then there are his expenses in going to London about the Town Cause.

This latter was probably the affair in which both he and William Treffry were implicated in 1596.[2] These two gentlemen, so stalwart in the cause of defending the port of Fowey, absolutely refused to contribute money towards the fortification of the town of Plymouth, thirty miles up the coast. The money was to be raised by means of a tax laid on pilchards brought into Fowey and Rashleigh and Treffry went so far as to persuade other merchants in the town not to pay. Eventually the Privy Council were constrained to send down a letter rebuking them both and ordering them to pay up all arrears or, failing that, to come to London and furnish an explanation.

In another two years they were partners in another cause which also affected the well-being of the town. Although Fowey had for long been merely a part of the possessions of St. Andrew's Priory, it is clear that the inhabitants always enjoyed a good deal of freedom in the management of the town and this may conceivably be set down to the prosperity and standing of the burgesses in the Middle Ages, which enabled them to stand up to the Prior. Their chief officer seems to have taken the title of Mayor from common usage and was addressed as such in numerous proclamations. "Mr. Mohun—the Mayor" is mentioned in a communication written in 1595.

He was, in effect, the "Praepositus" provided for in Prior Theobald's

[1] Henderson MSS.

[2] A.P.C., 349. As late as 1607 the Fowey merchants, John Rashleigh, Peter Holman, John Robyns and Henry Peters were named in a list of those who had refused to pay the tax levied four years previously.

charter, just as the free burgesses were now become "the chief men of the town or parish". The chief men met from time to time to decide how the town should be governed and what monies would be required for various purposes.

In one respect the townspeople were in a very fortunate position, for they had no parish rates to find. When the inhabitants of another Cornish town were having to provide money for the upkeep of roads and the maintenance of the poor, householders at Fowey paid nothing for these services, the cost of which was met from the income of the "Town Lands". These properties are reputed to have been given to the town by Thomas Treffry during the reign of Henry VI: in 1598 they consisted of 24 tenements, including houses, shops, gardens and meadows.[1] Seven of the houses were situated in and near Lostwithiel Street, one adjoined John Rashleigh's house, two lay at the lower end of the Churchyard, three in Fore Street and four in North Street. Of the meadows and gardens, five lay between Lostwithiel Street and Whitehouse, and another half a mile to the north. The position of the two shops is interesting. One stood on the Town Quay, with a dwelling house attached, and was kept by Joan Stephens, widow; the other, kept by Rowland Jennings, stood next to the present "Globe" in Fore Street and its site is still occupied by a shop. Master Jennings could probably have directed an enquiring customer to the "Velgeze"—an open space between the top of Lostwithiel Street and what later became known as Brown's Hill. Adjoining the "Velgeze" were the two houses of Rowland Jacob and another held by John Garland. Only one house and a portion of land are in "Langorthowe" and, from the position of the property, it is clear that the ancient manor of that name impinged on the town and manor of Fowey on the west side.

In 1598 the responsibilities for the Town Lands were transferred by legal deed. The feoffment was between William Treffry, John Rashleigh of Fowey and his namesake of Coombe, John Cobbe the elder, Thomas Peter the elder, Francis Colquite, William Hunckinge, John Davye, William Richard (Rickard) and others on the one hand and Ursula, wife of Thomas Treffry, her son John and daughters, Jane and Emelyn; the younger brothers of William Treffry, namely John, Thomas, Matthew, Abel, Henry and Benjamin; John and Jonathan, sons of John Rashleigh of Fowey; the younger John Rashleigh; Robert, John and Thomas, sons of John Rashleigh of Coombe; Henry Peter the younger, Thomas Peter the younger, John Cobb, John and William Colquite, sons of Francis Colquite, and John Hunckinge, on the other hand.

The duties of the trustees were clearly laid down: they were, after consultation with three or four of the chief men of the town or parish, and with the churchwardens, to spend the rents received from the Town Lands on the relief of the poor in Fowey, the repair of the church, the maintenance of the town's bulwarks and fortifications and

[1] Report of the Charity Commissioners: 1838.

JOHN RASHLEIGH (1554–1620) AND HIS WIFE

(Photo by Graham Gullick, Fowey, from the portrait in the possession of W. S. Rashleigh, Esq.)

in general for the use, profit and commodity of the townsmen or parishioners. When by the process of time only 3 trustees still survived they were to appoint others to make up the original number.

Thus the "chief men" found available not only the tolls of the market and quays, the burial fees, etc., but also a considerable sum from the Town Lands. Although the income from the latter was at first in the hands of the trustees, in the course of a few years it seems to have been included with the tolls and fees and the whole then used for the purposes mentioned above and also for repairing the market house and quay, paving the streets and to settling up with the overseers, the constables and the churchwardens. In other words the trustees became merged with the unofficial body which managed parish and town affairs.

William Treffry was born in 1559, represented Fowey in Parliament from 1584 to 1588 and in the following year married Ursula, daughter of William Tremayne of Upcott in Devon. In 1595 Sir Robert Cecil recommended his appointment as a justice of the peace and in this capacity he examined suspicious characters landing at Fowey and also transmitted to the Queen's advisers in London such intelligence on foreign affairs as might have come to the ears of travellers arriving from abroad. There was actually quite a complicated intelligence system in operation and little happened in the ports of Spain or even at the Spanish Court, of which the English Privy Council was not very soon aware. Treffry was a correspondent of Cecil and many of his letters are preserved in the Hatfield Collection. Possibly the introduction to Sir Robert may have come from a younger brother, Thomas Treffry, a counsellor at law, who was lodging in Fleet Street in March, 1594,[1] and evidently acquainted with the Cecil household. It is easy to imagine Thomas making his way down to the water gate on the Thames and taking a barge to Southwark, where the Globe and the Swan Theatres were attracting great crowds every day. As a lawyer he may even have seen Shakespeare at the opening of "Twelfth Night" in January, 1600, when the play was performed in the great Hall of the Middle Temple.

The elder brother at home had more serious matters to deal with. Although the Armada had been dispersed, Spain had not yet relinquished all hope of invading England, and several expeditions were planned, the rumours of which frequently reached Fowey through the media of roving Irish soldiers of fortune, Flemish and Breton sailors and English merchants. Thus in 1593 some fishermen of Fowey, including one named May, were just outside the harbour entrance when a Spanish ship of war bore down on them and carried them off to St. Anderes in Spain, where they were thrown into prison.[2] The relatives were naturally concerned and employed a Frenchman living in Fowey to seek news of the captives. Unhappily he failed in this task but did bring back some news of the state of preparation of Spanish ships which he duly handed to William Treffry.

[1] Cal. S.P. Dom., 31. [2] Cal. S.P. Dom., 463–4.

In August, 1595, the latter explained to Cecil that "our haven of Fowey being opposed (i.e. opposite) to that part of Brittany possessed by the enemy,[1] we understand daily the affairs of those parts and, I think, sooner than any other part of England": he also mentioned the fact of a Bristol ship being chased into the harbour by two Spanish "fly boats" or frigates.

A few weeks later Treffry was voicing the general alarm of the district at the presence at Blavet of a Spanish squadron,[2] the Commander of which boasted that they would burn all the country as far up as Dartmouth. (That the enemy's threat was no idle one, nor the fears of the Fowey men unjustified, may be seen by the actual raid which the Spaniards made on Mousehole and Penzance this very same year.) Treffry also made the sensible suggestion that some men of war might be stationed off Blavet to intercept and capture the ships which brought victuals from Spain for the garrison there. Among other intelligence is the news of the arrival of a Dutchman in the harbour after a running fight with four galleys and a great Biscayen ship seven leagues south-west of the Lizard.[3]

There were also religious intrigues to be watched: the Jesuits in particular seemed to attach great value to the use of propaganda to disseminate Catholic views, and tried many devices to get their letters and pamphlets smuggled into England. When a little Irish bark of 16 tons was driven into Fowey harbour one Friday in August, 1599,[4] it was discovered that she carried a great store of swords and some French pistols. Treffry suspecting that they were designed for the use of the Irish rebels, gave orders for the arms to be sold publicly in the town and instructed that a more thorough search be made. Surely enough, hidden in a cask of salt, was found a quantity of Popish books and papers. Another suspicious factor was the presence on board of a man named Autson who claimed to be merely the agent of a St. Malo merchant, although Treffry found him to be of gentlemanly bearing and fluent in the Spanish and Italian tongues. The Privy Council were informed and, being undecided, deputed Doctor Julius Cæsar, a relative of the vicar of Lostwithiel, to go into the legal aspects.[5] He advised that Autson—believed to be a seminary priest—should abide the rigours of the law but that as the cargo was being sent by a merchant in a friendly alien port to a town (Waterford) within the Queen's domain, the Irish vessel should be freed. No doubt there was more in it than met the eye—the original idea would seem to have been to put the priest ashore with his papers at some prearranged spot where Catholic friends would have been ready to take him to a safe place—perhaps to one of the "priest's holes" with their secret panels and doors, occasionally found in old mansions.

[1] Hist. MSS. Comm.: *Hatfield, V*, 322.
[2] Hist. MSS. Comm.: *Hatfield, V*, 360.
[3] Hist. MSS. Comm.: *Hatfield, V*, 443.
[4] Hist. MSS. Comm.: *Hatfield, V*, 326.
[5] Cal. S.P. Dom., 325.

In the same month it was decided to send a small vessel to Brest, Blavet and finally to the Groyne to spy out what the Spanish fleet were up to, and a Fowey ship, commanded by Captain John Fleming, was fitted for that purpose.[1] She had fifteen men aboard but was chased by a Spanish man-of-war and forced to return with but very scanty news. However, £16. 18s. 10d. was paid to the master to cover his expenses and it was only some time later when the Fowey man was fitting out for a trip to the Straits that it was discovered he had made use of his mission to rob a poor Breton fishing vessel—a throw back to the heyday of piracy !. Perhaps Fleming remembered what had happened to Edward Rawes nearly twenty years before.

More sinister is the hint that there was someone in Fowey ready to play the traitor.[2] An agent in Spain described how one Richard Cooke (who dared not show his face in England, where he was suspected of coining) had been coming and going freely in Spain until a time came when the Spaniards decided to use him. He was approached by Don Juan d'Idiaques, who offered him employment to go to Fowey in Cornwall, taking ten engineers with him to spy out the place and confer with someone they knew. Cooke said that he refused and was then put into prison and endured such misery that he finally agreed to the plan, which included the burning of the Queen's storehouses at Fowey. However, he managed to communicate the plot to an English secret agent in Spain, to whom he also promised to disclose more information when he arrived in England. Maybe there was some truth in Cooke's tale, but there is also the possibility that he was playing a double game.

Carew, writing about 1585 (although his Survey was not published until 1602), says that Fowey harbour[3]

> "is guarded with Block-Houses, and that on the town's side as also the town itself, fortified and fenced with ordinance. The commendation of which industry is principally due to the providence and direction of Mr. Wil. Treffry, a Gent. that hath vowed his rare gifts of learning, wisdom and courage to the good of his country and made proof thereof in many occurrents".

Of Hall Walk and the view of the harbour, Carew has this to say: "It is cut out in the side of a steep hill whose foot the salt water washeth, evenly levelled to serve for bowling, floored with sand for soaking up the rain, closed with two thorn hedges and banked with sweet scenting flowers. It wideneth to a sufficient breadth for the march of five or six in front and extendeth to not much less than half a London mile: neither doth it lead wearisomely forthright but yieldeth varied and yet not over-busy turnings, as the ground's opportunity affordeth, which advantage increaseth the prospect and is converted on the fore side into platforms for the planting or Ordinance and the walkers sitting: and on the bank part into Summer houses for their more private retreat and recreation.

[1] Cal. S.P. Dom., 121.
[2] Cal. S.P. Dom., 8.
[3] Carew: *Survey of Cornwall* (1602).

In passing along, your eyes shall be called away from guiding your feet, to descry by their farthest kenning the vast Ocean sparkled with ships that continually this way trade, forth and back, to most quarters of the world. Nearer home they take view of all sized cocks, barges and fisher boats hovering on the coast. Again contracting your sight to a more narrower scope, it lighteth on the fair and commodious haven, where the tide daily presenteth his double service of flowing and ebbing, to carry and re-carry whosoever the Inhabitants shall be pleased to charge him withall, and his creeks (like a wanton lover) fold about the land with many embracing arms.

This walk is guarded upon the one side by Portruan, on the other side by Bodynick, fishing villages. Behind, the rising hill beareth off the cold Northern blasts: before the town of Foy subjecteth his whole length and breadth to your overlooking: and directly under you ride the home and foreign shipping, both of these in so near a distance that without troubling the passer or borrowing Stentor's voice, you may from thence not only call to, but confrere with any in the said town or shipping."

SIXTEENTH CENTURY BRASS IN ST. FIMBARRUS CHURCH—
ALICE RASHLEIGH (DIED 1591)
(*Photo : British Museum*)

CHAPTER 6

(i) General

By the end of Queen Elizabeth's long reign the whole county of Cornwall was well prepared against invasion. Years of mustering, drilling and inspection had wrought the Trained Bands and individual companies such as that of John Rashleigh at Fowey into a reasonably efficient force with leaders drawn from the well-to-do merchants and landowners. However, by this time it was evident that Spain was weary of the idea of invading England.

But if the landsman drew breath again and returned his pike or halberd into the parish store, the seaman and shipowner gained no respite, for at sea a new menace had arisen. Algerian and Tunisian galleys now drove out of the calm waters of the Mediterranean and attacked merchant ships in the Bay of Biscay and even within sight of the English coast.[1] In 1608 it was estimated that five hundred of these craft hunted in English waters and at one time they dared to use the island of Lundy, off the Devon coast, as a base. Cornish ports and fishing villages were constantly alarmed and in 1625 Penzance petitioned for a fort to protect the town. Next year it was reported that thirty Turkish sail were off the Spanish coast and that they intended to attack Pendennis and Fowey[2]. The Mayor of Plymouth wrote to London begging definite authority to collect money required for suppressing pirates from the merchants and shipowners of Fowey and other places.[3] Perhaps he remembered the unpopularity of the Pilchard Tax in Fowey a generation before: in any case, the measures taken against the pirates were ineffective. By 1631 it could be said of Fowey that it was "so decayed in shipping, mariners, fishermen and all sorts of people living by trade being spoiled by Turks and pirates,[4] and daily sustaining infinite other losses at sea that through poverty, many people have abandoned the town and gone to other places to seek their living", and three years later "it hath now lost the lustre of its former greatness by reason of the great piracies, spoils and decays it hath often sustained".

A Fowey seaman named John Davies was among the crews of the "Nicholas" and "George Bonaventure"[5] which were boarded and surprised by pirates in November, 1621. The Englishmen were taken to Algiers and sold into captivity. In such miserable conditions it was not unusual to find a small number of captives who had been prevailed upon to change their religion in return for a certain amount of freedom, but Davies must have been surprised to recognise one of these "renegades" as a Fowey man named John Goodall. Goodall

[1] Cal. S.P. Venetian, 192.
[2] Cal. S.P. Dom., 231.
[3] Cal. S.P. Dom., 112.
[4] Hamilton Jenkin: *Cornish Seafarers* (1932).
[5] *Purches His Pilgrimes*, 151 *et seq.*

had adopted a Turkish name and was then employed as master of a ship being fitted out in the port. The owner of this ship wanted a navigator and Goodall was pleased when Davies recommended a fellow slave named Rawlins. Eventually the pirate ship sailed with Davies, Rawlins and fourteen other European slaves aboard, together with a Turkish crew of sixty-three. Once at sea Rawlins plotted a daring escape and at a moment when the master and most of the Turks had gone below he gave a prearranged signal and the slaves rushed to batten down the hatches. At the same time Davies seized a culverin and fired at those of the enemy who remained on deck. Some of the Turks were flung overboard, others taken prisoner and the Englishmen headed the ship for Plymouth, where they arrived safely. It is comforting to know that John Goodall the renegade earnestly desired to be reconciled to the Christian religion and was presumably restored to his family at Fowey.

Many years later—in 1669—another Fowey man, Philip Major, was redeemed from captivity at Algiers, but not before a considerable ransom had been paid.[1] As for the horror with which seamen regarded this fate, there is the statement of a master mariner who brought his ship into Fowey after becoming separated from the rest of his convoy—"Having tasted of the cruelty of the merciless Turk by whom I have been in captivity, if I should ever again come into their hands there were no hope of redemption".[2]

Charles FitzGeoffrey, born at Fowey in 1575, the author of a life of Sir Francis Drake and a poet of some distinction, had a sermon published in 1636 entitled "Compassion towards captives, chiefly towards our brethren and countrymen who are in miserable bondage in Barbary".

According to one account, a ship owned by John Rashleigh was taken by these pirates but was later re-taken by Capt. Whitbourne of Dartmouth, who complained that he received neither thanks nor reward for this action. Possibly Rashleigh was by this time less concerned with shipping matters and devoting his attention to Menabilly and his other lands in Cornwall. Out at Menabilly a fine new mansion was nearing completion—a fitting residence for the prosperous merchant venturer who had now turned landed gentleman. At Fowey he provided almshouses for twelve "decayed widows". This group of dwellings, built into the hillside close to the church, still fulfils the founder's intention and adds a touch of serene beauty to the town when in season the whitewashed walls are relieved by a gay show of fuchsias and geraniums.

John Rashleigh died on the 12th May, 1624.[3] His elder son John died nine days later and the estates passed to the second son, Jonathan, then aged 32.

The following year was a time of great mortality in the closely packed town: many inhabitants died from the plague and the burial

[1] Cal. S.P. Dom., 454.

[2] Cal. S.P. Dom., 448. (1655).

[3] Henderson MSS.

register is sadly full of entries during the winter of 1625–6.[1] Towards the end the burial of the Vicar is recorded. Plymouth also suffered badly from this visit of the plague and the outbreak is usually attributed to the billeting in these parts of hundreds of ill-clad, starving English soldiers evacuated from La Rochelle, where they had vainly attempted to aid the French Huguenots.

On November 26th, 1625, some Huguenot ships dropped anchor in Fowey harbour and were soon followed in by several ships belonging to the King of France.[2] It was a dangerous and delicate position—a sort of cat and mouse game—and Sir John Eliot rightly considered that, should Catholic and Protestant come to blows at Fowey, the town would stand exposed to much danger. Alarm also filled the townspeople and the Trained Bands were hurriedly mustered. The French Admiral was warned to desist in his threats against the Huguenots whilst in English waters and was also reminded that Fowey was no healthy place owing to the pestilence. By early December the Rochelle squadron was safely away to the westward and the danger averted.

As a result of this incident, a petition was submitted by the inhabitants of Fowey to the Deputy Lieutenants of Cornwall,[3] drawing attention to the fact that Fowey, a safe port to receive a great fleet of ships, was open and unfortified. Meanwhile, in every letter to London, Captain Bonython,[4] a relative of the Rashleighs, was anticipating matters by persistently begging for command of the proposed new fort at Fowey. In the end, nothing came of the scheme—probably owing to lack of funds.

A brief spell of privateering followed. Ships were fitted out in many ports and granted "letters of marque". The largest ship from Fowey was the "Trial" of 150 tons; the "Sparke", next in size, was commanded by John Sparke, a cousin of Jonathan Rashleigh and member of a notable seafaring family of Plymouth. The remaining Fowey privateers were small craft—the "Hopewell" of 30 tons, the "Barnard" of 60 tons and the "Mary", owned by Peter Holman and others, of 25 tons burden. In addition, two Frenchmen, probably Huguenot refugees, took out letters of marque from Fowey in 1629 and 1630: Captain Daniel Galliard Le Cave sailed in the "Grace of God" and Peter Neau in the "Barnaby". Their success as a whole was meagre—the prizes often being small and difficult to dispose of. In the autumn of 1626, for instance, a Fowey privateer sent a small carvel manned with a prize crew right across to the Irish coast in an endeavour to sell her cargo of salt.[5]

[1] Cann: *St. Fimbarrus Church.*
[2] Cal. S.P. Dom., 160.
[3] Cal. S.P. Dom., 190.
[4] Cal. S.P. Dom., 214, 282.
[5] Cal. S.P. Ireland, 178. It was off the coast of Ireland that a Fowey fishing vessel, master John Weymouth, met with the starving mutineers of Hudson's "Discovery" and piloted that ship into Berehaven on 6th September, 1610. "Henry Hudson": L. Powys: Bodley Head, 1927.

The account book and journal of Jonathan Rashleigh provide some details of his domestic affairs.[1] Between travelling up to London to represent Fowey in Parliament, he arranged for a tutor to teach his daughter Alice to sing and play the viol, and in 1637 sent his son John to Oxford with instructions that he should have a poor scholar to wait on him, that he should learn to dance, and above all avoid lewd company. Like most Cornish squires of the period he engaged in law suits—one with his relative Simon Clotworthy over a will made by John Rashleigh forty years previously.

Another native of Fowey, a contemporary of Jonathan Rashleigh, was at this time dwelling in New England. Hugh Peter (or Peters as he is more generally known) was the son of Thomas Dykewood the younger, who had married in 1594 Martha, daughter of John Treffry of Place.[2] The Dykewoods are believed to have been refugees from the Low Countries and they lived at Hillhay, half a mile out of Fowey. They had connections with the family of Peter of Exeter and the elder Dykewood, who was a prominent merchant at Fowey, assumed the name of Peter some time before 1586. He had married in 1568 Alice Penheale (Penhale, a small farm in the parish).

Hugh studied for his degree at Cambridge, subsequently taught at a school in Laindon, Essex, and was ordained in 1621. He became curate at Rayleigh in the same county but was suspended in 1627 on account of his preaching, and crossed over to the Netherlands. Two years later he was in England and subscribed £50 to the Massachusetts Bay Company. Returning to Holland he was appointed minister of the English church at Rotterdam. In 1631 he wrote a pamphlet, containing an account of the battles then being fought in the Low Countries, which he dedicated to his cousins, John Treffry and John Trefusis.[3]

In 1635 he followed in the tracks of the Pilgrim Fathers and emigrated to New England, where he was appointed pastor of the church at Salem. Here Peters became prominent in politics, religious affairs and commercial undertakings. At that time a movement was afoot to found a college in New England, although the site had not been decided upon.[4] Peters was appointed one of the trustees for the new undertaking and he went to some trouble to persuade the committee to utilise some land near Salem with a frontage of three quarters of a mile along the rocky shore of Massachusetts Bay: at the same time he appears to have bought a house in Salem to temporarily house the college.

The proposed site lay alongside land which had been granted to Peters and was within a mile of the new settlement named "Foy" (or Marblehead). The latter name was eventually adopted for the

1 Henderson MSS.

2 Marriage Registers: Fowey (pub. Phillimore).

3 B.M. 9406, b. 27.

4 *The Founding of Harvard College:* Morrison (1936), pub. Harvard Press. Today Marblehead has a population of nearly 10,000 engaged in shoe manufacturing, boat building and fishing.

THE NOAH'S ARK—SIXTEENTH CENTURY HOUSE IN THE FORE STREET

(Etching by George Kitto, Fowey)

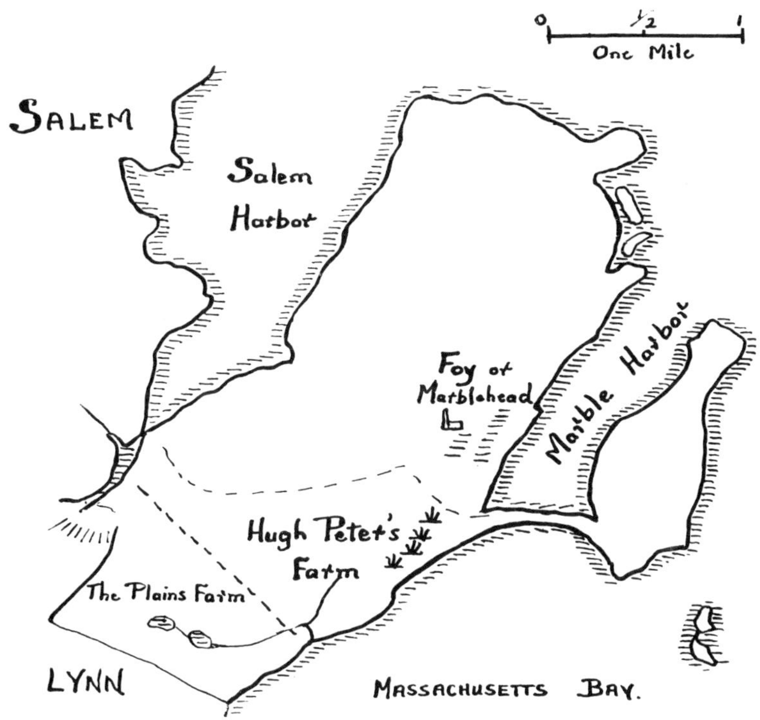

SKETCH MAP SHOWING THE SETTLEMENT OF MARBLEHEAD, *alias* "FOY" AND HUGH PETER'S FARM

(From "The Founding of Harvard College" by S. E. Morison.—Harvard University Press)

growing town and Marblehead became a flourishing sea-port in the colonial period and claims to have been the birthplace of the American Navy. There seems reason to believe that Hugh Peters, a Fowey man, was concerned with this early settlement which adjoined his small estate and that but for some fortuitous circumstance there would have been a "Foy" in the United States.

But the site advocated by Peters was rejected and the college named after John Harvard was established instead at Newtown. Peters became one of the Overseers and when in 1641 he was sent to England on behalf of the colonists, one of his tasks was to collect money for the new school. He was still here when the Civil War broke out in the following year. Without question he joined the side of Parliament and his fiery, eloquent sermons on the eve of a battle or siege did a great deal to inspire their troops.

Jonathan Rashleigh, on the other hand, was a staunch Royalist from the start. When recruiting for the new volunteer army was progressing in Cornwall during the first year of the struggle, he lent £104 in silver plate to help in the maintenance of the new corps and stood surety for another £600 worth of plate which his neighbours contributed.

Whilst the majority of the Cornish gentlemen decided, like Rashleigh, to support the King, there were many who joined the opposite side, one of the foremost being Lord Robartes of Lanhydrock, later Governor of Plymouth. The merchants of Plymouth came out strongly for the Parliamentary side and the stout defence of that city throughout the war contributed to Cromwell's ultimate success.

John Treffry, unlike his neighbour, belonged to one of those unhappy families whose members found themselves divided. His nephew, John Trefusis,[1] who sat in Parliament, was wholeheartedly for the constitution and earlier in the year was one of those who signed a petition urging a stricter observance of the sabbath, together with other improvements in the religious field. His cousin, Hugh Peters, had joined the Parliamentary side. Even his brother-in-law, Henry Stephens, seems to have supported the same party. Hence it would not have been at all surprising to find Treffry joining his friends and relatives, yet when war broke out he was active in organizing the defences of Fowey—for the king. With a colonel's commission he supervised the setting up of twenty guns which were to defend the harbour—most of them probably relics of the preparations made against the Spaniards some fifty years earlier.

During the first two years of the war the Royalists managed to export a considerable amount of tin from Cornwall to France,[2] where Queen Henrietta Maria was relentless in her efforts to find assistance and funds for her husband, and although most of the cargoes left from the more westerly of the Cornish ports, Fowey seems to have had some part in it and to have been a haven for the privateers which

[1] Coate: *Cornwall in the Civil War.*
[2] Coate: *Cornwall in the Civil War.*

the Royalists fitted out to defy the Lord Admiral, the Earl of Warwick, who was based on Plymouth. Nevertheless, the south-east of Cornwall was rather out of the limelight after the first excitement had died down and the inhabitants of Fowey, no doubt, read the news-sheets which came down from Oxford and London, and discussed the latest rumours on the quays and in the taverns, with the detached interest of those who are not actually at close hand with war.

In the middle of summer, 1644, things began to take a more serious turn, so far as the West was concerned. The Earl of Essex, partly on the advice of Lord Robartes, whose new house and estate lay close to the upper reaches of the river Fowey, brought the Parliament's army westward to relieve besieged Plymouth. Sir Richard Grenville, who had once represented Fowey at Westminster and now commanded the scanty force of Cornish militia, retreated into Cornwall, and Essex foolishly followed him. On the 2nd August, 1644, the Royalists in Fowey were dismayed to see armed men, detached from Essex's force, then at Bodmin, riding into the town. Soon the larger houses in the port were selected for billets and the fortifications around the harbour taken over and manned by the Parliamentarians. On the same day Essex moved his quarters from Bodmin to Lostwithiel, as the enemy had already reached Launceston, but two days later a small Cornish boy told the Royalists that "there were a many gay men in Lord Mohun's house at Boconnoc", with the result that a party hastily set out from Lanreath, slipped through park and woods, surprised and took prisoner several important Parliamentary officers and seized the mansion.

By the 11th August Sir Richard Grenville was ordered to advance from the west and this he did, occupying first Bodmin and then Lanhydrock. Essex grimly held on at Lostwithiel, evidently hoping to last out until a relief column reached him or until it became possible for sufficient ships to arrive to evacuate his army from Fowey to Plymouth. Unfortunately for him, the former was waylaid by the king's forces and scattered, whilst his own neglect in not keeping the east bank of the river Fowey sufficiently guarded made the second alternative hopeless. On the 13th of the month the enemy seized the ford over Penpoll creek in the parish of St. Veep and next day entered the gates of the Mohuns' old house at Hall, above Bodinnick Ferry. Most important, they also succeeded in reaching Polruan and seizing the blockhouse which, situated on a point of rock near the harbour entrance, commands the entry to the port. A battery here would have found a sitting target in any vessel, deeply laden with men and stores, trying to work out to sea.

Let Richard Symonds, an officer in the king's army who was present and kept a diary of the happenings,[1] continue the story:—

"Satterday 17th August. His Majestie, attended with his owne troope, Queene's troope, commanded by Captain Brett and sixty commanded troopers, went to Cliffe, a parish on this side of the

[1] Diary of Richard Symonds: Camden Soc. (1859).

river that runs to Listithiel, where Colonel Lloyd, the Quarter-Master Generall's regiment lyes to keepe the passe. The enemye keepes the passe on the other side at the parish of Glant. From thence his Majestie went to Lanteglos to the manor howse belonging to the Lord Mohun just over against Foye, where his royall person ventred to goe into a walke there which is within halfe musket shott from Foye, where a poore fisherman was killed in looking over, at the same time that his Majestie was in the walke and in the place where the King a little afore passed by. A little below are some of our great pieces that command the towne of Foye and beyond that, a fort of ours that commands the entrance into the mouth of Foye haven in the parish of Perwyn [Polruan], this howse and walke being gotten by the vigilant care of Sir Jacob Astley, Major-Generall of his Majestie's army, three or four days before, which is now mainteyned by 200 commanded foot of ours under Sir Jacob's command."

Meanwhile the desperate and starving Parliamentarians were now shut up in a narrow strip of land extending from Fowey to Lostwithiel, for their adversaries had seized Par and St. Blazey. Although both sides were short of provisions for the men, and forage for their horses, Essex's army was by far the worse off, since a great part of the Fowey peninsula consisted of woodland and bracken and contained few farms to provide sustenance for the ten thousand dispirited and harassed soldiers. During these last days they seized everything they could lay hands upon.[1] Jonathan Rashleigh suffered the heaviest and although the manuscript notes of his losses are possibly exaggerated, they are probably correct enough so far as the livestock and foodstuffs are concerned. On his new estate at Menabilly he reckons he lost five hundred large sheep and one hundred lambs, eighteen draught oxen, twenty milch cows and a bull, thirty fatted bullocks, sixty store bullocks, forty horses and eighty hogs. In addition, they took a whole year's supply of butter, cheese, beer, wine, beef, pork and bacon, as well as corn and "my hay, grasses, gardens, orchards all spoyled". His house in Fowey, next to the old gateway at the bottom of Lostwithiel Street, they seem to have used as billets, for Rashleigh reckons that 1,500 bushels of salt were taken out of the cellars, as well as other goods. On the 16th August, Essex wrote that the country people were violent against his men and that if any scouts or soldiers fell into their hands they were "more bloody than the enemy".

During the next fortnight the fighting continued intermittently around the town of Lostwithiel and at one stage the Royalists nearly succeeded in blowing up their enemy's ammunition train, the burning fuse only being discovered when it was two inches away from the powder! On the 30th August, Essex held a council of war and decided to allow the horse to attempt to break through the Royalist positions whilst the foot should fall back on Fowey, Menabilly and Polkerris and be evacuated to Plymouth. At seven o'clock that evening two

[1] Coate: *Cornwall in the Civil War.*

deserters made their way into the king's camp and revealed these plans. The Royalist parties at St. Blazey, Polruan and St. Veep were warned of what was afoot and whilst the army was ordered to stand by, fifty musketeers were stationed in a cottage between Lostwithiel and Boconnoc. Perhaps the king's men were too confident, perhaps they assumed that the enemy would never make the attempt in the black and misty night—at any event, two thousand Parliamentary horsemen, no doubt with their horses' hoofs well padded, trotted past the cottage without a shot being fired at them. When their escape was discovered, a small force was sent in pursuit, but by the evening of the 31st August they had safely reached Saltash, having beaten off their attackers. On the morning of the next day, a Sunday, they were riding safely into the town of Plymouth.

Early on the Saturday morning the Parliamentary foot were observed leaving Lostwithiel and marching along the road and over the adjoining fields leading back to Fowey, so that they had the river on their flank; their baggage and artillery had started off in the night and soon found themselves in difficulties—the guns and heavy waggons sticking in the mud.

Essex himself said:—

"The wayes were so extreme foul with excessive rain and the harness for the drought horses so rotten that in the marching off, we lost three demi-culverins and a brass piece, and yet the Major General (Skippon) fought in the rear all day, he being loth to lose those pieces, thirty horses were put to each of them, but could not move them, the night was so foul and the soldiers so tired that they were hardly to be kept to their colours."[1]

By breakfast-time the Royalist advance guard were entering Lostwithiel and hanging on to the heels of the retreating enemy, while the King with two troops of horse, crossed the Fowey river on the south side of the town and came upon a cartload of muskets and another great pile abandoned by the roadside. Later they passed five cannon, whereof two were very long ones, which had resisted all Skippon's efforts, and then caught up with their own forlorn hope and continued the advance together. For two miles the pursuit continued, the Parliamentarians resisting stoutly, their musketeers stopping from time to time to set up their rests in the muddy ground and aiming a volley of shot at the charging Cavaliers.

Meanwhile, Essex had reached the old hill fort at Castle Dore and there he determined to make a last stand. Two of his ordnance officers wished to know what should be done with the ammunition train and the General first advised that it should be taken on to Menabilly but if that could not be managed, to draw the army up around the powder waggons and make conditions with the enemy or threaten to blow up the whole train. As it was, the artillery were placed in the centre, Essex's own regiment and Colonel Butler's musketeers on the left towards Par, whilst the regiments of Colonel Weare, Lord Robartes

[1] *Lives of the Admirals:* Deane.

and Colonel Bartlett formed the right towards Golant. All through the Saturday afternoon and early evening they stood at bay, knowing full well what the end would be. In broad daylight they behaved like men and although extremely weary, withstood two charges in the early afternoon, but as the darkness came on Colonel Weare's regiment on the Golant side lost heart—men straggled away and soon the whole flank was in disorder. Soon after daylight on the Sunday morning, Essex saw that it would be only a matter of hours before the end came and with Lord Robartes and one or two officers, he slipped back upon Fowey and went aboard a fishing boat which carried the party to Plymouth.

The Earl has been condemned for not staying with his men, yet it is difficult to see what good this would have done, and Parliament later exonerated him and testified to their confidence in his leadership. The great fault seems to have been that he allowed his army to be drawn down into Cornwall in the first place.

Essex and Robartes having departed, Major-General Skippon was left in command. He called a council of his officers on the Sunday morning and suggested that an effort should be made to break through the enemy's lines, as the horse had so successfully done on the Friday night. But the men were completely exhausted and the council decided to surrender. Next day the formalities were completed—all fit men were to be allowed to march to Poole and Wareham, with an escort to see them on their way, and all officers above the rank of corporal were to keep their arms. The sick and wounded were to be convoyed into Fowey and there be put aboard ship for Plymouth.

So, in a downpour of rain on the Monday afternoon, the remnants of the Parliamentary army marched away from Castle Dore—"prest all of a heap like sheep—so dirty and dejected as was rare to see, none of them except some few of their officers that did look any of us in the face". Their fate was a miserable one, for after being abused and reviled by the Royalist rank and file and plundered of cloaks, hats and coats (despite the king's orders to the contrary), they suffered worse when they reached Lostwithiel. Even their boots and meagre supplies of food were taken from them. The Parliamentary journals of the time are filled with accounts of their sad plight—of the 6,000 men who left Castle Dore, only a thousand reached Poole.

So all Cornwall became the king's again, but only for a short interval. In 1646 General Fairfax was steadily marching down through the West Country and meeting with little opposition from the exhausted and defeated Royalists.

The next few years were troublesome ones for both Rashleigh and Treffry. The former had given heavily to the king's funds at the beginning of the war, lost much stock and valuables when the Parliamentarians occupied Menabilly in 1644 and was now forced to pay large indemnities to the victors. He was no longer permitted to sit in the House of Commons but by reason of the property he owned in Fowey could still command the voters. Consequently there was the strange position of the Commonwealth candidate, Gregory Clement, a Plymouth merchant, having to beg the defeated Royalist, Jonathan Rashleigh, for his support. In 1650, for not paying a debt alleged against him, the latter was imprisoned for some months in St. Mawes Castle. John Treffry escaped more lightly because of his connection with Hugh Peters and John Trefusis, and in 1654 his estate was cleared of any claims upon it.

As for Peters, he had been present at the trial of Charles I and in 1650 was appointed Chaplain to the Council of State. In this capacity he regularly preached before Cromwell. In 1654 his elder brother, Thomas Peters, died at Mylor, of which parish he had been minister since 1628. He had gone to New England during the Civil War but had returned to Cornwall in 1646.

During the Dutch War of 1651–4,[1] Fowey was used as a base for the new frigates which were being built for the Navy and some fine prizes were brought in by the "Hopewell", "Warwick" and others. Nor were the privateers idle. They captured many Dutch wine ships and were evidently never at a loss for men: a complaint went up from Plymouth that the seamen "came tippling on shore and then marched away in their mad fits, some to their homes and some to privateers at Fowey". The latter were occasionally a source of trouble to the local inhabitants, an instance being that of Captain Diamond who, in 1655, fitted out a ship called the "Little Diamond" as a privateer without obtaining the necessary letters of marque and then sailed from Fowey with twenty sheep stolen from the people there.[2]

But if the privateers sometimes manned their ships with runaway Navy men, they themselves received the attentions of the press gang at times. The same year no less than a hundred men at Fowey[3] who had been in privateers and lay temporarily idle were pressed for the Navy, and in May a lively picture is painted in the official records of a meeting at Fowey at which the representatives of two parishes failed to make an appearance and following which the Press Officer took matters into his own hands, hired a boat and manning her with musketeers, sent her along the coast towards Coombe and the Gribbin.[4] Meanwhile, another party set out to scour the cliffs. Sure enough, they found the poor wretches, hiding in caves and behind rocks. There were doleful partings from wives and sweethearts in Fowey that day. Fishermen were also impressed, although the local Justices were sympathetic and endeavoured to have them exempted.

During the Commonwealth the affairs of the town and parish devolved upon the merchants, yeomen and tradesmen, the names of Rashleigh and Treffry being noticeably absent. In 1653 the committee which elected a Registrar consisted of Philip Tingcombe, Nicholas Hicks, Richard Cotton, Mark Collins, Lewis Colquite, Thomas Rose, Humphry Smith, Peter Baker,[5] William Donkyn,

[1] Cal. S.P. Dom., 93/4, 476.
[2] Cal. S.P. Dom., 135.
[3] Cal. S.P. Dom., 158.
[4] Cal. S.P. Dom., 281, 338.
[5] Cann: *St. Fimbarrus Church.*

MENABILLY—PROPERTY OF THE RASHLEIGH FAMILY SINCE THE TIME OF QUEEN ELIZABETH
(Photo by Graham Gullick, Fowey)

Ambrose Sawle, Reginald Dyfield, Jonathan Castell, David Toms and Gregory Giles. Philip Tingcombe held the rank of captain and in April, 1655, was instructed to appoint guards and watches at Fowey for its better security.[1] Hicks, together with John Major and Henry Stephens, were merchants, as also was Stephen Epps, whose business sometimes took him as far as Rotterdam. From another source the names of some of the tradesmen in Fowey at this time are given: John Ede, cordwainer; Richard Jacob, tanner; James Dingle, tailor; Thomas Hewitt, glazier. Henry Puckey was a "saynor", that is he managed and worked a pilchard seine-net and boat. John Nicholls and Francis Lambe were husbandmen.

The "mayor" of Fowey—Mr. Peter—was involved in an affair during September, 1658, which certainly showed that he was a man of spirit.[2] It seems that pipe, or barrel staves, being urgently required for the use of the Navy, an officer had been sent down from Plymouth to board a vessel then lying at Fowey and reported to be laden with staves. Whether this officer performed his duties with tact is not certain, but the Mayor, who was owner of the staves and also of the ship, resented the visit and threatened to throw the official overboard if he dared remove the cargo. The Navy Commissioners were accordingly requested to send a messenger down to bring Peter before them for punishment "as a stubborn knave and thus strike terror for the future into such malignant fellows".

But Cromwell was dying, the Navy Commissioners had more pressing business and it is unlikely that the mayor of Fowey was again disturbed. In 1660 Charles II landed at Dover and shortly afterwards was crowned at Westminster Abbey. The Commonwealth was at an end and many of those who shortly before had been high in office and dignity were now put on trial. On the 16th October in this year Hugh Peters was taken to Charing Cross for execution.[3] His death was a barbarous one and a few minutes before the end he was forced to witness the execution of one who had been his friend. To the sheriff standing by Peters exclaimed "Sir, you have slain one of the servants of God before mine eyes, and have made me to behold it on purpose to terrify and discourage me, but God hath made it an ordinance to me for my strengthening and encouragement!" Next day Gregory Clement, late member of Parliament for Fowey and one of those who had signed the death warrant of Charles I, met a similar end.

And so Jonathan Rashleigh, now well over seventy years of age, lived to see the king's restoration and took his place in the first parliament of Charles II. For the remainder of his long life he seems to have lived peaceably enough at Menabilly, although the lazy thunder of cannon must have scared that household one summer day in 1667.[4] The firing came from the direction of Fowey and from out on the headland could be seen a fleet of over fifty ships flying Dutch colours. Twenty-nine merchant ships, homeward bound from Virginia, were

[1] Cal. S.P. Dom., 302.
[2] Cal. S.P. Dom., 455.
[3] Coate: *Cornwall in the Civil War.*
[4] Cal. S.P. Dom., 213 *et seq.*

sheltering in Fowey harbour, having had news that the Dutch fleet under De Ruyter was off Plymouth and bearing to the westward. The countryside was roused and Sir Jonathan Trelawny lost no time in bringing his troop of horse and a thousand militia into the town. The guns from the merchant ships were taken ashore and mounted in batteries so that within a short time the defences were increased to a hundred guns, three thousand men and two troops of horse. On the Wednesday afternoon the enemy fleet was off Fowey and De Ruyter sent in a small vessel or galliot to sound the depth of water at the harbour entrance. She was encountered with such heavy fire from the land batteries that she heeled over to the wind and turned back to rejoin the main fleet. Altogether, the guns on shore did good work, placing their shot in the Dutch hulls and damaging their rigging. The enemy replied and managed to kill one old lady in the town but most of their cannon balls seem to have lodged in the rocks, where they occasionally come to light today. Soon afterwards the whole fleet drew off and the Earl of Bath and Sir Thomas Allen, after maintaining the precautions for another week, gave orders for the Trained Bands to be dismissed and the ships to take their guns on board. By the 30th August the Virginia convoy had left Fowey and passed safely up Channel.

What of the town itself in these days? In 1684 the burgesses drew attention to the decayed state of the fort (St. Catherine's Castle) and of the two blockhouses. Only two years previously Dr. Young of Plymouth had visited the port and found:—

> "A very pretty harbour, much like Dartmouth, hath a narrow going in but a great inlet.[1] In the Dutch warr, a fleet of Virginia men saved themselves here and some of them ran soe farr up ye River as 2 or 3 myles. The town is very small—many Ruined houses in it, hath a pleasant walk on the sea side from ye town to the outpoynt, by ye way there is an old castle wch at the distance of about 100 yards makes the distinctest eccho I have ever heard, ye castle (i.e. the Fowey blockhouse) doth stand under the hill on wch ye walk is and the eccho perfect and distinct in ye space of 7 yards only."

Possibly this is the "rampire called Jericho" which was mentioned in a lease a few years previously; if so, the townsmen had a pretty sense of humour.[2] The blockhouse was then three centuries old and stood in a very exposed position, great seas lashing against its rocky base in winter so that it hardly needed the noise of trumpets to complete its downfall!

A chart made a few years later shows the old disused chapel on St. Catherine's Point as a low building with a ruined tower arising from the centre[3]—it would seem that it had been converted into a dwelling house for a time and that later its stones were used to renovate

[1] J.R.I.C, 1878.
[2] Henderson MSS.
[3] Chart by Capt. Greenvile Collins: a copy is in the Harbour Master's Office, Fowey.

HUGH PETERS (1598–1660)—CHAPLAIN TO OLIVER CROMWELL

(Photo by Graham Gullick, Fowey, from the original portrait painted at Charing Cross in 1660, *now in the possession of Mrs. A. Treffry, Place)*

the castle below. The windmill is also depicted with sails intact, a fine mark for passing ships. Farther up the river is a house at the head of Caffa Mill Pill and at its entrance a partly-submerged obstruction labelled "Foy Rock". Most interesting of all are the several detached houses and gardens, one being of some size, which are shown at Carn—remains of the mediaeval "vill of Carn", of which almost every trace has now disappeared. Bodinnick is marked as "Pendennick" and the point of land projecting from Hall Walk as "Polleeth Point".

The ruined houses which Dr. Young encountered on his visit were probably some of those owned by the Duchy Manor of Fowey. Cromwell had dissolved the Duchy and it was many years before it could be properly reorganised. In 1695 the Steward, when petitioning for the grant of certain property which included a burgage and garden within the borough of Fowey, mentioned that it had so declined in value since 1660 that no-one had bothered to take up the lease. On the other hand this may well have been a bid to acquire burgage rights without payment.

(ii) Shipping : the Merchant Families: the Customs

The decline of Fowey during the early part of the century has already been described. It was not until after the Civil War that any considerable improvement took place. The ancient link with Brittany was still maintained (even at the end of this period it was normal for a Fowey merchant to send his son across the Channel to learn the language), although by that time ports in Spain were their principal destination. The Port Books show that it was the usual practice during the summer months for Fowey vessels to sail down to the French and Spanish ports in the Bay of Biscay and bring back salt. In 1670 Philip Goodall testified that his father had six ships bringing this commodity into the port[1] and that it was customary at Fowey for the salt to be taken out of the ships into boats "wherein it was carryeth to Polkerryes distant from the said harbour about one league and there cellared in another cellar".

A Breton ship which made several voyages to Fowey in 1660 with goods consigned to Mr. Goodall, used to load out tin, combed wool, etc.

It is also recorded that "John Mayowe did yearly sell and dispose of very great quantities of salt from his said cellars in Polruan, likewise great quantities of salt (were) sold to pilchard men from on board the said vessels".

In 1681 the imports of salt into Fowey amounted to 1,396 hogsheads.[2]

[1] *et seq.*, Port Books, Fowey. P.R.O. Also Exch. D. and C. E. 134.

[2] Hals says:—"After the engagement (i.e. the repulse of the Dutch fleet in 1667) the cargo of the whole Virginia fleet was landed at Fowey (its owners at London fearing the hazard of the sea in time of Dutch war, to transport it there by water) and gave opportunity to the townsmen to buy much tobacco at a very cheap rate, which, instantly upon the conclusion of the peace between England, France and Holland, was sold in this Kingdom, France, Spain and Holland at a dear rate, and much enriched the townsmen, thereby, as Mr. Major, one of these merchants informed me".

Spanish wine, aqua vita, brandy and iron were also brought in from the Bay ports. From Spain and from the Breton ports came soap, tallow, pitch, hemp, canvas and cork and small quantities of raisins, honey, salad oil and prunes. Two or three ships sailed out to Newfoundland each year, although that trade was fast declining, and the same number brought home valuable cargoes of tobacco from Virginia.[1] "Sea Coales" from the Welsh ports and a certain amount of salt and hogshead staves were re-exported. In 1681 there were twenty-six ships belonging to Fowey engaged in the home and overseas trade; they ranged in size from the "Willing Maid" of 60 tons (old measure) down to the little "Jonathan" of 10 tons. Very few ships from the port seem to have put to sea during the winter months, for most owners up to the end of this century preferred to keep their vessels snugged down in harbour at this season of the year. In November, 1675, there is news of the "Providence" of Fowey, laden with French wines from Bordeaux and bound for Bristol, being driven by fog and bad weather into Swansea Roads; this vessel, however, was one of the largest sailing out of Fowey.

Tin formed an important export and there is indication that in 1678 several persons had set up "kettles" in their private cellars at Fowey,[2] Truro and Penryn where, under pretence of re-melting into bars tin duly coined in the block, they could run down uncoined tin and defraud the revenue. In 1709 230 blocks of tin were salvaged from the "Betty" of Fowey after she was driven ashore on Dungeness beach by a French privateer. The following year the Admiralty arranged a convoy to escort the vessels which in July carried the Queen's tin from Fowey and Falmouth to London.[3]

In addition to the seagoing commerce there was also a considerable barge traffic with Lostwithiel six miles up river from Fowey. Salt, coal and timber were conveyed inland by this means. It was also customary for the Lostwithiel bargemen to dredge sand from the harbour. This was carried up to Lostwithiel and there sold to farmers for spreading over their fields.

Shipping at Fowey was in the hands of a small number of merchant families—the Goodalls, Stephens, Tollers, Williams, Majors and Cottons. They were closely linked by marriage and their ships were more often than not commanded by sons, nephews or other relatives of the owners. The Goodalls had been in Fowey since the time of Queen Elizabeth and had their large brick-built mansion at Bull Hill, where it commanded a view of the harbour and shipping. From this house they could descend through a steep terraced garden right into the Fore Street. In 1654 John Goodall acquired Hill Hay Farm and let it to the Majors, whilst three years later he was in a position to issue his own trade tokens. He died in 1684 and is buried near the altar in St. Fimbarrus Church below a small but elaborate monument

[1] Establishment Book, 1671. Custom House Library, London.
[2] Cal. Treasury Papers, 524.
[3] Cal. Treasury Papers, 345.

depicting him and his son William kneeling at a desk. Another son, Philip, was a non-conformist. Later the Goodalls had the good fortune to marry into the Coryton family and their combined wealth and estates descended to Peter Goodall, who adopted the name of Coryton.

The Tollers were also a family of some standing in Fowey. William Toller the elder had married Joan Holman, daughter of a local ship-owner. Peter Toller issued trade tokens and was buried in the church in 1667. William Toller the younger married a daughter of John Treffry of Place and it was his son who succeeded to that estate in 1731.

Members of these families were not averse from taking part-time posts in the local Customs Service—and they provided many an "extraordinary" landwaiter or searcher.

* * * * * * *

One of the changes brought about in the reign of Charles II was the reorganisation of the Customs. Since the sixteenth century a system of farming out the Customs revenue had been followed, but in 1671 six Commissioners were appointed to manage affairs.

In that year the officers at Fowey consisted of Abraham Biggs (connected with the Rashleighs by marriage), Collector of Customs with a salary of £40 a year; Samuel Weale, Surveyor with £35 a year; John Major, Tidesman, and Ralph Thomson, Waiter and Searcher at Polruan, each with £15 a year, and Bennet Pedlar and Anthony Biggs each with £10 a year.[1] Next year Mr. Collector Biggs died and Samuel Weale took his place; Ralph Thomson became Surveyor, but in 1674 was replaced by Richard Fisher.

Weale held office as Collector for only a short period. Just before Christmas, 1675, the Commissioners of Customs received a whole list of complaints which are worth recording for the light they throw on local affairs.[2] He was said to be infamous as a petty attorney; next, "for his more advantageous ensnaring the simple he pretends to be religious and being excommunicate from the church he uses the Customs house boat to carry persons to Conventicles or meetings"; thirdly, he had refused to enter a ship called the "Mary" which belonged to Fowey and arrived there from Virginia with a cargo of tobacco, on pretence that she was a foreign-built vessel and therefore liable to additional duty. Moreover, his accusers said that Weale was perfectly aware that the "Mary" was a prize ship which the owners had bought from the Commissioners of Prize Goods and therefore eligible to be entered free, but that he had demanded £100 from the merchants as a bribe to enter her, and this failing, had delayed the vessel for five weeks until the merchants had parted with a smaller "gift" of £10. Finally, they contended that he had taken bribes to dispense masters of ships from taking the usual oath declaring the contents of their cargoes, whereby the King had been deceived of his

[1] Cal. Treasury Books, 319.
[2] Cal. Treasury Books, 559.

customs, and that when he had made seizures of smuggled goods he had privately shared them with his companions. Affidavits and letters were produced in evidence.

Mr. Weale was ordered to answer these charges. He did so, but to no purpose, for by February, 1676, he was out of office and on the 30th August following, Andrew Cory was appointed to succeed him. Strenuous efforts were also made to get rid of Harris, Parker and Fisher; in the February the Rashleighs—Jonathan, John and Philip—together with William Courtney, accused them of going to the meeting house on Sundays, but met with less success. Fisher, it is true, was suspended, but in June, 1679, having been "formerly surveyor at Fowey and put out without cause", he was made Surveyor at Poole. Whatever Weale's faults, there was undoubtedly a strong bias against him on religious grounds.

Some years later this religious discrimination resulted in the removal of John Pising, the Catholic Surveyor, Waiter and Searcher in Fowey,[1] and his replacement in March, 1689, by Thomas Smith.

Relations between the newly reorganized Customs at Fowey and the merchants of the place at first seem to have been rather strained. In 1675 a warrant was issued for the taking into custody of William Williams of Fowey who had apparently abused an officer of the Excise.

It is only too evident, however, that there was a good deal of laxity in the Custom House at Fowey. In 1684 the Commissioners sent down William Culliford to investigate certain complaints here and in other Cornish ports.[2] Culliford found that Captain Andrew Cory was an old man, understood little of Custom house business and had allowed goods to be landed without examination. On one occasion Culliford detained several slabs of tin and a quantity of tin and pewter plates from the ship "Mayflower" and ordered them to be locked up in the Custom house store. Later when the store was opened there were found only lumps of rock and stone hewn in the shape of plates and dishes.

On another occasion Mr. William Williams, merchant of Bodinnick, had gone alongside the ship "Endeavour" in the harbour and brought off a number of casks of brandy and wine and bales of linen cloth in a boat which was "as deep loaden as she could swim". The Excise officer, standing on the Customs quay, waited for an opportunity to examine the casks in the normal course of his duty. Cory refused to allow this and without any examination declared the boat discharged. Thereupon Williams caused half a dozen bottles of wine to be drawn from the casks in the boat, which he drank with the Collector, Surveyor, Landwaiter and other inferior officers on the quay. Cottle, the Surveyor, was charged with allowing ships to be brought alongside the merchants' private quays "and back dores" instead of compelling them to come to the legal quays: Edward Parker had left his post as Landwaiter at Polruan to reside at Fowey.

[1] Fowey "Oath Book": Custom House Library.
[2] Culliford's Report: P.R.O. T. 64/139–140.

There was another shuffle round, of course. Cory, however, was allowed to resign—it seems that he had been a domestic servant to the Earl of Bath at one time and this influential connection and consideration for his advanced years saved him from dismissal.

Occasionally the officials were too zealous, as was the case in 1693, when a complaint reached the Treasury of the severity of the Customs Officers at Fowey in searching for prohibited goods supposed to have been brought ashore out of Captain Cotton's ship. As a result the officers were to be directed to do nothing contrary to the peace or to exceed their powers, although at the same time it was hoped that they would find all due encouragement for making seizures as the law directed.[1] Subsequently William Cotton of Fowey, mariner, was paid £561. 16s. 10d. under sign manual as royal bounty without account. Cotton was actually a secret agent employed by the government to bring intelligence from France, and the goods in question had apparently been brought in to camouflage his activities, but these facts were, of course, unknown to the officers at Fowey.

(iii) Local Government : The First Royal Charter

Both the organisation and methods of local government in Fowey up to the seventeenth century are obscure. Plymouth first had an officer known as the Praepositus prior to the appearance of the first recorded Mayor in 1370. The royal charter of incorporation was not received until 1430.

Fowey, a port not greatly inferior to Plymouth in the first half of the fourteenth century, also had a Praepositus—Thomas Taillour held this office in 1403. Proclamations are frequently addressed to the "Mayors" of Fowey and other places in the fourteenth and fifteenth centuries. A letter of 1597 refers to the "Mayor" of Fowey and as late as 1659 one of the Commonwealth officers visiting Fowey reports the ill-behaviour of "Mr. Peter the Mayor there". Neither these references nor the fact that Fowey was created a Parliamentary borough in 1571 can be construed to mean that the town possessed a Mayor and Corporation in the true sense of the terms.

The Town Lands ensured a source of income to Fowey and from the feoffment of 1597 it is clear that the more prominent men of the parish acted as trustees, although the actual business was transacted by the churchwardens. The Charity Commissioners, who had access to a number of account books and documents now lost, found that :—[2]

> "It would appear that the whole management of charity as well as the legal estate, was vested in trustees, subject to the approval of 3 or 4 of the chief men of the town, and of the churchwardens, yet from the entries in an ancient book of accounts, commencing as early as 1608, it seems that the churchwardens alone took any part, either as it regarded the letting of the tenements or the disposal of the income. That this was also the case before the execution

[1] Charity Commissioners' Report, 1838.
[2] Charity Commissioners' Report, 1838.

of the deed of feoffment before alluded to will appear from the following entry, made in the year 1606, which will also show the mode of letting at that time adopted.

"1606. Mem.—That Abraham Cotton, of Fowe, hath taken at the present account of the parish, the house that Robert Harris dwelt in, and took of the parish in anno. 1594 and the moiety of the town park, with the appurtenances, which Robert Donnell and his assigns lately held until this account, from the date of this account, for and during the full time and term of 21 years from henceforth fully to be complete and ended, to have and to hold the same house and moiety of the town park, with the appurtenances, to the said Abraham Cotton, his executors, administrators, and assigns, during the said term, and to pay yearly during the said term 16s. per year at the parish general account, and to repair the same yearly, upon view, and is to pay for a fine £32 betwixt this account and Whitsuntide following to the church wardens for the year present."

The rents and fines thus obtained, together with the rents received for the market and quay, monies derived from fees for burials in the church, and other sources of parish income, according to what appears to have been a common practice in the Cornish borough, were carried to one general account, and expended in payments for chief rents, repairs of the church, market house, quay and fortifications, paving the streets, distributions to the poor, the general disbursements of the overseers, constables and churchwardens; and no rates for any of those purposes appear to have been required or levied in the parish for a very considerable period. The account seems to have been rendered at Easter, before the inhabitants at large, till the year 1626, when as appears from the following entry, taken from the before-mentioned book, a kind of select vestry of eight men was constituted to manage the affairs of the parish:—

"Mem.—That for the better ordering of the affairs of the town and parish of Fowye, with the consent of the inhabitants of the said town and parish assembled, it is, this 20th day of December 1626 ordered, agreed and consented unto, that there shall be an election made of eight men in the said town and parish, (that is to say), Robert Rashlighe, esq., John Colquite, gent, John Joseph, gent, Mr. Peter Hollman, Mr. Thomas Crowe, Mr. William Byrde, Mr. Henry Stephens, Mr. Thomas Phillips.

"It is agreed and consented unto, the day above said, by the said inhabitants, with the said eight men, that if any of the said eight men, on due warning given, shall absent themselves and show no reasonable cause, shall, for every such default, pay unto the churchwardens 2s. to be distributed to the poor at their discretion."—Signed by the above-named eight men and nine others.

The "Eight Men of the parish" was an institution common to other parts of Cornwall. At Antony, for instance, they were responsible for the rates, maintenance of the church and "placing the inhabitants

THE SEAL OF THE TOWN OF FOWEY

William Goodall
Mayor

SIGNATURE OF WILLIAM GOODALL, MAYOR IN 1685.

of the said parish in such degree and order in the church as they thought fit". The "Eight Men" at Fowey were probably also the custodians of the fine set of brass measures which are still in existence. The largest measure, which bears the date 1661, is engraved with a ship in full sail and the inscription "The Armes of Fowy";[1] another is stamped "Beer" on the base and they were evidently the standard parish measures.

Local government was often involved with local trade and in 1670 a dispute arose between the merchants of Fowey and the Corporation of Lostwithiel over the ancient right of the latter to levy "bushellage" on salt and grain imported by ship and sold in the port. The bushel measure varied in capacity in different parts of the country and even at the same place. At Fowey twenty-four gallons to the bushel were taken of all salt and grain sold aboard ship in the harbour, but only twenty gallons to the bushel when the same commodities were landed.[2] An Act of Parliament attempted to regularise the matter by fixing a common national standard of eight gallons to the bushel. This suited the Fowey merchants and they refused to pay more. The Lostwithiel Corporation then prevailed upon their Recorder, Lord Mohun, to take up the case, and by a further Act, for the purpose of levying this local custom, the old rate was held to apply. Two Fowey merchants, Charles Rundle and William Williams, led the opposition which continued for some years. From the mass of evidence produced it seems that during the Commonwealth bushellage on ships entering Fowey had not been exacted.

This affair probably had the effect of stimulating the desire for municipal incorporation at Fowey: the benefit of an influential Recorder to any contemporary Corporation is very apparent.

In 1670 it was thought desirable to set out the duties of the "Eight Men" more fully. The town and parish accounts were made up every Easter Tuesday and passed at the annual meeting in the church, when officers were also to be elected. The churchwardens then chosen were to see to the repairs of the church and discuss such matters with the "Eight Men" if necessary; they were also to pay the parish clerk his £4 a year for attending upon the minister and ringing the eight o'clock bell, not forgetting the winding of the clock in the church tower (the clock which Jonathan Rashleigh is said to have brought down from London about 1620), and the sexton his 30 shillings a year for cleaning the church and ringing the four o'clock bell. The overseers of the poor were to make up their accounts and produce them to the "Eight Men" every Easter Monday in the church. (It is likely that the panelled room over the church porch was used for these purposes). Every Whit Monday the "Eight Men", or the major

[1] The earliest example of the use of the Ship of Fowey as the Town Arms appears to be the seal dated 1605 with the inscription "Sigillum Offici de Fowy". The ship in this case is a typical Elizabethan vessel, possibly intended to represent the well-known "Francis".

[2] Historical MSS. Comm.: Lostwithiel Corporation Records.

part of them, were to meet together and survey all the parish lands to see that they were kept in proper repair. All rents for the Town Lands were to be paid yearly to the churchwardens at the account table. The market stalls and the Town Quay were to be let on account days only and the rents paid quarterly to the churchwardens, who were to keep the stalls and quay in good repair. Every ton of timber lying on the quay for longer than a month should be charged at four pence and every barge load of sand landed there, the same amount. Every vessel not belonging to the town and unloading salt, coal or any grain at the Town Quay was to pay a bushel of the commodity to the lessee of the Quay.

In 1684 these rules were slightly revised to allow for the letting of the Town Lands to the best bidder and fixing a penalty (to be forfeited to the poor) for anyone who should ship or land any goods at the Quay which were not really his own, with intent to defraud the parish of the duty. More important, it was then ordered that the accounts should be taken and other parish business transacted in the town hall, instead of in the church as had hitherto been the custom.

During this same year the town was hard put as to how to answer the impressive "Quo Warranto" which was now being sent around to many harassed boroughs in the kingdom. As its title implies, the order demanded to know by what legal right the borough held its privileges, and was an attempt to bring the corporate boroughs under the closer control of the king.

Eventually the "Humble Answer of the Towne and Burrough of Fowy to his Majestie's Quo Warranto" was put together and despatched to London. The text continued:—

> "Whereas your Majestie hath lately been pleased by a Quo Warranto to summon us to render an accompt how wee came to enjoy such priviledges and immunities;[1] wee, with all humble submission to your Majestie's demand and Royal Authority herein answear that wee have always, tyme out of mynds, enjoyed them; whether by the Bounty of your Majestie's Royall ancestours they have been confirmed to us by a Charter, or not, wee cannot resolve. Thus farre we humbly conceive, that the Incursions of the French and Spaniard, by whom our Towne hath been twice burnt, may have occasioned the losse of it amongst other great damages sustained. We have been dutifull and loyall subjects, both to your Majestie's Royall Ancestours and Selfe, whom wee have been ready on all occasions to serve with the hazard of our persons and families, particularly in the late unhappy wars, in which wee had our share of sufferings (as the Narration subscribed will demonstrate).
>
> Our priviledges are so small; wee know no more than sending two Burgesses to Parliament and a small markett once a weeke (which is much predjudiced by a newly erected markett at Saint Austle) with the keeping of a Court which wee always enjoyed until the late Rebellion (the Civil War). Wee humbly submit ourselves

[1] Henderson: Essays.

and sufferings to your Gracious favour and consideration, not doubting, but firmely hopeing your Majestie will not only ratify what wee have but also adde such previledges as in your Bounty and Goodness you shall think fitt and we shall ever pray for your Majestie's continuance in a long and happy Reigne over us. Wee shall ever continue to approve ourselves (as hitherto wee have done) your Majestie's most loyall and obedient servants."

This document was signed by John Treffry, Robert Rashleigh, William Toller, John Goodall, Richard Cotton, Henry Stephens, John Pomeroy, Abraham Stephens, Jonathan Rashleigh, Jonathan Toller, Jonathan Tingcombe, John Billing, William Rawe, John Rashleigh, Philip Goodall and John Toller.

Nevertheless the king's ministers were determined to have their way in deciding how Fowey and other towns should be governed and in 1685 the "portreive", burgesses and commonalty duly surrendered all their possessions. A new charter, however, was granted, and William Goodall was the first Mayor. In the second year of the new king, James II, it was decided to pay the Mayor a yearly salary out of the town revenues and in December, 1687, Richard Cotton, the Mayor, and seven aldermen of Fowey acknowledged the receipt from Jonathan Rashleigh of Menabilly of £100 "that was in his hands and was formerly given by the Lords and Ladyes". Although this Charter disappeared at a later date, the Corporation did go to some trouble to commemorate its grant. They evidently had made the two black-framed pictures which hang in the Town Hall—one bearing the royal coat of arms supported by a very bold rampant lion and equally fierce unicorn, with the cipher "JR" (Jacobus Rex) and the date "1686". The second has the legend "The Armes of Fowy 1686" and depicts a frigate of two decks and 38 guns, painted black, with a broad band of buff and yellow between the lower gun ports. She carries the old-fashioned lateen sail on the mizen mast.[1]

Another board was obviously intended to record gifts made to the Borough, the single entry reading:—

"Sir Bevill Grenvile—Knight, Gave to this Burrough of Fowey two Guilt Maces in the Maieralty of Mr Richard Cotton of this Towne. And in the yeare of our Lord God 1685."

The two maces are of silver gilt, each being surmounted by a crown and engraved with the emblems of the kingdom—thistle, harp, rose and fleur-de-lys—along the barrel. Winged figures support the head, the flat top of which bears the royal arms and cipher. The base bears the inscription "Ex dono Bevilli Grenville, Arm. & Burgensis 1685" and the Ship of Fowey. The donor was a grandson of the famous Sir Beville who fell in the Civil War. Under the charter of James II

[1] An interesting discovery was made during the restoration of the "Noah's Ark" in 1948. A framed canvas, bearing on both sides the painting of an Elizabethan ship came to light. It is supposed to have been the old sign of the Lugger Inn but seems more likely to have been the Town Arms prior to 1686. The ship is very similar to that depicted on the Town Seal of 1605.

the Earl of Bath was appointed Recorder of Fowey, with Jonathan Rashleigh as his assistant.

The western counties were much involved in this short but troublesome reign. Monmouth's rebellion had its beginning in Somerset in 1685 and was stamped out with vigour and unnecessary cruelty—after the battle of Sedgemoor. Sir Jonathan Trelawney, Bishop of Bristol and Wells, whose home was at Trelawne near Looe and less than a dozen miles from Fowey, was one of the seven bishops whom James II ordered to be detained in the Tower of London and even John Rashleigh was dismissed from his office as Deputy Lieutenant for Cornwall. In 1688 there were few who were genuinely sorry to hear that William of Orange had landed at Torbay and that James had fled into exile.

The charter granted to Fowey by James II being now declared void, a new one was obtained from King William and Queen Mary on the 28th April, 1690.[1] The new charter commences with a wordy preamble:—

> "William and Mary, by the Grace of God, King and Queen of England, Scotland, France and Ireland, Defenders of the Faith, etc., TO ALL to whome our present Letters shall come, greeting:—
> WHEREAS our Borough of ffowy in our County of Cornwall is an Ancient Borough and is situate on the Sea Coast
> AND WHEREAS the Burgesses and Inhabitants of the same Borough have used and exercised many ancient Liberties franchises and Priviledges by reasons of divers prescriptions, Uses and Customs in the same Borough from a time whereof the memory of man runneth not to the contrary"

and goes on to state the names of the first Mayor and Corporation. Jonathan Tingcomb, gentleman, was to hold the former office until the feast of St. Matthew the Evangelist and was also to be Guardian of the Gaol, Clerk of the Markets and Coroner. The aldermen were Jonathan Toller, Richard Cotton, John Pomeroy, Philip Goodall, John Billing, Arthur Strybbs, John Toller and Peter Major. In addition John Treffry, Abraham Stephens, William Rowe, Stephen Wenmouth and Nathaniel Tingcomb, gentlemen, were nominated as the first and modern Free Burgesses of the Borough.

John Rashleigh was appointed Recorder for the duration of his life and it is significant of the influence which both families then held in the town, that a clause is expressly included in this charter to ensure that nothing therein shall be construed to the loss or prejudice of the titles, rights or liberties belonging to John Treffry or Jonathan Rashleigh, Esquires.

The Recorder was to be assisted by a Common Clerk and to complete the number of officials, the Mayor and Aldermen were to nominate two or more upright and honest men who were to be called Sergeants-

[1] After the extinction of the Corporation in the early nineteenth century this Charter disappeared. It was purchased on behalf of Ald. Simeon Rowe of Fowey at a London sale in 1916.

at-Mace and also others as Constables, Guardians and Supervisors of poor and needy persons within the borough, and Assistant Beadles.

The mayor might collect the tolls on produce sold in the markets and in particular, authority was given for a common beam and scales, called the "King's Beam", for the weighing of cloth, wool and other commodities, to be erected. For the use of these scales the Corporation might charge whatever was the custom in the Borough of Plymouth, and the proceeds were to go towards keeping the Town Quay in good repair. From this time onwards the separate authority of the "Eight Men" seems to have been completely merged in the Corporation.

One of the most praiseworthy activities of the new Corporation—the foundation of the Grammar School—took place in these years. In January, 1692, John Treffry handed over to John Rashleigh and Shadrach Vincent[1] about three quarters of an acre of ground situated at the head of the town and comprising a house, garden and meadow, at a nominal rent of six shillings and eight pence a year, on the understanding that a free school should be erected on the site. On the 10th November of the same year the members of the Corporation and others entered into a subscription to pay for the cost of building this school, making it quite clear that it would be "for the good and benefit of all the corporation in general, which consists of the parish as well as the town and for the particular advantage of the landlords, for increasing the rents of their houses within the town, as well as for the benefit and convenience of all neighbouring gentry that desire their children may be educated near them".

Shadrach Vincent then made it known that "he knew where there was a sum of £500 available for charitable and pious use" and that as soon as the school was built, he would guarantee that the money should be laid out to bring in an income of £30 a year for the express purpose of educating 30 poor children of Fowey and adjacent places. It is a pity that a composite portrait of the Corporation was not painted and hung in the school—as was the frequent custom in Holland—if only to preserve a likeness of the gallant Shadrach, who had distinguished himself whilst serving as a volunteer in the Navy under the Earl of Ossory and afterwards as a major of horse in Flanders.[2] He had come home to Cornwall, settled down at Roselyon in St. Blazey as a country gentleman and respectable burgess, and no doubt often rode over to Fowey to view the new school and perhaps drink a health with his cousin Rashleigh and with friends of the Corporation.

The powers which the Mayor and Aldermen wielded after 1690 were extensive. They had the income from a considerable amount of property in the town. They possessed the tolls from the markets and the Town Quay; and now they controlled the new Grammar School. Under the new Charter the Mayor was also a Justice of the Peace. Officers of the Customs were sworn in before him and he was

[1] Charity Commissioners' Report, 1838.
[2] Lysons 25.

responsible for law and order in the town. His duties covered a wide field. Thus "a poor souldier of Collonel Duglas' regiment disbanded and put ashore at Foy" received a certificate and pass from the Mayor which enabled him to make his way to London and to receive charitable contributions on the road.[1] On the 26th August, 1703, the Mayor wrote to London that he had apprehended one, John Rowe, and confiscated certain papers, on suspicion of treason. Rowe's father was postmaster at Fowey and early in September the Mayor received instructions to remove him from office.[2] The main post road ran from Plymouth along the south coast of Cornwall and inland places such as Lostwithiel were served only by means of "bye-posts". Hence the appointment of a postmaster at Fowey. After 1703 a new post road was organised running inland from Exeter to Truro.

Moreover, it must be remembered that the Corporation was elected by no more than perhaps thirty or forty of their townsmen, since the rights were restricted to those who possessed burgage property in the town. When these electors were friends and relatives of the aldermen, it is not surprising to find that the Corporation soon became the real autocrats of the place, particularly when the gentry withdrew from the somewhat mercenary business and only made an appearance when their own interests were involved. The Corporation had a powerful influence.

It was from the Duchy manor of Fowey that the new Corporation found its first opposition. The tenants of this manor had the power of electing one of their number as "portreeve", in which capacity his duty was to summon the manor court and to preside over its proceedings. He could, moreover, admit new tenants and enter them on the manor roll, adjudicate on minor disputes, and, with certain qualifications, was to the manor of Fowey what the mayor was to the corporate borough of Fowey.

The trouble came to a head at the parliamentary election which was held in 1698 when Jonathan Tingcomb was the Portreeve. Some fourteen years before he had been among those who had petitioned the king for a new Charter and he had held the office of Mayor in 1690; but by taking up the office of Portreeve he seems to have fallen foul of his brethren on the Corporation. In this year of 1698 he was appointed to decide which of the parliamentary candidates had been truly elected and in due course he sent up the names of John Williams of Bodinnick and Sir Bevil Grenville.[3]

The unsuccessful candidates—one of whom was Shadrach Vincent, the other Harry Ashurst—forthwith presented a petition which came before Parliament on December 12th of the same year. In this petition Shadrach and his partner complained that, although they had been duly chosen by a large majority, such was the partiality of Jonathan

[1] Hist. MSS. Comm.: Bridport Corporation.
[2] Cal. S.P. Dom., 108, 113.
[3] Carew, T.: An historical account . . . . Parliamentary elections—London (1755), 243.

Tingcomb, portreeve of the borough, that even before the elections he had openly boasted that he would not return Vincent and Ashurst, had they never so many votes, but that he would return Williams and Grenville if they had only four votes! When Tingcomb was reminded that he might be sued for damages if he persisted in making a false return, he had, according to the petitioners, said that far from losing money "he hoped to get £500 by the bargain".

The parliamentary committee appointed to investigate the disputed Fowey election slept upon the case and in November, 1699, the irate Shadrach put up a second petition. Alas, within another twelve months he was dead. In February, 1700, the committee could heave a sigh of relief and report that, Shadrach Vincent being dead, they were proceeding no further with their investigation.

In the same February another unsuccessful candidate presented a petition to Parliament. This was Thomas Vivian, who complained that, although he was duly chosen and ought to have been returned for Fowey, yet by many illegal practices used by and on behalf of John Williams, gentleman, and by the partiality of his uncle, Jonathan Tingcomb, Williams had been declared successful. For some reason Vivian withdrew his petition in April, 1701, but in the meantime the Mayor, Recorder, many of the Aldermen and the majority of the voters paying scot and lot, had joined in the battle and had themselves laid their grievances before Parliament. In brief, they stated that the Portreeve had publicly said that the right of voting belonged to the inhabitants of the town who paid scot and lot and taxes for the relief of the poor, yet at the last election he had allowed several persons to vote at the polling booth who, far from being independent, tax-paying inhabitants, were rather "objects of charity"—paupers in fact! (He had probably enrolled them as "manor tenants" just previously.) The Corporation then put up the ubiquitous Edward Parker who said he had lived in Fowey for fifty years and that to his knowledge the rights of election were vested in the Prince's (manor) tenants, one of whom was always chosen as Portreeve, and in such inhabitants as paid scot and lot.

Here, then, are the two rival parties in Fowey—the Mayor and Corporation leading the inhabitants who are scot and lot men, but not manor tenants, on the one side; on the other side the Portreeve, commanding the manor tenants.

The voter, perhaps a quiet, hardworking master shipwright or husbandman, finds himself a highly important fellow and much sought after during election times. He has a word in quiet with one of the Aldermen and thereafter may drink and eat as much as he pleases. Each candidate feasts his supporters and the taverns are never so busy as at these times. The Corporation have carefully vetted their friends and those tenants of the Town Lands who are voters; to make sure of their men they have made lettings at very low rents and now sip their glasses of Madeira with the reflective countenances of those who could say a lot if they had a mind to and the guineas were forthcoming.

The anxious Candidate, whose wine they are drinking, is rather worried about the four or five thousand pounds he will have to lay out on this election—a good deal on the gentlemen opposite if they are to engage for him—but consoles himself with the thought of the pickings to be made once he is returned to Parliament. Yet nearly all are honest, patriotic men in their own way of thinking.

Even peers of the realm were anxious to gain an influence in the small parliamentary boroughs. Here is the almost obsequious letter which the Earl of Radnor addressed to the Mayor and Corporation of Fowey in the first year of the reign of Queen Anne:—[1]

"Mr Mayor and Gentlemen,

The very kind reception I lately met with from you not only requires my hearty thanks but has increased in me the desire of cultivating a friendship with my good neighbours of Fowye and claims the offer of my service, on the late occasion of the death of your Recorder.

I doe assure you, Gentlemen, there is no man in England that shall more zealously promote the honour and interest of your Town, whenever you shall think fit to make it my duty, as 'tis my inclination to demonstrate myself,

Mr. Mayor and Gentlemen,
Your very affectionate and faithful Servant,
RADNOR.

Wimple Sep. 12, 1702.
For the Worshipfull Mr Mayor of Fowye and rest of the Members of the Corporation."

Despite Marlborough's victories, the war with France seems to have been unpopular at Fowey: the merchants complained of ships "taken and lost by this unhappy warr so that wee have noe trade at all". Young Jonathan Stephens of Fowey had his studies interrupted and it was not until June, 1703, that he received a pass allowing him to return to Morlaix. At the same time, two French boys, Francis Sabatier and Peter Lucas, who had been to Fowey to learn English, were permitted to return home aboard a transport. A Frenchman who stayed on in the town was Mr. Rene Contusin, possibly a Huguenot refugee and one of many who settled in the Westcountry. He married Mistress Elizabeth Andrewes at the parish church in 1724 and was a burgess of Fowey three years later. Other names of likely French origin which appear locally about this time are Bunny (Bonnet) and Cundy (Condé).

(iv) Church and Nonconformity

In 1603 Edward Basil was installed as Vicar of Fowey. There is a record of the beating of the Parish bounds during his incumbency. John Fletcher, M.A., who succeeded Basil, gained repute as a critic, scholar and writer. He was accused of speaking or writing against

[1] Bodmin Register (1827), 328–9.

the government, tried at Launceston assizes and sentenced to leave the realm but on applying for a new trial was acquitted. On the 31st October, 1656, John Tutchin was instituted, the patron being John Treffry. A letter of the time mentions that at Fowey, "there were some good souls but that the grandees (presumably the Rashleighs and Treffrys) were unreasonable men" who wished to drive the Puritan minister from the town. Fowey also received an augmentation of £10 to the minister's income in 1655. Tutchin seems to have been deprived in 1662, for John Atwill was vicar in the following year.

In these days the returning Cavaliers viewed the new religious sects—Puritans, Presbyterians, Anabaptists and Quakers—with suspicion. They had, as in the case of Hugh Peters, been very much to the fore in Cromwell's time and it was feared that they were secretly plotting rebellion, and the downfall of the king. Hence the Five Mile Act of 1662, which forebade nonconformists to hold their meetings within that distance of a town. The dissenters had gained a hold in Cornwall and at Fowey there were many in sympathy with them. The seeds of this nonconformist growth may well have been sown in earlier years by refugees from the Low Countries.

On the 14th November, 1664, Thomas Tregosse, a prominent nonconformist and ejected from Mylor in 1662, visited the town and before long it became known that he had privately baptised a child of Richard Baker and another of William Hoskin, "after the presbiterian or the independant way". Another inhabitant refused to have his child baptised by the vicar and even carried the baby up to St. Winnow where the ceremony was undertaken by Mr. Philip Leach, an independent. These delinquents were duly reported to the Archdeacon of Cornwall, and Thomas Luney, Anthony Owen (*alias* Humphrey) and one Edward Parker (whose name crops up again as a dissenter) were indicted for not coming to church on the 5th April and for spending part of that day in sporting and gaming (this last seems to have been a rather malicious charge).

As with the Quakers at Lostwithiel and St. Austell, these dissenters were invariably men and women of some standing and well respected in the community. Walter Tingcombe, an anabaptist, came into Fowey one day according to evidence supplied to the Archdeacon "to seduce some of the Towne from their conformity to the discipline of the Church of England". When told that Philip Goodall, the merchant, had been in trouble for insisting on keeping his hat on during sermon time in church, Tingcombe asked "What made the fool there?" Goodall's attendances at church then became less frequent.

The prejudice against Samuel Weale, the nonconformist Collector of Customs, has already been mentioned. Such were the trials and tribulations of those who would not conform at Fowey. In spite of persecution they seem to have kept some sort of meeting place; for a few years before Wesley passed through Fowey there were still a small number of nonconformist families, although at that time (1746) they had no minister and occasionally attended the parish church.

CHAPTER 7

A VISITOR to Fowey in the time of Queen Anne must have found it a place smelling strongly of fish curing and packing. For some unaccountable reason the pilchard appeared off Cornwall in immense shoals in these years and at intervals throughout the whole of the eighteenth century. Fowey shared in these temporary periods of prosperity, when the old Cornish toast of "Fish and Tin!" was particularly applicable. At the same time the trade in Newfoundland fish dropped away until in 1710[1] the Mayor found it necessary to inform the Council of Trade and Plantations that the port was "entirely unacquainted with the Newfoundland trade". Instead, Cornish shipping was kept increasingly busy with the export of pilchards, chiefly to the Mediterranean countries. During 1718, 13,182 hogsheads of pilchards were sent away from Fowey alone; the busiest months were January, February and March, when thirty-six ships sailed from the port carrying 10,867 hogsheads to Venice, Genoa, the Canaries, Barcelona, St. Sebastian and other southern ports.[2]

In good seasons a large quantity of salt was required for the fish curing. A certain amount came from Guernsey duty free, but by far the greater part was brought in from France and it was a bitter grievance with fishermen and merchants alike that a tax should be levied on this foreign salt. In 1717 the Treasury were advised that a Supervisor of Salt should be appointed at Fowey to control the district from Plymouth to Penzance.[3] Boats having permits to convey salt from Fowey to Mevagissey were also taking salt which had paid no duty from ships at sea and the appointment of a resident Salt Officer at Mevagissey was also suggested.

Smuggling continued to give the authorities a great deal of trouble. For some years smacks had been employed by the Customs to watch the coast but it was now decided that the Fowey smack and three others could be dispensed with as they seldom made seizures and were not able to watch close in to the shore. Riding Officers were appointed to keep an eye on the coastline, each with a salary of £30 per annum and an allowance of £10 to keep a horse. The Customs establishment in 1716 consisted of the Collector—Charles Lambe—and twelve other officers.

Occasionally the Navy made a seizure. In June, 1719, the smack "Mary" in command of Lieutenant Dilke put into Fowey to impress seamen for the Royal Navy. On going ashore Dilke was met by the

[1] Cal. S.P. (Colonial): 24.

[2] Port Books: Fowey: P.R.O. *cf.* Thomas Fuller, writing in 1662 of Cornish pilchards—"Their numbers are incredible, imploying a power of poor people in polling (that is, beheading), gutting, splitting, powdering and drying them: and then (by the name of Fumadoes) with oyle and a lemon, they are meat for the mightiest Don in Spain". *History of the Worthies of England.*

[3] Cal. Treasury Papers: 104–5.

Mayor, who informed him that a suspicious looking brigantine had been observed in Mevagissey Bay.[1] The "Mary" slipped out of harbour at three the next morning and within a few hours had seized the vessel which turned out to be a well-known Irish smuggler armed with two swivel guns, five muskets, a musketoon and a blunderbuss.

Par seems to have been a favourite place for making a landing and in 1724 two Customs officers intently watching a boat making its way up the inlet were set upon by five men disguised and armed with sticks and clubs.[2] Two of the assailants were recognised as apprentice servants belonging to George Fox, into whose house they had afterwards run. One of them, Julian Laugherne, was arrested and later received a heavy fine. Two years after this affray the Mayor of Fowey, Fox and other leading merchants were writing to London begging for a removal or mitigation of the fine.

Fox himself was implicated in a seizure of salt at this time but as the evidence was not substantial it was thought inadvisable to bring proceedings against him. Nathaniel Couch, shopkeeper of Fowey,[3] and Thomas and John Couch, yeomen of Tywardreath, who were involved in the running of 230 gallons of brandy, similarly escaped prosecution. Between 1724 and 1732 there were 42 seizures of wine alone at Fowey, the worst year being 1725, when 1,132 gallons were taken. At Looe only 220 gallons were seized during the whole period.

There was an affair of a more serious nature in 1735 when excise men found a number of kegs of rum in a barn near Fowey. The kegs were being removed to the custom house when a gang of armed smugglers waylaid the king's officers and attacked them. So venturesome and confident had these smugglers become that the officers went in fear of their lives, the more so since it was reported that the gang had made an agreement among themselves to rescue any of their fellows who should happen to be arrested.[4] They could often rely on the good will of people of position, and towards the end of the century there is a hint that it was not altogether unusual for a keg or two to appear suddenly in the tower room at Place whenever a successful run had been made.

In 1731 John Treffry died at the age of eighty-one and Place passed to William Toller, his nephew. Toller had been Collector of Customs and was Mayor of Fowey in 1716. Polwhele the antiquarian tells a story to the effect that John Treffry, during his lifetime, lay down in a grave to show the sexton a novelty—"a man swearing in his grave". He also had a tablet placed in the church recording how the estate had descended, out of the direct line, to himself and that having no heir he had settled it on William Toller, his sister's son, and "incerted it here to Prevent all future disputes or cavils and that mine ancestors and my intent may allways be fulfilled". Toller assumed the name and arms of Treffry but within five years he also was dead. Of the

[1] Letters: Custom House to Admiralty: P.R.O., Ad/1.
[2] Cal. Treasury Books.
[3] P.R.O.: T. 64/143.
[4] V.C.H., 505–6.

eight children of William Toller Treffry and his wife Rebecca, four died before reaching the age of three and only one son survived.

After a long period of peace England went to war in 1739 and Fowey came in for some of the preparations being made to meet the possible threat of invasion. Whenever was war declared the Navy invariably found itself short of men and the press gangs were soon at work in the coastal towns and villages. In June of that year ships were ordered to call at Fowey and other places to take on board men pressed into the King's service. Years later a traveller was told that Fowey had been so depopulated by this war that "it had not left them above one man to seven women".

In Parliament, Walpole, the prime minister, had become unpopular and interest now centred about the elections of 1741. After the petitions and disputes of 1700 the Fowey elections seem to have been managed quietly for some years. Henry Vincent was member in 1710 and 1713 and Nicholas Vincent in 1722, when he sat with John Goodall, whose mansion then lay in Bull Hill. Both were dead by 1726 and Jonathan Rashleigh of Menabilly filled one of the seats and with William Wardour was representing the borough in 1740. It was at this time that the brothers Thomas and William Pitt, both opponents of Walpole, made a private survey of the twenty-one Cornish boroughs and weighed up the chances of the Prime Minister's supporters being thrown out at the next election. These Pitts were grandsons of "Diamond" Pitt, an Indian nabob and Governor of Madras, who had made a small fortune out of the sale of a famous diamond. In the time of Queen Anne he returned home to England and bought up the estate of Boconnoc, which Lady Mohun was forced to sell when her husband was killed in a duel. They were reasonably optimistic with regard to Fowey, being comforted by the idea that the Mayor or Portreeve would be chosen by the Prince's manor tenants. At that time the Prince of Wales was, in political affairs, at loggerheads with his father George II. The Pitts enjoyed the favour of the Prince and no doubt supposed that a little pressure would ensure that the Fowey electors voted as desired. It is true that in most of the Cornish boroughs Walpole's supporters were heavily defeated, but at Fowey, where the Rashleighs owned much of the property in the town and had interests in the Corporation, Jonathan Rashleigh and Wardour held their seats.

Six years later the Pitts again interested themselves in the Cornish elections.[1] On 19th June of that year Thomas was hopeful of getting enough support to win one if not both of the seats at Fowey,[2] but a fortnight later he was very doleful as to his party's chances there.

[1] A visitor to Cornwall in 1759 noted that Fowey supported itself by its fishery and trade with Norway in deals. He considered it "a poor mean place; its Harbour defended by four Batteries with 21 Guns which have no Gunner, Ammunition or Touch hole. . . . . Vessels of 600 Tuns can come up here light . . . . Town is rich in nothing but Members of Parliament." Article by Jack Simmons, p. 281, *Devon and Cornwall Notes and Queries*, Vol. XXIII, Part IX, January, 1949.

[2] Hist. MSS. Comm.: Fortescue MSS., Vol. I, 114, 119, 127.

Buck's print of Fowey in 1734

He had visited the town and had received promises of support from 26 out of 45 or 46 likely voters, but these had since gone over to the other side. He complains, ironically, "What general can command success when the men won't stand?" Writing from Boconnoc on the 2nd August, 1747, Pitt comes to the crux of the matter—"At Fowey Mr Rashleigh is an old man but healthy . . . I have gained a good footing at Fowey, which by bringing some kind of trade, may be established to be a prevailing interest. I understand there is a Club of West India merchants who make it a rule to promote the trade of any borough where a friend may be chosen. Could they not be prevailed on to order some of their ships to be victualled at Fowey?"

But the West India merchants preferred to victual their ships at London and Bristol, and in years when the pilchard seining was poor the decline in trade at Fowey was felt severely. The voters on this occasion returned Jonathan Rashleigh and George Edgecumbe and Pitt presumably lost the £2,000 which he had anticipated would be required as "expenses" for his candidates.

Polwhele mentions that the Cornish fishermen were never adaptable and that when the pilchards failed to appear they would lie about in the sun rather than cultivate other employment. Calls on the Poor Rate were probably heavy and it was with the intention of alleviating such distress that the various Fowey Charities were founded.[1] By the middle of the eighteenth century these were numerous. As early as 1652, Warwick, Lord Mohun had left fifty shillings to be divided among fifty poor people at Christmas and ten years later Thomas Rashleigh of Coombe made a similar bequest. The wording of Nicholas Sawle's legacy, probably written in the time of the Civil War, typefies what was in the minds of other of his fellow townsmen:—"I, the said Nicholas Sawle, compassionately and tenderly considering and bewayling the great decay and poverty of the town of Fowey, being the place of my nativity, and out of love of the said town, etc. . . . ." He left £200 for the benefit of certain poor inhabitants. Twelve poor people were to be selected by the "Eight Men" of Fowey and were to attend at church on Sundays when they would each be given two pennyworth of good white bread—a delicacy when ordinary loaves were dark and coarse in texture. The remainder of the money was to be expended in clothes.

Mention has been made of the almshouses built by Jonathan Rashleigh in the time of Charles I. In these galleried houses, eight poor widows found a home. At Christmas time each received fifteen pence, and the same amounts on New Year's Day and at Easter. Also at Christmas they had £8 divided between them in clothes, and on New Year's Day, four shillings each in bread and victuals. In 1704 his descendant, Jonathan Rashleigh, built an additional three almshouses as a thanksgiving for the family's preservation during the Civil Wars.

Among other benefactors were John Pomeroy, James Denbow, John Treffry, Henry and Abraham Stephens and Zachariah Taylor

[1] Charity Commissioners' Report, 1838.

(the last-named left £10 to the poor and enough to provide a vane for the church tower). The Grammar School was, of course, partly a charity foundation. Another educational bequest was that of Mr. John Johns who died in July, 1773. He gave to a schoolmistress the sum of £8. 10s. 0d. for ever for teaching 25 poor children to read, provided she took no other scholars on any pretence whatsoever (a wise precaution). The children were to be nominated by the vicar and if the schoolmistress proved negligent or guilty of any gross immorality, then the vicar should turn her out and appoint another. He bequeathed £1. 3s. 0d. a year to buy books for the 25 children and 10/6. to the vicar for the trouble he should be at in inspecting the conduct of the schoolmistress. In addition Johns left £5 a year for ever, to be distributed each Christmas by the vicar, who was himself to receive one guinea for preaching a sermon annually, for distributing the £5 and for keeping in a book the names of such poor persons to whom the money should be given, always preferring the aged and industrious.

In Georgian times two great boards, painted and varnished, hung in the church with inscriptions recording these charities, the intention being that there should be no disputes among later generations. Yet the truth of the matter is that those charities which were administered by the Corporation often failed to benefit the intended recipients. John Treffry's legacy was apparently never executed and the money was merely allowed to accumulate. Sawle's charity was neglected after a few years and the same seems to have applied to all the monies with which the Corporation was entrusted. An equally unsatisfactory state of affairs prevailed in connection with the Town Lands. Originally bequeathed for the relief of the poor of the town and parish of Fowey, and similar objects, this Charity had been used by the Corporation to further their own interests, the various tenements being let at very low rents to friends of that body.

Nearly a hundred years later members of the Corporation professed that they were ignorant of the proper mode of using the rents of the Town Lands. It had long been customary, according to their statement, for the mayor to receive all the tolls and dues, and having taken them for his private use, he subsequently paid the general expenses of the borough out of his own pocket, without accounting for them in any way. In 1728 Jonathan Rashleigh sent along £200 to the Town Hall to settle the various debts due to the former churchwardens in respect of the upkeep of the church and churchyard. The following year it was necessary, for the first time, to levy a Church Rate.

In the course of time the Corporation became almost a closed body. Son followed father in office and few strangers were admitted as aldermen unless they became connected with the more prominent Fowey families. No complete list of mayors has survived, but from the names which are available it is clear that the office rarely passed outside certain families—the Lambes, Stephens, Pomeroys, Rashleighs and Grahams. Even the appointment of Town Clerk descended from

John Kimber the elder, who held the post in 1755 to John Kimber the younger, who was Clerk in 1783.

Although the Fowey Corporation never possessed the wide bargaining powers of some Cornish corporations, owing to the presence of the Duchy Manor with its tenant voters, as a body it exercised a great influence at the parliamentary elections and when trade declined it seems evident that the members interested themselves far more in the elections than in looking after town affairs. In the end this was the ivy which pulled down the house.

During the latter half of the eighteenth century the Corporation made a brave appearance. A small girl, staring open-eyed from the depths of her pew, could not help admiring their appearance each Sunday at church, and recalled the scene in later years:—

> "Well I do remember our thinking the Mayor and Aldermen[1] above all superior and their dresses so imposing—cloth cloaks, trimmed with fur, Winter or Summer, their hair fully powdered; large stiff sausage curls, one row on another above their ears, the hair behind in a black silk bag with a large rosette of black ribbon; small cocked hats stuck on the tops of their heads and large buckles on their shoes completed the visible part of the costume of these Dignitaries. Nor must Ralph Paine the Mace-bearer, who walked before them, be forgotten, for in his own opinion, as well as ours, no doubt, he was a great character in his large brown cloak with a cape and cocked hat trimmed with gold lace—who could be greater in his own estimation? And what an air of authority it gave to the whole Corporate body when Ralph placed the large Mace at the head of their Pew as a terror to all evil doers!"

In 1755 John Wesley passed through Fowey and his diary records:—
"August 25th 1755. At Fowey a little company met us and conducted us to Luxillian".

Little is known of the early Methodists in Fowey nor of the earlier dissenters except that in 1746 the latter had no resident minister and occasionally attended the parish church. The first Methodist chapel seems to have been built in 1801 in North Street.

The Parish Registers show the trades and occupations of many inhabitants of Fowey about the middle of the century. The majority are, as might be expected, connected with sea-faring:—

William Nicholls and John Willcock—Shipwrights.
William Beare—Ropemaker.
William Collins and John Bone—Cordwainers.
Richard Hingston—Blockmaker.

Many occupations have since died out:—

Richard Willington, John Hawkins, Alexander Hoskings—Peruke Makers.
Henry Lukey—Hatmaker.
Thomas Courts—Scrivener.
Thomas Lanyon—Salt Officer.

[1] Memoirs of Susan Sibbalds (1926).

Many family names which have long been associated with Fowey are mentioned, for example:—

Thomas White—Tailor.
Thomas Jago—Mason.
William Carne—Maltster.
Richard Coplestone—Miller.

It was an age in which almost everyone—from the nobleman down to the tradesman—maintained a keen interest in party politics and was either Whig or Tory. The Corporation of Fowey was predominantly Whig and time after time a Rashleigh represented that party as one of the borough's representatives in Parliament. Philip Rashleigh represented Fowey for nearly forty years and eventually acquired the dignity of "Father of the House of Commons". At Menabilly he formed an extensive collection of Cornish mineral specimens.

The Rashleighs still held a great deal of property in Fowey and were on good terms with most of the merchant and professional families. John Rashleigh was Mayor in 1783, William Rashleigh in 1805 and Philip Rashleigh in the following year. The Kimbers have already been mentioned. John Kimber the younger was Collector of Customs in 1799 and held office as Mayor ten years later. About the middle of the century Thomas Graham, "a gentleman from London", married Susannah, the sister of Charles Lambe, the Collector of Customs. A nephew, Thomas Graham, established himself at Penquite, became Sheriff of Cornwall in 1806 and Mayor of Fowey in 1814. These were some of the leading Whigs.

There was opposition, of course. The Treffrys were Tory.[1] A letter from John Coryton to Philip Rashleigh in 1770 refers to the methods then in use for the upkeep of the roads and continues:—

"Returned from Fowey where we appointed new Way Wardens. I subscribed two guineas, one for you and one for myself, towards the expenses of the old one. Treffry says if you and I will make roads we may maintain them and would give nothing."

This Thomas Treffry died in 1776. He had married Susannah, daughter of Thomas Pipon, merchant and alderman of Fowey, and was Sheriff of Cornwall in 1766. During his lifetime Place seems to have been neglected, the old tower in particular falling into decay. His son, William Esco Treffry, survived him by only two years and the estate then passed to a daughter, Susannah Ann, who had married Joseph Austen of Plymouth. Mrs. Austen was now a widow with one young son, named after his father. She was a lady of decided personality and ruled her circle of acquaintances at Fowey. One of this circle was Thomas Mein, a native of Scotland and a surgeon in the Royal Navy. When not employed afloat he lived with his growing family in a large brick house which still stands in the North Street.

Dr. Mein was keenly interested in politics, art and literature and enjoyed social life. He was no doubt glad to make the acquaintance

[1] Henderson MSS.

PETER PINDAR (DR. JOHN WOLCOT), 1738–1819, POLITICAL SATIRIST AND POET,
PATRON OF JOHN OPIE THE ARTIST
(Photo : National Portrait Gallery, London)

of the celebrated Dr. John Wolcot, who sometimes came down to visit his sisters at Fowey. All the fashionable world knew Wolcot from his caustic writings and verse and from his recent discovery of the young "Cornish Wonder"—John Opie, whose portrait painting he had encouraged and introduced to London society. Wolcot was familiar with Fowey. He was a grandson of a brother of Alexander Wolcot, who was Mayor of Fowey in 1713. The elder branch of the family was settled at Dodbrooke in Devon but when the boy's father died, he and his sisters were brought up by their uncle, John Wolcot, a surgeon at Fowey. One sister married Dr. Robert Stephens in 1765. The young Wolcot acted as assistant to his uncle, subsequently travelled to Edinburgh and London, qualifying as a doctor of medicine and also entering holy orders. After some time in Jamaica he returned to Cornwall, lived for a little while at Truro, where he was at loggerheads with the local Corporation, and then settled in London. Here he soon fell out with his protégé, Opie, but made something of a sensation with his witty, satirical verse. He was interested in art and his "Odes on Royal Academicians", first brought out in 1782 and repeated in subsequent years, were very popular. Elizabeth Fry, the great Quaker reformer, mentions in her journal spending "a pleasant merry day with Peter Pindar" when she and her father visited London in 1798. She was a friend of John Opie's second wife and it is evident that the friendship between Dr. Wolcot and Opie had been re-established at that time.[1]

At Fowey, Wolcot seems to have entered into the political contests with gusto, taking the side of the "Blues" as the Tories were popularly known. In 1790, Mrs. Austen, Mein and Wolcot all held shares in the sloop "True Blue", a vessel of 12½ tons recently built at Fowey.[2] The registration entry at the Custom House describes Wolcot as "Doctor of Phisic of the City of London": the "True Blue" was probably a pleasure boat.

At the election of 1789 the "Blues" managed to give the Whigs a run for their money and Dr. Mein took a leading part in the campaign. The Tory candidates were Lord Shuldham and Sir Ralph Payn and it was hinted that the Prince of Wales had given them his blessing. Thomas Mein knew enough about the Fowey elections to realise the possibilities that lay behind the Duchy Manor of Fowey, whose tenants were among those who had the right to vote. From somewhere or another he produced fifty-one new "tenants". Their names having been duly entered on the Duchy Manor Rolls, these new "tenants" gathered together on the 26th November, 1789, and at the Manor Court chose Thomas Mein as their Portreeve. This was probably the occasion on which Mein had a great box of millinery sent down from London, so that on the very next Sunday the young Miss Meins[3] minced sedately to church in bonnets boldly trimmed with "True

[1] *Elizabeth Fry:* Whitney (Guild Books, 48).
[2] Registration Books: Custom House, Fowey.
[3] Memoirs of Susan Sibbalds.

Blue" ribbons. That same night the Whigs broke the windows of the doctor's house in North Street.

Mr. Stackhouse, who had been elected Portreeve in 1788, was a Rashleigh adherent and he now declared that Mein had been chosen by fraud. Mein set up his hustings,[1] probably at the King of Prussia Inn (where the Duchy manor courts were customarily held) and declared the poll open. The results, as might be expected, showed a majority in favour of Shuldham and Payn, the actual voting being:

Shuldham	77
Payn	76
Valletort	74
Rashleigh	69

At the Ship Inn, Stackhouse also opened the poll. The fifty new "Duchy tenants" were naturally absent and the results were announced as:

Rashleigh	75
Valletort	74
Shuldham	18
Payn	17

In the end a parliamentary commission had to unravel the legal points arising from the Fowey election and on the 7th March, 1791, it was decided that Viscount Valletort and Philip Rashleigh had been duly elected.

Although his candidates did raise an appeal against the finding of the commission it was rejected and Mr. Mein's efforts had been in vain. The importing of voters was, of course, no new election dodge and upon occasions the use of such "fagot" votes, as they were derisively called, did turn the scales at Cornish elections. Blackguards brought down from London or paupers hired for the occasion often enough had their names inscribed on a manor roll or were registered as the holders of property within the borough and were then allowed to vote. Even the genuine voters expected to be treated and plied with wine and good food whilst the elections were on, and the rival candidates might expect to find themselves poorer by a few thousand guineas by the time the rowdy affair was over.

The outbreak of war in 1779 renewed the fear of invasion and plans were made for cattle, carts and other removable material likely to assist the enemy to be driven inland, first to Lostwithiel and then, if necessary, to Bodmin. The invasion never came to anything but a number of privateers were sent out from Cornish ports to harass enemy shipping.[2] The Quillers of Polperro obtained letters of marque for the "Swallow", 80 tons, and the "Alert", 150 tons. Captures at sea were frequent and at times exchanges of prisoners of war were effected with the French. In 1796 the Borough Constable at Fowey, Edward Stocker, assisted by Walter Colmer, had the task of escorting

[1] Peckwell, R. H., Cases of Controverted Elections, 512–25.
[2] Registers of Letters of Marque. P.R.O., Ad/7.

a man named Crossfield by chaise to Bodmin gaol.[1] Crossfield had been one of a party of exchanged prisoners brought into the port and had aroused suspicion by his loose talk. In May of that year he was tried at the Old Bailey on a charge of treason but was acquitted, the evidence showing that he was more fool than knave.

A chart made by Lieutenant James Cook (a namesake of the famous navigator) and printed in 1786 shows the seaward defences of the town.[2] St. Catherine's Castle housed six cannon, whilst a watch-house and battery of three guns stood on the cliffs above Mundy's Rocks, where Point Neptune House was afterwards built. Another five-gun battery stands at the Fowey blockhouse which was, judging from a print published in this same year, surprisingly intact after four hundred years. Whitehouse was still a rocky cove, with one ridge jutting out into the harbour. Above the battery of five guns which defended this point was a group of small trees and farther up again "Mr. Hewitt's Rope-House and Yard". From here to Lost-withiel Street were a number of pleasant gardens with here and there a solitary house. At the other end of the town, past the Sailors Return Inn which overlooked Passage Slip was Caffamill Pill, then a busy place with three quays or slip ways—one being on the Carn side.

A "List of Men enrolled to serve as Sea Fencibles"[3] in the town and neighbourhood of Fowey shows that in 1798 there were 150 men in training. They were divided into six companies, their local officers being Thomas Graham, Benjamin Bloomfield and Richard Dugger. By 1803 Captain Shuldham Peard had succeeded to the command of the district. The Petty Officers at Fowey were then Walter Colmer, John Willcock, John Easlick, George Beer and Robert Good. Exercises were held weekly. Captain Peard resided at Fowey although his command extended from Rame Head to the Dodman and included companies of Fencibles at Fowey, Looe, Polperro, Mevagissey, Gorran and Charlestown.

These were years in which the small Cornish shipyards, particularly those of Mevagissey, were busy turning out sloops and luggers in large numbers. At Fowey the principal builder was Thomas Nicholls.[4] The luggers were fine seaworthy little vessels ranging from 20 to 100 tons and their simple fore and aft rig made them ideal for coasting, as certain individuals in Jersey and Guernsey well knew when they bought them for smuggling. During the French wars many were converted into privateers and were launched complete with twelve to sixteen gun-ports and deck stanchions. For privateering a high turn of speed was necessary and so the sail area was often increased by fitting a longer bowsprit. This was all very well so long as the lugger was engaged in legitimate cruising against the enemy, but if and when she indulged in a little smuggling and was chased, she could

[1] B.M.: Trial of R. T. Crossfield.
[2] A copy is in the Harbour Commissioner's Office, Fowey.
[3] Pay Lists—Sea Fencibles. P.R.O., Ad/28.
[4] Registration Books: Custom House, Fowey.

easily outstrip the slower Revenue cutter. Hence the official precautions taken to ensure that these luggers should, unless actually in commission as privateers, be fitted with shortened or "legal" bowsprits. In addition to building new craft, Nicholls occasionally attended at the Fowey Custom House where smuggling vessels which had been seized and condemned were put up for auction. In 1793 he bought up the "Harriet" and "Nancy" at such auctions and re-built them.

In spite of the penalties some of the smugglers were bold enough to openly defy the revenue officers. In April, 1780, the "Hawke" in the service of H.M. Customs surprised the cutter "Active", armed with ten carriage guns and eight swivel pieces off Mevagissey.[1] The "Active's" master refused to allow an officer to board her, maintaining that his vessel was a privateer. Leaving a boat to watch the suspected smuggler, the "Hawke" made for Fowey and obtained permission to embark a sergeant, a corporal and twenty-two privates of the 1st Battalion Royals then stationed in the town. With these reinforcements he put out again and chased the "Active" up Channel. Shots were fired on either side but the sight of the "red-coats" seems to have daunted the cutter's men and they surrendered. When the "Active" was searched in Fowey harbour fifty pounds of tea in small bags, one anker of Geneva and fifty-seven pieces of china-ware were discovered and handed over to the Collector of Customs.

The almost continuous wars between 1786 and 1815 saw no less than thirty-four foreign prizes brought into Fowey harbour and sold, chiefly to local inhabitants. The greater number had been captured from the French by privateers such as the "Brilliant", commanded by Captain John Quiller, the "Phoenix", "Matchless", "Mars", "Hero" and others. Their fitting out must have occupied a good many local hands, for they were usually well provisioned and armed. The "Valiant", a private ship of war licensed at Fowey to "cruise against the enemy" in 1793,[2] for instance, was a small vessel of 111 tons, but she boasted an armament of 12 carriage guns (3-pounders), 26 muskets, 4 blunderbusses, 20 pistols and 40 cutlasses. Only eleven Fowey vessels were lost to the enemy and three of these were prizes previously taken from them. The heaviest blow was the loss of the "Virtuous Grace" of 235 tons, captured by the French in 1806—a blow which brought her owner, John Kelly Graham, into difficulties.

In Nelson's time the English Channel afforded a picturesque and stirring sight, ships of all nationalities, rigs and sizes crowding the panorama. With the leisurely speed of sailing ships days, vessels were often in sight of one another for hours at a stretch: men of war with their rows of gun-ports and elaborate, gilded figure-heads, bluff

[1] Letters from Custom House to Admiralty. P.R.O., Ad/1.

[2] Registration Books: Custom House, Fowey. Privateers were usually fitted out and licensed entirely for warlike purposes: letters of marque, on the other hand, were granted to armed merchant vessels, enabling them to make captures whilst bound on trading voyages. The term "privateering", however, was often used for the latter activity.

THE TOWN TAP

East Indiamen, trim fast-sailing privateers and slower trading brigs, pinks and snows, together with numerous armed luggers, Revenue cutters and other small craft, all kept the look-out busy. To the West, great three-deckers and frigates were constantly putting out from Plymouth, ploughing through the seas to join the blockading squadrons off the French ports or to strengthen Nelson's fleet watching the enemy in the West Indies. To mark Nelson's victory and death at Trafalgar the space between the "Ship" Inn and the Town Hall was subsequently named after the battle.

Even with the aid of the press-gang, men-of-war often went to sea very short of men and were glad of any opportunity of gaining recruits.[1] In the autumn of 1805 H.M.S. "Melampus", cruising in the Channel, fell in with a Fowey lugger named the "Hope", some five leagues off the Lizard. It was an unfortunate encounter for the Cornishmen, since their vessel had below over five hundred casks of spirits as well as bags of tobacco, pepper and salt, all contraband. The lugger was, of course, seized but the crew were offered the choice of standing their trial as smugglers or of volunteering for the Navy. With the exception of the master, all hands accepted the latter alternative and it was probably months, perhaps years, before they saw their families again.

Others were more fortunate than the crew of the "Hope". Many made smuggling a paying game and consistently sailed close to the wind yet escaped the penalty. Occasionally a smuggling trip was combined with the more legitimate occupation of privateering. Polperro men were among the more successful privateers and it was the "Unity" belonging to Polperro (and also well known as a smuggler) in company with the "Hero", which captured and brought into Fowey harbour the much battered Danish East Indiaman "Constantia Maria". She was an extremely rich prize,[2] being homeward bound from Mauritius with a cargo of cotton, coffee, sugar and ebony. An Act of Parliament had to be passed allowing the goods to be exposed for sale in the Port and Town of Fowey by the captors or their agents, since by law all produce from the East Indies had normally to be unloaded in the River Thames and the Danish ship was far too disabled to make the journey round to the London river.

Captain William Quiller, another Polperro man, was well known in Fowey. In the spring of 1811 he was in command of the "Pheasant". She was a schooner, at that time considered a fairly modern rig, but better adapted for coastal sailing than the old square-sailed brigs and much easier to manœuvre during a fight. On 20th March Quiller brought her into Fowey after a cruise off the coast of France, where he had taken two prizes. These captures—the "L'Assomption" and "L'Aimable Barbe"—were put up for auction at the "Ship" Inn early in the following month, together with two tons of white rosin, "the whole being condemned as a prize to the private ship of war

[1] Letter Book: Custom House, Plymouth.

[2] Article by C. K. Croft-Andrew—*Old Cornwall* magazine, 1941.

Pheasant, W. Quiller Commander". Whilst the "Pheasant" was off in search of fresh booty, her owners, no doubt wishing to make the most of the vessel's high reputation, auctioned part of her shares at the "Rose and Crown".[1]

Another successful privateer seems to have been the "Chase", captain Sleeman. She arrived at Fowey in January, 1813, having already sent in a French prize laden with wine; on the same cruise she had slipped in close to enemy shores and had driven an American vessel flying French colours right into the hands of the British blockading squadron.

Besides the usual repair work a certain amount of ship-building was being carried on in the Fowey yards. A print dated 1811 shows the hull of a small vessel, half completed, on the slip-way where Captains Row joins with North Street, and in April of the same year Messrs. Richard and Hugh Polgrain advertise that they have a fine schooner "which will shift without ballast" ready for launching at Fowey.

The long years of war, however, played havoc with the pilchard export trade. Richard Warner, who passed through Fowey in 1808, wrote:—

> "Complaints of the decay of commerce from the continuance of the war and the shutting up of the Mediterranean ports were as loud and general here as at Looe. The stock of pilchards, the fruit of the toil of several seasons, was decaying on the hands of the inhabitants."[2]

Lysons confirms this. Whereas before the war 60,000 hogsheads of pilchards caught in St. Austell Bay had been exported from Fowey in one year, from 1800 not a third of that quantity was sent away annually. Between 1807 and 1811 the trade slumped badly and in 1808 and 1810 no pilchards were exported, except coastwise. There was some improvement in 1811 when shipments were made to the West Indies. During this period great quantities were sold for manure after the oil had been extracted.

Another traveller who was in the district a few years earlier described how in bad seasons the fishermen became dependant on limpets and other shellfish for their support.

Nevertheless the population increased steadily—from 1,155 in 1801 to 1,319 in 1811.

Two natives of Fowey attracted public attention during these years, both being the victims of a merciless justice. Mary Bryant, a young servant girl from Fowey, received in 1786 a sentence of transportation for stealing a cloak. The terrible conditions of the trip out to Australia were equalled when the convicts were put ashore at the settlement of Port Jackson. With her husband and baby, Mrs. Bryant joined in an attempt to escape by boat, but the party were recaptured. Boswell, Dr. Johnson's friend, was instrumental in

[1] *West Briton*, 1811–13.
[2] Warner: *Tour through Cornwall in* 1808, 94.

saving her from an even harsher sentence of life imprisonment, and she ended her days in peace. Some years later Elizabeth Fry was able, after a long struggle with the authorities, to ameliorate the sufferings of the unhappy women convicts sent from Newgate to Botany Bay.

Robert Jeffery was still a youth when he was pressed into the Navy and found himself aboard H.M.S. "Ulysses" bound for the West Indies. During the voyage he was accused of theft and Captain Lake ordered that he should be put ashore on the desert island of Sombrero. Here he would have starved to death had not an American ship touched the island. The news of this inhumane punishment reached England and Lake was dismissed the service.

At the beginning of the nineteenth century an old inn named the "Rose and Crown" stood at the lower end of the churchyard. Considering the site it is possible that originally it was a church ale-house and later converted into a tavern. In 1811 it changed hands, the new landlord being a stranger to the town—he had previously kept a public house at Plymouth Dock (now Devonport). Towards the middle of November a Jew also arrived at Fowey and made for the "Rose and Crown".[1] He was apparently no mere huckster, was evidently well known to Wyatt and possessed a good stock of money, since within a few days he was changing a five-pound note with a customer at the inn. He stayed in Fowey nearly a week and then apparently left very suddenly.

Suspicion was aroused and by the following March the innkeeper was standing trial at Bodmin assizes for the murder of the Jew, Isaiah Falk Valentine. Witnesses attested that long before high water one winter's evening, Wyatt and his guest had been seen on the Broad Slip and shortly afterwards someone heard a shout, "Mr. Wyatt! Mr. Wyatt!" The Jew was never seen alive again but it was observed that his companion arrived back at the inn some time afterwards by a roundabout route (probably by way of Bull Hill). The body of the murdered man was later found in the water near the same quay.

At the trial it came to light that the deceased was an illicit dealer in guineas, with whom Wyatt had been acquainted at Plymouth. The publican wrote asking him to come to Fowey and hinted that a gentleman of the town had a quantity of "buttons" (i.e. guineas) to dispose of. He evidently planned to rob and murder Valentine for the money was found at the back of the inn premises beneath a heap of rubbish.

The jury returned a verdict of guilty and the judge sentenced Wyatt to be hanged on the following Monday. But the prisoner's counsel pointed out that by law execution must take place within 48 hours of sentence (or 72 hours if Sunday intervened), and the judge admitted that he had mistaken the day of the trial for Friday instead of Thursday. So on Friday the unhappy man was brought up again and this time ordered to be hanged on the following day. Other legal points arising,

[1] *et seq. West Briton.*

however, he was respited and removed from Launceston to Bodmin gaol.

For some weeks he remained at Bodmin, but early in May the authorities decided to carry out the sentence. The execution was in public, but once again the wretched business was to be drawn out. Wyatt was a large heavy man, the rope was not greased as was customary and for twenty minutes even the crowd gathered for amusement and excitement sickened at the grotesque struggle. Wyatt's "Dying Words" were afterwards printed and sold as a broadsheet.

The Fowey Bank was in existence at this time. A one-pound note issued in March, 1810, bears the names of Vevers, Robinson and Co. and is payable on a firm of London bankers, Prescott, Grote and Co. The Fowey seal of 1702 is also printed on the note.

A lighter note appears in the local paper for June, 1811, when it was announced that there had been quite an assembly of local beauty and fashion at a subscription ball recently held at Fowey, the dancing being kept up with great spirit until a late hour. As the town boasted no Assembly Rooms the event was probably held in the newly-built Town Hall.

CHAPTER 8

WELLINGTON's victory at Waterloo brought the war to an end, and one summer's evening in 1815 Plymouth townsfolk swarmed out into the Sound in boats to gain sight of the defeated Napoleon standing contemplative at the quarter rail of H.M.S. "Bellerophon", a few hours before his departure for St. Helena. Long afterwards panelling made from the timbers of the old "Bellerophon" was used for a room at Place.

With the advent of peace there was inevitably a change in everyday life at Fowey. Something of the colour faded and the tempo slowed. The signal gun at the harbour entrance no longer announced the arrival of a ship of war or of a privateer escorting her captures into the port. The comings and goings of naval and military officers ceased, and polite society in the town missed the company provided by the families of half-pay officers who, like the Meins, had found it economical to live here rather than at Plymouth. Doubtless the assembly balls were dull with only the local beaux to wait upon the ladies and young George Peard, whose father had been promoted to admiral after the disbandment of the Sea Fencibles, found the place tedious and was glad, one day in 1818, when the family took chaise for London, a journey which occupied them a full five days. The batteries at the Castle were neglected and became the promenade of such lovers and nimble-footed children as chose to climb the rocky path leading up from the pilchard cellars at St. Catherine's Cove.

There was lack of employment and expenditure on the poor of the parish rose from £309. 14s. in 1816 to £627. 4s. in 1820.[1] In June, 1819, it was advertised that the fast-sailing brig "Sceptre", Thomas Nickells, master, would take in goods and passengers at Fowey before departing for Quebec. During the next half a century many ships were to sail for America with Cornish emigrants aboard. In this year Dr. John Wolcot died at his residence in London.

The activities of the Corporation, as well as the Parliamentary elections—there were thirteen contests between 1800 and 1832—still provided outlets for controversy. Joseph Thomas Austen, son of Mrs. Austen of Place, was now a young man in the prime of life. Keen, capable and energetic, he soon took an interest in local and parliamentary affairs. He was a man of enlightened views and as early as 1811 was speaking at a meeting of the Friends of Parliamentary Reform at Bodmin; he detailed instances of abuses in some Cornish boroughs and commented upon the manner in which elections were conducted in these places. This was probably a tilt at the Fowey Corporation in particular.[2]

Politics and pleasure were refreshingly combined. In May, 1815,[3]

[1] *West Briton*, 1819.
[2] *West Briton*, 1811.
[3] *West Briton*, 1815.

"the Friends of Freedom at Fowey celebrated the anniversary of their jubilee. The utmost harmony prevailed during the day; the dancing was kept up with great spirits until near five o'clock the next morning, when Messrs. Austen and Fortescue, the Stewards, were conducted to their houses by the company preceded by an excellent band playing popular airs".

Two years later an information was laid on behalf of Mrs. Austen and Joseph Ham against the mayor and free burgesses of Fowey,[1] alleging that they had misused the Town Lands so that the rents only amounted to £8. 1s., whereas they should have brought in an annual amount of £250 and that the letting of the Lands had been deliberately managed by the Corporation in such a manner as to increase their influence at elections. In other words the Town property was being let to friends of the Corporation on ridiculously low terms in return for their votes at the parliamentary elections.

During the eighteenth century the abuses had not been so evident, as the Corporation were usually on good terms with the Rashleigh family, whose members were invariably elected to represent Fowey. In 1798 Philip Rashleigh bought the Duchy Manor of Fowey, no doubt to consolidate the position of his family at ensuing elections.

But when William Rashleigh sold his interest in the manor to George Lucy in 1816 and the latter, a complete stranger to the county, became patron of the Corporation, the battle began in earnest and the opponents of that body found a champion in Joseph Austen, who was already doing much to retrieve the Treffry family fortunes from the low state into which they had fallen in the previous century. The municipal reformers also had the backing of the most influential of Cornish newspapers—the "West Briton"—which praised the "Blues" and at the same time reviled their opponents, the "Greys". In November, 1817, the West Briton reported that "a most numerous meeting of the Inhabitants of Fowey was held at the Town Hall for the purpose of returning thanks to J. T. Austen, Esq.", but when the "Greys" held a meeting in the following month it was facetiously announced that they had had to resort to a house of entertainment named the "Mumpers Inn" where after much persuasion they managed to enlist the support of two travelling tinkers ![2]

At the election of 1818 the "Blues" alleged that supporters of the Corporation had been first primed with drink and then stationed at the windows of two adjacent public houses (probably the "Ship" and the "Rose and Crown"). From these vantage points "they commenced vociferating so as to render it impossible that any persons but those quite close to the speaker could hear a word he said. This posse was headed by a Mr. Nicholls, who, we understand, is a lieutenant in the navy. This pot valiant son of Neptune held a speaking trumpet through which he brayed hideous and unremitted discord". However, in spite of the efforts of Lieutenant Nicholls and his crew, the candidates supported by the Corporation failed to gain the seats.

[1] Charity Commissioners' Report, 1838. [2] *West Briton*, 1817–18.

THE OLD LUGGER INN
(From an old photograph)

Private individuals, as well as the Corporation, made capital out of the election issues. The fact that ownership of certain property carried with it the right to a vote ensured that it would fetch a high price when put up for sale. The "West Briton" for 13th January, 1815, contains a notice of the forthcoming auction of several tenements in Fowey, concluding with the inducement that "the above Tenements being Borough or Prince's Holdings, give the respective owners, on due admission at the Borough Court, a right to vote at elections without residence and the owner is capable of being made Portreeve of the Borough". The buyer stood a chance of recouping himself and making a good profit when an election came on.

In 1819 the Corporation neatly turned the tables by petitioning for and obtaining a new Charter; there seems reason to think that as in a previous election there was some influence at work with the Prince Regent. But their success was short lived. Between 1820 and 1825 there was much opposition (of which Mr. William Rogers of Trenant appears to have been a leader) to various proposals to add new names to the Poor Rate list. The names were invariably those of adherents of the Corporation and the significance was that inclusion in this list was one of the qualifications of a Parliamentary voter. Objections could be raised to a person being placed on the Poor Rate but as these were heard by the local magistrates, of which the Mayor was chief, the objectors rarely succeeded. Only when the appeal was carried to the sessions was there any hope of success. In 1825 it was ordered at the quarter sessions that the names of John Isbell, John Nicholls, John Couch, George Bate and four others should be removed from the Fowey Poor Rate.[1]

One of the contentions of those who petitioned for a new Charter in 1819 had been that without magisterial powers smuggling would increase. It was therefore ironical that in the summer of 1824 the Mayor, Mr. John Bennet, was himself involved in smuggling on quite a large scale.[2] According to the account which appeared in the local paper, the cutter "L'Union" of Brest arrived at Fowey on Saturday evening the 24th July and was visited by the Customs officers who found concealed a quantity of French brandy and wine. The master of the vessel attended at the Custom House on the following Monday morning, the Mayor also being present. Subsequently Mr. Bennet left and was speedily followed by the Customs officers, who repaired to his house and demanded admittance in order to search for contraband. This was refused, and a messenger being sent to the Collector he came along in person. The "West Briton" hastened to place the full particulars before its readers:

> ". . . . On his (i.e. the Collector's) appearance, the Mayor thought proper to open the door; when an active search commenced and in various parts of the house they found quantities of French wines of various kinds, and several casks of brandy. Whilst in one of the

[1] *West Briton*, 1825.
[2] *West Briton*, 1824.

rooms they heard a crackling as if made by the breaking of bottles overhead; they instantly proceeded upstairs and on forcing open the door of a room, against which a large chest was placed, they found an aspirant to aldermanic honours busily employed in breaking bottles filled with brandy and wine; on the floor of the room in some places these precious liquors were nearly three inches deep; we also learn that between the time the Mayor got a hint of what was intended, until the door was opened to the Collector, a great quantity of wine and brandy was spilled into the river. What has been removed is estimated at £300 . . . ."

About this time the Town Clerk sued the Mayor and Aldermen for various expenses and although Mr. Robert Hearle was chosen Mayor in 1826, no further business was transacted by the Corporation after that date.

Parliamentary representation only lasted another six years. In 1832 the Reform Bill was passed and Fowey, together with many other places, ceased to return members to Parliament. One of its last representatives, elected in 1830 and 1831, was Lord Brudenell, better known by his later title of Lord Cardigan and as leader of the famous charge of the Light Brigade at Balaclava.

The census taken in 1831 provides figures which illustrate the size of the town on the eve of the passing of the Reform Bill. The parish was 1900 acres in extent and contained 321 houses which were inhabited, as well as another 30 which were not. In other words, one house in every ten was either vacant or derelict. The population numbered 1769, made up of 801 males and 968 females. Of the former it is rather remarkable that only 20 fell within the category of "Capitalists, Bankers, Professional and other Educated Men". There were 75 labourers employed in agriculture and a further 86 in other work, whilst 20 were occupied as Male Servants. Another 159 men were engaged either as Workmen or as Master men. Of the female inhabitants no less than 66 were employed as servants. Under the heading of families, 46 families are shown as engaged in agriculture, 140 in Trade, Manufacture and Handicrafts, whilst the remaining 189 families are not classified.

The report of the inspector of Customs for the previous year also contains some interesting information concerning the trade of the port. From overseas, 21 vessels arrived with timber during the previous twelve months, 1 with salt from France and 17 with Bricks, Shot, etc. To foreign ports sailed 3 vessels with China Clay, 2 with Copper Ore and 1 with Salt.[1] Coastwise shipping provided the bulk of the trade—257 ships arrived with Coal and Culm, 1 with Slates and 184 with general goods. 751 vessels laden with general goods left Fowey for other coastal ports. These figures, of course, include Charlestown, Mevagissey, Par and Pentewan, which were included in the Fowey Customs district. 82 vessels were registered in the Port of Fowey.

China clay, discovered by William Cookworthy nearly a century

[1] Inspection Report: Custom House, Fowey.

before, was already being sent abroad and formed a considerable part of the coastal trade, whilst the mines around St. Blazey were still very active, and in the absence of main-line railways most of the minerals went by sea. The greater part of the timber brought into the port was for use in the mine shafts and buildings. At Fowey ship building and repairing flourished in a small way and the rope-walks on the open fields to the west of Lostwithiel Street employed men, women and children in laying out the rope yarn. Fishing also provided a rather precarious means of livelihood. although the Fowey sailing trawlers and luggers were often enough in demand when a smuggling run was being planned.

Considering the low level at which public standard of honesty stood during the time of George IV as exemplified by the corruptness of the Corporation and the bribery and mismanagement at the parliamentary elections, it is small wonder that the activities of the smugglers aroused little condemnation.

Smuggling in this part of Cornwall certainly does not seem to have been accompanied by the violence which characterised it in certain English districts. It is true there was the "Lottery" affair in 1798 and as late as 1815, when the commander of the "Hind", revenue cutter, surprised a smuggling vessel in Mevagissey harbour and was about to take possession of her, the smugglers fired at the cutter's crew and in the confusion managed to get the goods safely on shore. In the winter of the following year John Horner and John Chubb, two riding officers in the service of H.M. Customs at the port of Fowey,[1] met with a numerous gang of smugglers, armed with fire-arms and other weapons and carrying on horses a large quantity of smuggled spirits in small casks, at Polgooth in the parish of St. Mewan. When the riding officers attempted to make a seizure the gang attacked them, dangerously wounded Horner and carried off his sword and pistol. A reward of £200 was offered to anyone giving information to the Collector of Customs. These affrays invariably happened in some out of the way part where the smugglers had friends, for when in the same year the "Providence", revenue cutter, seized the open boat "James and Mary" in Fowey harbour, there seems to have been no resistance.[2] There being no justice of the peace at Fowey on this occasion the offenders were taken to Plymouth.

By 1830, however, determined efforts were being made by the authorities to limit the frauds. The revenue cutters sailed up and down the coast from Plymouth to Falmouth—at Fowey the "Hind" carried out this duty and was later replaced by the "Fox"—trim craft of about 160 tons and 16 guns, commanded by a Lieutenant. Ashore the Customs officers were assisted by the riding officers, who could call out a party of Dragoons if necessary to help them make a speedy capture. Finally a new force named the Coast Guard was formed to watch the actual coastline and patrol the cliffs and possible landing

[1] *West Briton*, 1815.
[2] H. N. Shore: *Old Foye Days* (1907), 4.

places. Prize money was held out as an inducement for making seizures and capturing smugglers. Stoppage of promotion threatened those who failed to prevent a "run" being accomplished. Guernsey, so long a favourite rendezvous for the smuggling craft, had to be abandoned owing to new and crippling legislation, although Roscoff, situated on the Breton coast and therefore outside English law, took its place and for some years prospered by the change.[1]

Careful and methodical planning were now imperative if these ventures were to succeed. The ringleader planned the "runs", dealt with the merchants at Roscoff and with the buyers of the goods here in Cornwall, and arranged freights with the masters of the vessel bringing the cargoes across. Such a man was Richard Kingcup, who joined the Coastguard at Polruan in 1824. He served four years as a Commissioned boatman and then set up as publican at Fowey.[2] For the next twenty years, during which time he moved to Plymouth and took over a shipbroking business, he was actively connected with smuggling enterprises. His every movement was carefully watched and noted by the Customs and his "dossier" includes the following entries:—

"1833 *October*. R. K. of Fowey, is believed to be mixed up with the 'Tam o' Shanter' of Fowey.

November. Has been seen moving about in a suspicious manner in company with Abrm. A— of Downderry, and Hicks of Fowey. Is supposed to be arranging a cargo.

1834 *July*. Reported to have hired the open boat 'Four Brothers' to bring over a cargo for the Fowey district as he has been absent from Fowey several days.

October. Is seen at Plymouth and reported to have engaged a Fowey sloop.

1835 *January*. Is believed to be concerned with Thompson of Lostwithiel in the 'Hope' of Devonport, seized in Yealm river with 317 tubs and 13 flagons concealed under dung.

July. Seen aboard the 'Jane' of Fowey. Is said to have a brother serving on board the 'Fox', revenue cutter, at Fowey.

1842 *July 1st*. Was seen near Fowey, on the road to Charlestown.

July 18th. Returned to Fowey; is still hanging about and is believed to be concerned in 'Le Oif' French smuggling cutter.

1844 *February*. Landed at Polkerris. A sharp look-out to be kept on his movements.

1848. Is somewhere in the Fowey district. To be strictly watched."

There was certainly a very adequate system of gaining information and it led to many craft and their cargoes being seized. In 1824 the "Elizabeth" and "Grace" of Fowey were caught, whilst five years later the "Lucy" was seized at Chichester with 100 half-ankers of spirits concealed below. In 1832 a budget of news reached the Customs authorities from someone who was evidently in the know at Roscoff

[1] Shore: *Smuggling Days*, 93–4.
[2] Shore: *Old Foye Days*, 59–61.

on the French coast. It was then reported that the "Rose" of Fowey, 11 tons, had taken across 100 tubs of brandy for Fowey and even then, with a larger vessel—the "Eagle", of 35 tons, was loading a cargo for the same district. Early in the following year the "Eagle" paid two visits to this locality, the first time with 300 tubs and the second with 150—she was evidently making some very successful trips. Another vessel, the "Love" sailed for Fowey with 150 tubs aboard. It was certainly a more paying game than fishing, although if caught red-handed the penalties were severe—impressment into the Navy for five years and seizure of the goods.[1] As for the boat, she might be taken over by the Customs or deliberately sawn into three parts and sold as firewood. It was a risky business. On the "Eagle's" last mentioned trip it is reported that she and two other craft had twice put back into Roscoff, having been chased by a revenue cutter which had fired upon them. Only by good sailing had the "Eagle" managed to escape.

Finally there was the actual landing of the goods. The usual method was for the smuggling vessel to take advantage of a dark, moonless night to evade the Revenue cutter (whose movements were carefully noted) and to stand in to the rocky coast at a prearranged spot. Here, in some quiet cove, the gang, which usually included one or two farm labourers with a thorough knowledge of the nearby country, would be waiting. With a look-out stationed on the cliff above to give warning of approaching danger, the work of landing the kegs went on as rapidly as the men knew how, and if all went well the kegs were soon safely stowed away in a farm outhouse or cave and the smugglers dispersed. For those not actually sharing in the "run", a guinea amply repaid a night's work, together of course with a sample of the liquor. If, on the other hand, the landing was interrupted, it might well mean a spell in Bodmin gaol—no healthy place in those days.

One such landing is said to have been made at Lantic Bay, close to Polruan, in 1835.[2] According to the story the "Daniel and William" landed a cargo of tubs one Friday night and the Revenue cutter "Fox" having sailed down to the westward on the Saturday morning, it was thought safe to fetch the tubs inland that night. Unexpectedly the crew of the "Fox", together with the coastguards, and the riding officer, Richard Barrett, burst upon them. Apparently the "Fox", hard driven, had reached Falmouth and with a favourable wind had got back to Fowey by ten o'clock the same night. A scuffle followed, during which some of the smugglers were secured; strangely enough, none of them was convicted when they appeared at Bodmin Assizes.

Another story is told of a landing in 1845 at Coombe on the Fowey side of the harbour entrance,[3] and the greater part of this is substantiated by official records. The original plan was to run boldly into Fowey harbour and land the goods at Bodinnick, but an informer

[1] Shore: *Smuggling Days*, 103-106.
[2] Shore: *Old Foye Days*, 19–31.
[3] Shore: *Old Foye Days*, 38–45.

had been busy and gaining knowledge of this the smugglers decided to drop their cargo in Coombe cove. This was the second method in use and enabled the vessel to get quickly away without having to lie too long off the land. It meant, however, that the tubs, sunk in shallow water with an unobtrusive buoy attached, had later to be located and dragged up. Their first plan having gone astray, it is said that the Bodinnick ferry boat was taken from her moorings and used to bring up or "creep" the cargo. However, the Polruan coastguard got wind of the affair and were soon pulling away in their galley to the spot. One of their number, named Piper, patrolling the coast, had meanwhile walked right into the hands of the smugglers waiting in the darkness of night for their companions to bring the boat in to the beach, and he was immediately seized and tied down to a rock, but not before he had managed to fire off one of his pistols. With the arrival of the Polruan coastguards the smugglers fled. The haul must have been a pretty big one, for over £200 was distributed as prizemoney in September, 1845.

But the end of large-scale smuggling was in sight. Within the next few years Government duties on spirits were greatly reduced, so that the powerful incentive of profit was much curtailed—it hardly paid a man to risk his capital and freedom—and since the accession of the young Queen Victoria, new standards of moral integrity were being built up, by the side of which smuggling became widely viewed as plain dishonest fraud. A third view is that the call for men to build the new railways drew away from the coast many of the daring but idle spirits who had been so ready to take part in smuggling ventures.

During the 1830's the Charity Commissioners visited many districts, investigating the management of local charity foundations.[1] At Fowey they found that the Quay and pavements were decayed, the salary of the master of the Grammar School in arrears, and the rents of the Town Lands not collected for many years past. Their detailed report described the various Charities, and some years later the income of the Town Lands was finally settled on the Grammar School and the maintenance of the church.

In 1837, when Queen Victoria was entering the first year of her reign, Joseph Thomas Austen of Place was one of the most outstanding figures in Cornwall. He had lived through eventful times and had seen the advent of steam engines on land and sea. No doubt he was among the spectators who watched the new steam packet "Sir Francis Drake"[2]

[1] Charity Commissioners' Report, 1838.

[2] In 1822 Austen had purchased three mines and smelting works in the parish of Tywardreath. These had commenced working in 1813 and stopped in 1819 after £50,000 had been expended upon them. Lanescot, an adjoining mine, was united with the other three in 1836, the whole being known as the Fowey Consolidated Copper Mines. The venture was a very successful one in these years—from 1815 to 1841, 234,486 tons of copper were extracted and sold for £1,422,633. Profits in the year 1837 totalled £15,820. There were then 1,706 persons (including 636 women, girls and boys who chiefly worked above ground) employed. Nearly two thousand tons of coal and 62,000 feet of timber were used in one year. Conditions were probably better here than in many other mines in Cornwall—

with her immensely tall funnel and engines of no less than 70 horse power, thrash her way into Fowey harbour in 1825. He was engaged in many commercial enterprises—the building of the harbours at Par and Newquay, the construction of the mineral railway which linked the two places, and owned ships and smelting works as well as shares in tin and copper mines. In 1838 he assumed the name of Treffry in place of Austen and held office as Sheriff of Cornwall. Through his influence the New Road leading into Fowey was constructed and he rebuilt a part of, and extended Place, which had become very dilapidated. In the latter work he employed a youthful sculptor named Neville Northway Burnard to carve some of the finer work. Burnard no doubt received much encouragement at Place, for he returned to his home at Alternun greatly advanced in his accomplishments. Subsequently he won the Silver Medal of the Royal Cornwall Polytechnic Society and went to London. He was successful as a sculptor and in 1852 completed the Lander statue at Truro. Through misfortune he took to drink and died in Redruth Workhouse in 1878.

In September, 1846, Fowey received a royal visit—that of Queen Victoria and the Prince Consort, who were then making a tour of the Channel Islands and the western counties.[1] On Tuesday morning, 8th September, the Queen and Prince Albert landed at Broad Slip from the royal yacht, and proceeded to visit the ancient castle of Restormel near Lostwithiel. The party then returned to Fowey and in the words of a weekly journal of the time—"entered Mr. Treffry's drive which commands a delightful view of the river and picturesque harbour of Fowey. On her arrival the Queen was received by the owner and Captain Davis, with every demonstration of loyalty, and Mr. Treffry had the honour of conducting Her Majesty and Prince Albert through the tesselated Porphyry Entrance into the ancient Hall where Mr. Treffry presented to the Queen a loyal Address from the borough of Fowey. On leaving the house her Majesty and suite ascended the steps on the left to view the sculptured effigy of the 'Heroine' (Elizabeth Treffry, who led the defence of Place against the French in 1457) before alluded to; and they examined the Porphyry Arch which is 22 feet high and very massive, and supports the eastern square of the tower, as well as the arches of jasper, amethyst porphyry and shorle in the hall connecting the western tower with the mansion. Previous to his departure Prince Albert announced his intention of having a porphyry arch constructed in a similar manner to that at

"Each miner in these well managed mines received thirty shillings a month during illness and has medical attendance with medicine provided for himself and family. For these allowances a deduction of one shilling and nine pence is made upon his monthly earnings; the least possible amount to secure such benefits".

"*J. R. L.*" *Cornwall & Its Mines*, 1854, pp..177–9.

The expansion of the railway put an end to the proposals for a canal across Cornwall to link the ports of Padstow and Fowey. Several notable civil engineers had carried out surveys for this and similar schemes, including Boulton, Telford and Brunel.

[1] *Illustrated London News*, 1846.

Place. Mr. Treffry had the honour to present to his Royal Highness a beautiful model of Restormel Castle made of cork; also a splendid drawing of Place House and another of the Viaduct; which the Prince was most graciously pleased to accept".

On leaving the southern entrance her Majesty, attended by Prince Albert, and their suite, walked through the streets of Fowey "*totally unguarded* except by her loyal and faithful Cornishmen". She was received on the Royal Victoria Stairs by a guard of honour composed of the Coastguard, under the command of Captain Holman. The royal yacht "left the harbour under a salute and was soon followed by the 'Fairey', 'Black Eagle' and 'Garland', when all proceeded eastward".

Four years later Joseph Thomas Treffry died and was buried at Fowey. His mother, the redoubtable Mrs. Austen, had long outlived her generation and passed away in 1842 at the great age of 94.

CHAPTER 9

THE port was at a very low ebb during the early 1850's. Tin and copper mining interests had moved away from the neighbourhood to the west of Cornwall and fishing was, as ever, a fluctuating business hampered by the distance from any good market. The new railways, although stretching out in all directions, had not yet reached Fowey. No Corporation had been in existence for thirty years past and the town seemed fated to continue as a decayed port, with memories of past glories.[1]

It happened that the newspapers of these times were filled with accounts of the thrilling passages of such clipper ships as the "Lightning", "Sovereign of the Seas" and "Challenger"—large, fully-rigged vessels usually owned in New York or Liverpool—and it was also well known that such fast ships were making a mint of money for their owners. In the last few years, spurred on by the Gold Rushes and the high market price for early tea from China, ship designing had shown a wonderful improvement which soon spread to smaller craft. The sailing ship, now built on finer, tapering lines was very much a match for the steamer—still somewhat unreliable and expensively hungry in her consumption of coal.

At all events the fever for ship-owning soon spread to the West-country ports, including Fowey. The shipyards in the Canadian provinces of Nova Scotia and Prince Edward Island, making use of their great supplies of timber, were turning out some fine small craft, and two of these sailed across the Atlantic to Cornwall in 1857. They were both brigantines: the "Ossena" of 150 tons was bought by Captain Thomas Dyer of Fowey and the "Polyxena" of 137 tons by James Hayes, innkeeper, of Bodinnick.[2] The latter vessel had a short career, being lost five years later, but the "Ossena" completed a very useful life under various Fowey owners, mostly in the coastal and continental trade, Runcorn, Newcastle, Dordt in Holland, Elsinore in Denmark and St. Petersburg were among the ports she visited. The "Ossena" was lost in September, 1887.

By 1863 a dozen or more of these Canadian-built vessels were owned in Fowey—by far the largest being the three-masted barque "George Arkle" of 553 tons, owned by William Warren Dingle. Then there were seven brigantines, ranging from 160 tons down to 111 tons in burden: the "Lydia", "Capella" (later re-rigged as a schooner), "Ossena", "Polyxena", "Kingaloch" (also owned by Dingle) and "Wild Wave" (owned by Captain J. H. Hocken); three schooners of approximately the same tonnage—the "Concord", "Muta" and "Chase" and a solitary brig, the "Carthaginian".

[1] A traveller to Cornwall in 1853 came to the conclusion that Fowey was a lamentably wasted town. He noted that the streets were full of angles with heaps of rubbish at each corner, but admired the natural scenery.

[2] Registration Books: Custom House, Fowey.

In the 'sixties the Cornwall Mineral Railway constructed a broad gauge line down from Lostwithiel to Fowey, following the course of the river, for the purpose of shipping iron ore from the mine at Restormel. Following closely came an increased demand for china clay and properly equipped jetties were built from Lower Carn Point upwards. So the call for shipping became greater and the old Fowey and Polruan shipyards were soon steadily employed once more, not only repairing but building new craft. There were yards at Caffamill Pill and Bodinnick; at Whitford's Yard, and across at Polruan three slipways, all capable of turning out seagoing vessels.

From 1840 to 1856 very few new ships left these slips, but after the Canadian brigantines had shown their paces, the local shipwrights set to work in earnest. Hardly a year went by from 1856 to 1881 without at least one vessel being launched from one side of the harbour or the other.

Curiously enough the honours were shared almost equally and in alternate years. Thus in 1856 the "Peter and James", a two-masted brigantine, was launched at Polruan for Peter Tadd and others. Next year the schooners "William Morgan Davies" and "Ann Beer", left the Fowey slips. The former had a very brief existence, being wrecked at Fayal in the Azores in January, 1858, but the "Ann Beer' 155 tons, gave many years of service. She was for some time commanded by Captain Jonathan Tadd, had a peculiar mishap in the summer of 1876, when a truck fell on her deck whilst she was loading at the Fowey jetties, and eventually foundered with all hands whilst bound down to the Bay of Biscay in the Newfoundland trade.

Polruan replied in 1859 with the schooner "Kate and Anne" in which John Henry Hocken and other members of that family had interests, whilst the "Albertus" laid down for William Warren Dingle was sent out from Fowey the following season. 1860 saw the "Thomas Aylan", a two-masted schooner of 123 tons, take the water. Her master for a number of years was Captain J. Salt. Two years later the brigantine "Perseverance" of 164 tons was launched at Fowey and the little schooner "Rebecca" of 87 tons at Polruan. In 1863 three schooners, the "Bessie", "Juno" and "Mary Barrett", all left the Polruan slips. Dingle had the brigantine "Rosebud" of 171 tons on the stocks at Fowey in 1865, but on completion she went around to London. Two schooners were launched there in the succeeding year, the "Eliza Annie" of 178 tons and the "Sparkling Wave" of 154 tons.

The latter seems to have set a new fashion in more interesting and appropriate names, for in 1868 the Polruan yards replied with the schooner "Silver Stream", a vessel of 163 tons. Strange as it may seem nowadays, the tiny village of Bodinnick had a building slip next to the ferry landing which in 1869 completed the "Rippling Wave", a fine little schooner of 130 tons. Then in 1870 Slade's yard at Polruan turned out the "Jane Slade". She was originally two masted, but as with many of these vessels it proved more economical

"Ocean Swell," of Fowey.

to fit a third mast and she was accordingly re-rigged in 1905. A proud woman Jane Symons Slade must have been when she looked over the quay wall in the seventies and saw her trim namesake fitting out in Polruan Pool. Captain Thomas Slade was her first master and he was succeeded by Captain T. H. Slade. Eventually the ship passed to William Geake and Co. of St. Columb Major, and for many years she was employed in the general coasting trade. Finally, whilst bound from Hull to a Westcountry port, she went aground and was later brought home to Polruan for repairs, but after being laid up in Pont Pill, she was gradually dismantled. Her remains may still be seen at low tide, a little distance up the Pill.

The "Gem", originally built as a two-masted brigantine in 1871, also underwent a change of rig to suit altered conditions and emerged as a three-masted schooner. In 1873 the schooner "Thetis" was launched at Fowey and next year the "Silver Spray", originally fitted out as a two-masted schooner, but later re-rigged with an additional mast, came from Polruan. Her masters were Richard Pearn and later, Captain H. Martin, who was in command when the vessel foundered off the coast of Brazil.

Three vessels were launched for local owners in 1875. The "Undine" was a two-masted brigantine of 194 tons, with the old-fashioned square stern (still favoured by certain French fishing craft to-day) and a female figurehead; the "Ocean Swell" was a large, three-masted brigantine, whilst the last of the trio was the "Little Beauty", a schooner of 90 tons, lost in 1889. Next year, also from Fowey, came the two-masted (later re-rigged) schooner "Katie Cluett". The three-masted barquentine "Koh-i-Noor" was launched at Polruan in 1877 and was wrecked some thirty years later off the Start. The "Spinaway", schooner, was also built at Fowey in this year, In 1879 the "E. S. Hocken", a three-masted brigantine of 296 tons, was launched at Polruan and the following year saw the last of the locally-built ships, when the "Zingari", afterwards re-named "Little Pet", took the water at Whitford's Yard.

Nor must the considerable amount of ancillary trade which came in the wake of the sailing vessels be forgotten. The Rillstons, besides holding shares in many ships, were also shipchandlers in Fowey. Before the Esplanade was built up the rope-walk was a feature of that part of the town and men and women were constantly employed in laying down the cables and smaller cordage for rigging. Block and pump makers, shipwrights, sailmakers and many others found employment whilst local shipping prospered.

Apart from the coastal trade, in which china clay from Fowey itself, and miscellaneous cargoes of coal, salt and stone picked up at other ports, predominated, with an occasional load of limestone for the farmers in the district, many Fowey and Polruan vessels found a lucrative employment in fetching fruit home, first from the Mediterranean, and later from the West Indies and South American ports, and when steamers gained the monopoly of that trade from 1880 onwards they turned to the Newfoundland fish trade—as their predecessors had some two hundred and fifty years before. There was still a great demand for the Newfoundland cod in the Catholic countries around the Mediterranean. No larger than the ships in which Drake made his voyages, and entirely dependent on the elements, these little Fowey vessels took great risks at times. They sailed dangerously close to the Northern limit of navigation and were often in sight of ice which had broken away from the packs and was drifting southward.

A glimpse of the life is given by Captain John Phillips, who served aboard the ships managed by Messrs. Stephens of Fowey in the 1890's. Of the Fowey vessels he says:—

> "I often now marvel how they stood the strain. I vividly remember one voyage in the 'Little Minnie', in the dead of winter, when halfway across (the Atlantic) we were head reaching, under close-reefed storm trysail and double reefed fore staysail,[1] the mate and I (a boy) on deck about 11.30 p.m. and a dark, dirty night. A big wall of water came hurling towards us, when the mate yelled 'Look out!' It broke aboard just abaft the main rigging and filled her level with the rails; the sea was all lit up with phosphorus. The mate and I picked ourselves up from somewhere for'ard, and when we crawled away aft to see what damage was done we found the skipper was on deck asking what was the matter, as he had been washed out of his bunk.
>
> We found the cabin skylight and companion washed away, and the cabin full of water, port bulwarks gone. We then got tarpaulins and lashed around the combings. The captain and mate then lived for'ard in the foc'sle for the remainder of the passage out. A lot of our stores were damaged, and the fresh water tainted by salt water.
>
> That was a memorable year for casualties in the Western Ocean on both the passage out and home. Out of five vessels that left home that voyage the 'Little Minnie' was the only one that arrived at her port. The 'Daring', of the same firm (Captain Jack Daniels) left Glasgow, bound out but never arrived. The others drove back home and fetched either Falmouth or Plymouth. The 'Little Wonder', of the same firm, homeward bound got dismasted and was abandoned in the Western Ocean. Some of her crew were drowned, washed overboard, the rest lashed themselves to the stumps of the masts and were eventually rescued by a steamer."

A notorious grouse in big ships and small ships of the time was the matter of provisioning. The difficulty of keeping food tolerably fresh during the trip was always a problem, and where the captain was also a part owner in the vessel and as sometimes happened, "careful" in the matter of stores, the men suffered. It was such a master who, when his ship was just out of Fowey harbour at the commencement of a voyage, sent a great part of his sea-stock ashore.

[1] *Sea Breezes.*

In the Tropics the crew, half starved, refused duty and were put ashore where they spent some time in the local gaol and eventually reached home as "distressed British seamen".

The following letter tells of the difficulties experienced in keeping bread or rather ship's biscuit aboard ship:—

"New York October 15. 1884.
10 p.m.

Dear Sir,

I have just finished up on shore . . . . I had to sell 230 lbs. of my bread here for 4/6d per cwt for dog biscuit, it being full of maggots and I allmost starved coming up from Brazil for when I saw the maggots I could not eat the Bread. The Bread was good quality enough, no Fault there. The Fault was with Mr. Tre—— for not baking it enough . . . . but one could hardly expect any other from a man that had been a ship carpenter all his days and then turning Baker . . . . !"

Although the building of seagoing vessels came to an end at Fowey and Polruan in 1880, local owners continued, as they had done in the past, to buy up ships built at other ports. Thus William Warren Dingle, perhaps the greatest of the Fowey shipowners in the 'sixties and early 'seventies, owned, in addition to the vessels already mentioned, the brigantines "Adelaide", built at Padstow in 1869 and altered to schooner rig in 1917, and "Carrie Dingle" and the three-masted barque "Emilie Dingle" of 284 tons.

The numerous Hocken family of Polruan and Fowey (there were 19 brothers and sisters !) had shares in or managed, in addition to their locally-built vessels, the "Ocean Traveller", a three-masted brigantine lost in 1878, and the "Ocean Ranger", a three-masted brigantine of 280 tons with an elliptic stern and woman's bust as a figurehead. John Henry Hocken bought the Austrian-built brigantine "Maria Luigia" and John Edward Hocken the "Italian Gudrun". Richard, Nathaniel and William Hocken also had shares in many other ventures.

Edward Rillston, grocer, bought the schooners "Island Maid" and "Spring" in 1886: the latter was actually a topsail schooner built at Kingsbridge in 1867 of oak and designed especially for the Mediterranean fruit trade. A very fast sailer, she drew only 14 feet of water when loaded. Rillston employed her chiefly in the china clay trade, but in 1891 she went ashore at Gravesend, was sold to a ship-chandler there and for several years was well known in the London river, under her new name of "Gravesend". In 1888 he also had the schooner "Constance". Of his two later ships, the "Victoria", a two-masted brig of 211 tons, was abandoned at sea, whilst the "Beatrice Rillston", a brigantine of 399 tons, stranded at Kiprena Island and was sold as a wreck in May, 1891.

Perhaps the name which survived longest in the local shipowning business was that of Stephens. William Stephens was the postmaster at Par, some three miles from Fowey, and in 1875 owned the "Bessie

Stephens", a schooner of 119 tons, built at that place. He also had interests in the small schooners "Harvest Maid" and "Crystal Stream", the latter also built at Par in 1877. John Stephens had shares in the "Pass-by", a Kingsbridge-built schooner, and in 1886 was managing owner of the "Little Wonder". During the ensuing years he managed a small fleet of schooners, including the "Little Mystery", "Little Secret", "Little Pet", "Little Minnie" and "Daring".

In later years a member of this family bought the famous "Waterwitch"—the last barquentine to fly the British flag. She was originally a brig built at Poole in 1871 of seasoned oak, but in 1885 was re-rigged as a barquentine and for years was in the coastal trade. In 1914 she was driven ashore at Newlyn and was sold for breaking-up purposes to Mr. Edward Stephens, but after a survey she was deemed worthy of repair and was practically rebuilt at Tregaske's yard, Par. Captain Deacon subsequently commanded her on many voyages and she made some very good passages—Fowey to Antwerp in 32 hours, for instance. In 1939, after being laid up for some time, she was sold to Esthonia.

It was a great day when a ship was to be launched. Flags and bunting were displayed and the cheers echoed across the harbour as the vessel glided down and slapped into the water. Nor had ancient superstitions entirely departed. When, on one fine afternoon in 1875, two ships were to be launched at the same time, the "Undine" moved down the slipway at Fowey and in a moment was smoothly riding on the water. Everyone looked expectantly across to the Polruan side, but there the "Little Beauty" refused to budge. Some of the wise ones who watched the shipwrights sweating to release her may have tightened their lips and nodded, for they had seen a little old woman with ringletted curls stand against the seawall, muttering: for long it was vowed that she had cursed the ship, in payment of a grievance she harboured against one of the owners.

Another occasion—this time the excuse for a good Cornish spread—was the "share-out". Notices were sent out in advance and at the stipulated time the various parties, male and female, who held shares in the vessel, stepped into the parlour of a convenient public house, sat down to the "dinner" and then heard the managing owner's report on the ship's activities during the past year and eventually the result of the "share-out" of the profits she had made. In the 'seventies, particularly on the Polruan side, the 64 shares into which the ship was divided were often held by as many as thirty individuals. Thus the original shares in the "Jane Slade" were held by various persons whose occupations or standing included those of Blacksmith, Butcher, Sailmaker, Master Mariner, Grocer, Gentleman, Cabinetmaker, Farmer, Yeoman and Widow.[1]

* * * *

The appearance of Fowey in 1846—the year of Queen Victoria's

[1] Registration Books: Custom House, Fowey.

SCHOONER "LITTLE MYSTERY" IN CAFFA MILL PILL
(Photo lent by Mr. H. Stephens)

visit—included a number of features which have since been swept away. Three or four of the old brick mansions of Stuart and Georgian times still survive, although sadly decayed, but a great many of the more modest cob-built dwellings, which existed a hundred years ago, with their thick irregular walls whitened with lime wash, have now gone. The majority of the arches or bows which then spanned the narrow streets and courts have long since disappeared. One of these was at the Passage end, next to the "Sailor's Return" Inn, and was evidently the site of the North Gate. Beyond this point the road continued up to the old Caffa Mill, keeping close to the little stream which then flowed unhindered into the Pill. A few houses stood on the right-hand side and at one point a cart track led down to the beach. At the mouth of the pretty, wooded little valley were the slipways and quays of the ship-yard with great logs of wood floating in the briny water until they were properly seasoned. A quay projected from the Carn side of the Pill and with the present quay formed a small basin where vessels were repaired. The revenue cutter underwent her overhaul here. This was essentially the maritime quarter of the town and from the "Sailor's Return", Captains' Row led from the Passage, past another small slipway, with a tall old house with granite foundations and brick upper storeys on the left. Fish cellars extended all the way from Pottery Corner almost as far as the Custom House on the seaward side. In North Street were the Bible Christian Chapel, a little school kept by John Godbeer and at the top of Custom House hill an open spring (which may have been the "Blynde Well" in North Street mentioned in 1497). Adjoining was the large 17th-century brick "mansion house" which Dr. Mein and his family had occupied, and at the foot of the steep Custom House hill were two somewhat later residences—the one with dormer windows and a carved porch—the other Waterloo House. Between them in a snug corner, the old Custom House fixed its glassy eye right down the length of Fore Street. In this year Broad Slip was renamed Albert Quay (the original proposition was "Victoria and Albert Quay"). Dolphin Court, leading off from Fore Street, is said to have had a "Dolphin Inn" and was entered, as it is today, under a built-over "bow". Farther along, opposite the "Globe" Inn, was the establishment of Mr. William Lane, printer. The "Lugger Inn" at this time resembled the "Noah's Ark" in its outward appearance and was probably a private house long before it became an inn in the eighteenth century. On the Town Quay were the old fish stalls and the "King of Prussia", an inn dating from early Georgian times and built on to a house some three centuries older. Another "bow" overhung Webb Street, named after John Webb, one of the Overseers of the parish in 1832. The "Rose and Crown" tavern was pulled down following the murder there. The fashionable part of Fowey seems to have been Trafalgar Square with its stately row of large brick and granite residences unmarred by shops. Opposite and adjoining the Town Hall were three older houses, one being occupied by Mr. Phillips, Ropemaker, and another by Mrs.

Bartley, Straw Bonnet Maker. The "Ship Inn" was very much as when it was built in Elizabethan days and a door led through the old oak-panelled upper chamber to the room above the arch, which spanned Lostwithiel Street. Across the way a covered-in alley led down to the yard—Refuge Court—where Mr. Lukey made tallow candles. Next to the "Ship Inn" was the Postmaster's office, where the inhabitants might call for their letters. About this time John Easlick used to bring in the mail on horseback from Par and would sound a horn as soon as he reached the head of Lostwithiel Street to give notice of the arrival of the post. The streets, of course, were cobbled.

This was the town in the early part of Queen Victoria's reign. In April, 1864, the great Garibaldi sailed from Fowey after a triumphant journey down through the west of England to visit his friend, Colonel John Peard of Penquite. Peard was the younger son of Admiral Shuldham Peard and was born at Fowey in July, 1811. He graduated at Exeter College, Oxford, and in 1837 became a barrister at the Inner Temple. It is said that as a young man he weighed fourteen stones, had the "shoulders of a bull" and that on one occasion he drained at a single effort a loving cup containing two quarts of wine. In 1859 he had gone out to help the struggling Italian patriots and soon made a name for himself as a tough fighter, becoming known as "Garibaldi's Englishman". He commanded the English legion and was awarded the Cross of Valour by Victor Emanuel.[1] Returning to Cornwall he lived until 1880, having served as a justice of the peace and deputy lieutenant for the county. He is buried in Fowey cemetery.

In the following summer the Prince and Princess of Wales visited Fowey in the "Osborne". They landed at the "Victoria stairs", where they were received by Lord Vivian, Lord Lieutenant of the county, and the Rev. Dr. Treffry, vicar of the parish and owner of Place. They inspected the "handsome obelisk" at Albert Quay and then proceeded to Place, where a large party of the neighbouring gentry were in attendance. Later the royal party visited the Par Smelting Works and Fowey Consols before continuing their tour to St. Michael's Mount.

Another distinguished visitor was Alfred Lord Tennyson, who came here first in 1849. There is this note of his visit in the journal of Dr. Jonathan Couch, the naturalist, of Polperro:—[2]

> "1848 June 20. I received a visit from Mr. Alfred Tennyson the Poet. He came to Polperro in a boat with Mr. Peach and others, and after viewing the scenery in all directions and taking tea at our house they all rowed back to Fowey late in the evening."

The "Mr. Peach" mentioned in Dr. Couch's journal was Charles William Peach, Customs Searcher at Fowey.[3] He had a very great knowledge of marine fauna and fossils and in 1845 obtained the post

[1] D.N.B.; also article on Peard, *The Listener*, 1946.
[2] Quoted by Sir A. T. Quiller-Couch in *Memories and Opinions* (1944), 6.
[3] The King's Customs: Acton and Maitland.

at Fowey as a result of representations made to Sir Robert Peel. Four years later he moved to another post outside Cornwall.

The usual method of reaching Fowey in those days was by road, either crossing the Ferry at Bodinnick or coming in from Par or Lostwithiel, past Four Turnings and down the recently-constructed New Road hill. The construction of the main line through Par then brought Fowey less than half an hour's journey by carriage or gig and in 1883 the broad gauge mineral line which skirted the river from Lostwithiel to Fowey was reconstructed for passenger traffic. In addition a line was made from Par into Fowey. The result of this construction was to change the old Caffa-mill valley. The mill disappeared, the stream was diverted through pipes and the Pill was partly filled in to provide the foundations for a stone-built station which was never used, the present timber building close by taking its place. In these years the arches at Passage and Lostwithiel Street were taken down (on one occasion the fire-engine had become wedged for many hours under the latter).

A monument in Fowey cemetery commemorates a certain Miss Sarah Jukes and after relating her numerous good qualities adds that she was the first person to reside to the west of Whitehouse. She died in 1871. From then onwards the crews of incoming vessels would perceive a number of changes going on to the west of the town. Private houses, detached and in terraces, hotels and boarding houses were rising in quick succession and some forty years later extended almost to Readymoney Cove.

Some years before this William Rashleigh (1817–1871) had Point Neptune built at the entrance to Readymoney Cove and lived here in preference to Menabilly. After travelling extensively abroad he represented East Cornwall in Parliament from 1841 to 1847 and during the Crimean War went out as a volunteer in H.M.S. "Leopard". He died in 1871 when Menabilly passed to his brother, Jonathan Rashleigh (1820–1905), and Point Neptune became the home of his daughter, Edith Frances, who in 1875 married Sackville George Stopford-Sackville. Mr. and Mrs. William Rashleigh and their daughter were buried within the Mausoleum built for them on the other side of the Cove, close to where St. Catherine's Chapel formerly stood.

A list of tradesmen and merchants in Fowey between 1875 and 1877 includes the following:—

A. Dingle. Flour Merchant.
E. & W. Lovering. Plumbers, Bellhangers, Ship Chandlers.
William Lowry. Wine merchant.
Thomas Richards. Commercial Hotel and Posting House.
John P. Isbell. Painter, Glazier, etc.
G. B. Brokenshaw. Coal Merchant.
Henry Lamb. Manchester House. Silk Mercer, Draper.
E. Gould & Son. Post Office, Dispensing Chemists & Family Grocers.
A. W. Hicks. Sadler, Harness Maker.
J. Wellington. Chemist and Druggist, Stamp Office.

In 1864 a branch of the South Cornwall Bank (Williams, Treffry and Co.) was established here and later the Commercial Bank of Cornwall opened an agency, their representative in 1881 being John Henry Hocken.

The medical practitioners included Dr. Illingsworth and subsequently Drs. Arthur and Percy Davis. The latter lived in the brick house (formerly inhabited by the Meins) before moving to the Scallop Shell House.

In 1856 a scheme was approved for the management of the Town Lands, the Free School and the two charities endowed by John Treffry[1] and Nicholas Sawle. The income was to be applied to altering the existing boys' school and to building or altering premises to serve as a girls' school. A master and mistress were to be appointed at salaries of £80 and £30 respectively. The school was to be open to paying children of all denominations, but the thirty Vincent scholars were to be taught the Church catechism. £30 was to be allocated for repairs to the church, £10 for distribution amongst the poor and £8 for distribution in Bread. In 1879–80 new School buildings were erected above the site of an old quarry near Daglands and in 1890 a new wing was added. Navigation was included in the subjects taught.

Mention has already been made of Godbeer's school in North Street. John Godbeer came originally from Tiverton, where he had been assistant master at the Grammar School. He wrote a pious discourse (printed by William Lane at Fowey in 1830) on the drowning of two men off the harbour entrance and for fifty years taught French, navigation and other subjects. He died on the 15th November, 1867.

There were also a number of private schools. One was kept by a Miss Nicholls. She was a daughter of Lieut. Nicholls, R.N., who was a prominent figure in Fowey during the early part of the century. Miss Netherwood kept a small school in a house farther down the Fore Street, afterwards the offices of Graham, Couch & Co., solicitors.

At Polkerris the village children were taught in a small school maintained for some years by the family at Menabilly. William Rashleigh, F.R.S., F.L.S., F.H.S. (1777–1855), also erected and endowed a chapel-of-ease at Tregaminion. He had been a Member of Parliament for Fowey prior to the passing of the Reform Bill, wrote a number of papers on seaweeds, botany and fishes, and had the Grotto constructed at Pridmouth to house a number of interesting geological specimens and curiosities of natural history.

Most of the existing public buildings were erected during the latter half of this century. As in other parts of the country, the settled conditions and steady increase in prosperity of mid-Victorian times encouraged new building. The parish church was extensively restored in 1870 and the old gallery removed. A new Bible Christian Chapel was built in the Fore Street in 1883 and three years later the Congregational chapel was erected in Lostwithiel Street (in place of an earlier structure dating from 1797 and situated in Bull Hill). In 1894 the Methodist church in North Street was built.

[1] The Charities of Fowey, Cornwall Scheme, 1856.

There was no regular water supply in the town. Water was drawn from wells: one being in North Street, another reached by an open passage way under the "Noah's Ark", a third at Cobb's Well, and a fourth above Union Place. The Fowey Gas Co. was established near the railway station in 1876.

A Cottage Hospital came into being in 1860 and was put on a new footing some thirty years later: the premises were in North Street. Sailors from incoming ships were among the patients and often recuperated at the "Sailors Rest" in Fore Street. This latter institution was a great blessing to seamen and at Christmas time a dinner and entertainment were always provided. The lifeboat station was at Polkerris and it was not until the turn of the century that it was transferred to Fowey.

The Foresters (Court Treffry) were established here in 1863 and five years later the Working Men's Institute was built on the site of the old fish stalls on the Town Quay. A Masonic lodge was opened in 1882 and is situated in Lostwithiel Street. There were various recreational activities such as the Cricket Club—in existence as early as 1856 and dramatic societies flourished in their season. The Regatta was always popular and in 1894 the Royal Fowey Yacht Club was founded with premises in Whitfords Yard. Horse races were held in the fields opposite Lawhyre.

The Volunteers had their drill hall in part of the "Noah's Ark" which had earlier in the century been in use as a beer shop and later as bottling premises for the "Lugger Inn", then kept by Mr. George Varco. Two floors were removed and a new ceiling put in to adapt the house for the Volunteers.

As the result of representations made to the Board of Trade an Act of Parliament was passed in 1869 which provided for the setting up of The Fowey Harbour Commissioners to undertake improvements to the harbour, including dredging and the laying down of buoys and moorings. One of the first tasks of the Commissioners was to arrange for the cutting of a channel through the bar at the harbour mouth, which was threatening to become a serious obstruction. In 1875 Trinity House was prevailed upon to erect a light at Whitehouse Point.

In spite of many changes, Mr. Quiller Couch found much that was still charming and quaint when he first came here in the 1880's. He was a grandson of Dr. Jonathan Couch of Polperro. Writing fifty years later of this first visit he said:—

> "That night I stood long and gazed on the harbour, the track of the moon on its water, the riding lights of two or three small schooners at anchor in the shadow of the farther shore and decided that this were no bad place in which to live.[1] And that is all I need say here of my first acquaintance with the upper and lower reaches of an estuary the tides of which time has since woven so close into the pulse of my own life that memory cannot now separate the rhythms."

[1] *Memories and Opinions*, 66.

In 1887 this young man of twenty-four wrote a novel, "Dead Man's Rock". Following in narrative the style of R. L. Stevenson but with a Cornish background, it was an immediate success and stimulated "Q" (which pseudonym he had adopted) to complete "The Astonishing History of Troy Town" in the following year. "Troy" was, of course, Fowey and a number of the characters in the book, as well as the descriptions, were drawn from local sources. Emra Holmes, who had been Collector of Customs at Fowey, and who was something of a poet and the author of a little booklet on the port entitled "An Unknown Watering Place", is said to have been the original of the love-sick "Mr. Moggridge".

During the next twelve years Mr. Quiller Couch became known for his romantic novels, mostly dealing with Cornwall. In August, 1889, he married a Miss Hicks from Fowey and a few years later the young couple moved into "The Haven" at Whitehouse. Here, during the last years of the century, were entertained a number of famous writers, among them J. M. Barrie and Kenneth Grahame. Towards the end of that time "Q" was turning to more serious literature and in 1900 he completed and had published that greatest of anthologies "The Oxford Book of English Verse".

"Q"—SIR ARTHUR QUILLER COUCH (1863-1944)
(From the portrait by Henry Lamb now in the Royal Institution of Cornwall, Truro)

CHAPTER 10

THE story of Fowey during the last fifty years has been full of change and it will be convenient to take four standpoints during the period and recall what was then happening and what had taken place in the intervening years.

1902. To celebrate the coronation of King Edward VII, the streets of Fowey were decorated with arches and, according to a contemporary account, fashionably attired ladies and gentlemen, entering into the spirit of the occasion, walked alongside farm wagons and distributed loads of silver fir, laurel and larch at suitable points. Holes were made in the cobbled streets and the saplings set up to give the town a pleasant verdant appearance. The festivities, delayed for a month owing to the King's illness, included a procession, a tea for the children in a field at the top of Rawling's Lane and the planting of young trees in the Church Yard. At night great bonfires crackled and roared on the hills above Bodinnick and Polruan. "The Haven" was illuminated by numerous gas lamps, with a four pointed star and "E.R." as the set piece and the newly-built villas, hotels and boarding houses along the Esplanade followed suit, until, with the lights of vessels anchored below and the lamps of Polruan across the water, the whole harbour was aglow.

In general, life in Fowey was still marked by the strict observance of the Sabbath and the soberly attired parishioners who attended the Rev. Purcell's sermon at church or the retired master mariner and others who toiled up Custom House Hill to the newly-built Methodist chapel, usually ruled their households with a strict regard for what in Admiral Buzza's circle was termed "cumeelfo" or as they themselves would have expressed it—"right and proper".

Despite increasing modernisation, Fowey was still the little grey sea town, where, as Kenneth Grahame wrote at the time:—[1]

> "through dark doorways you look down flights of stone steps, overhung by great pink tufts of valerian and ending in a patch of sparkling blue water. The little boats that lie tethered to the rings and stanchions of the old sea wall are gaily painted . . . . the salmon leap on the flood tides, schools of mackarel flash and play past quay sides and foreshores, and by the windows the great vessels glide, night and day, up to their moorings or forth to the open sea."

1913. In the autumn of this year Fowey received a new municipal charter and was restored to the ranks of corporate boroughs. For some years there had been a growing dissatisfaction with the town's meagre representation—three seats out of a total of forty-five—on the St. Austell Rural District Council. A small committee was elected in 1907 from members of the Parish Council and the Fowey Chamber

[1] Kenneth Grahame: *The Wind in the Willows.*

of Commerce, to investigate the possibility of regaining the lost charter rights. Local enthusiasm speeded the project and in 1912 an official enquiry was ordered. Mr. Colquhoun Dill, a barrister, came down from London to preside at this enquiry, which was held in the Town Hall and lasted for two days. It was then shown that since 1871 the population had almost doubled, the export of china clay had increased tremendously and as a holiday resort Fowey was attracting many visitors. Sir Arthur Quiller Couch (for "Q" had been knighted in 1910 and was now Professor of English Literature at Cambridge) also supported the petition.

Eventually it was learned that Fowey's petition had been granted and on a Wednesday in October, 1913, all shops were closed, houses were decorated with flags and a whole day of festivities was planned to celebrate the restoration of borough rights. In front of the Town Hall was emblazoned the Fowey coat of arms—a ship in full sail and underneath, the dates 1295–1913. From the steps above, the acting Town Clerk, Mr. N. P. Jaffery, proclaimed the Charter at 9.30 in the morning.[1] A fanfare of trumpets followed and a service was held in the parish church, where the preacher recalled the close historical connections between the town of Fowey and the Priory of Tywardreath.

Arrangements had been made for the Mayors of the principal Cornish boroughs to visit Fowey, and despite the dull weather an imposing procession formed up in the Station Yard. When the Mayors arrived, wearing their gowns and chains of office, the whole assembly, headed by the Territorial Band and comprising the local Coastguards, boy scouts, fire brigade and other bodies, moved off down the narrow streets.

During the afternoon Place was the centre of affairs and here General Sir Reginald Pole-Carew—a Cornishman who had distinguished himself during the Boer War—handed over the Charter to the first Mayor under the new constitution—Mr. Charles E. Treffry.

The first meeting of the Council of the Borough was held at the Town Hall on the 19th November, when the following were elected:—[2]

Aldermen. Walter Harvey Launcelot Shadwell.
Dr. William Henry Boger.
Captain William Cornish.
Henry Paull.

Councillors. Albert Bartlett.
Robert Vincent.
George Varco, jnr.
Isaac Singleton.
Simeon Rowe.
William Henry Arthur Tucker.
William Hawken Northcote.
Hugh James Nimmo.
John Lewarne.
Frederick H. Knight.
John Pain Isbell.
John Henry Hannan.

[1] *Western Morning News.*
[2] Minute Books: Fowey Borough Council.

Within another twelve months a meeting of this council was interrupted by a messenger bearing a telegram. The telegram was for the Town Clerk, Mr. H. S. Graham, and ordered him to arrange for the mobilisation of the Fowey detachment of Territorials. In many a town and village, peaceful routine was being interrupted in such a manner. Men from Fowey made up the first Territorial unit to land in France.

1925. Five years previously, during the brief post-war spell of prosperity, clay importers in the United States had been pressing for increased loading facilities at Fowey and the completion of the great No. 8 Jetty with its belt conveyor and electrical equipment now enabled a thousand-ton coasting vessel to be loaded in a single day. Larger ships of British, American and Japanese nationality, as well as a host of Scandinavian, Dutch, Belgian and French tramp steamers, used the port. Among the British coasters, the "Rose" line of Richard Hughes & Co. of Liverpool were the most regular callers. The jetties worked right through the night, the ships alongside looking like ghost craft with the whole of their upper works smothered with fine white china clay dust, under the dazzling glare of arc lights and the black velvet pall of darkness framing the entire picture. At times there were a dozen or more vessels lying out in the stream waiting their turn to load, and even the surviving schooners and barquentines were still able to scratch a living in this trade and occasionally make a smart passage reminiscent of their youthful days.

There always seemed to be something of beauty or interest in the harbour. On one occasion the two large Finnish barques "Elakoon" and "Varma" were in port together and a fine picture they made with their white hulls, varnished masts and yards standing out so clearly against the green slopes of Hall Walk, with a cloudless azure sky above.

In the Church Yard a cross of Cornish granite recorded the names of forty-two Fowey men who had not come home when the Great War had ended. During the war years the port had been engaged in sending coal and other supplies to France and there remained vivid memories of Territorials and naval reservists hurrying to the railway station in August, 1914, of the arrival of a thousand men of the Worcester Regiment and their temporary billeting in the town, of the regime of the resident Naval Officer and his ruthless suppression of naked lights which might aid German submarines lurking off the coast. Sir Arthur Quiller Couch had acted as recruiting officer and a pioneer battalion of the D.C.L.I. had been raised and equipped at Fowey. In 1917 "Q 's" only son, Bevil, had been wounded, and two years later whilst serving with the Occupation Forces in Germany he was suddenly taken ill and died.

Soon after the war a public meeting took place at the Armoury, when Sir Charles Hanson presented the Borough with the gold chain and badge which he had worn as Lord Mayor of London. Sir Charles came of local stock, had emigrated to Canada, where he made a fortune and returned to London, of which City he became Alderman in 1909 and Senior Sheriff two years later. In 1917 he was chosen Lord Mayor and created a baronet. He built and resided at Fowey Hall, on the high ground near the old windmill which overlooks the harbour.

In the first years of peace Fowey had, in common with most other towns, enjoyed a short period of commercial activity. There was a great demand for shipping and two or three schooners lay in Caffa Mill Pill at a time, waiting for the repairs which would send them to sea again to earn valuable freights. Yet the boom had died and for months, dragging into years, men steadily tramped up to the jetties and finding no ships to load, tramped back to the Labour Exchange to queue for the "dole". By 1925 however trade was recovering and better times were in sight. In this year a new recreation field was opened at the top of New Road Hill—a bequest from the late Squire and former Mayor of Fowey, Mr. C. E. Treffry.

1935. The greatest apparent change to Fowey in the years following the Great War was undoubtedly the building of the new suburb on the heights above the old town. Opposite the ancient farm of Lawhyre, there sprang up within two decades nearly forty "Council" houses and an even greater number of privately-owned dwellings. The names of Polvillion, Langurthow and Park Roads were given to the thoroughfares fronting these houses. Prior to 1939 a number of old properties—the majority dating from the fifteenth and sixteenth centuries—in the old part of Fowey were demolished. Damp, insanitary and cramped—often built right into the oozing rock, these had been the homes of families through many generations, only their fœtid snugness providing some illusion of comfort.

The general amenities of the borough were increased by several gifts from Mr. Stenton Covington who, about 1920, heard of a scheme to build bungalows on St. Catherine's headland. He promptly bought the property and presented it to the National Trust. Some time later Mr. Covington assisted the Town Council in the purchase of the adjoining woods and garden by providing one-half the cost and as a compliment to him these were named Covington Woods. Another benefactor to the town was Dr. R. T. Cann, who died in 1935. He was a member of the 1907 committee which had performed the groundwork for Fowey's re-incorporation and took a great deal of interest in the history of the locality (his guide to St. Fimbarrus Church being an admirable authority on the subject). In his lifetime he was a friend of the sick and needy and by his will made provision for a number of pensions to be paid to certain aged inhabitants as part of the "Ralph Thomas Cann Charity", an action perhaps inspired by his antiquarian knowledge of the Fowey Charities.

Amongst a number of improvements to the town, the old lime kiln at Readymoney Cove was converted into a bathing shelter, a children's pool and other facilities were provided at Whitehouse and the Town Quay frontage was extended by the removal of old buildings—this work being carried out by the Council. Arrangements were made to increase the water supply and after 1925 a private company supplied the town with electricity. The roof of the church also received a thorough overhaul after it had been discovered in 1930 that the death watch beetle had been destroying the beams. An appeal for funds was launched by the Vicar and Parish Council and fortunately the visible parts of the ceilings, together with the carved angels and ornamental bosses, some five hundred years old, were saved.

Nor was the lighter side of life neglected. A great feature in the summer months had for long been the annual regattas. Fowey Town Regatta is more than a century old—a handbill of 1839 exists, describing the various contests and the prizes offered in that year. After 1919 these regattas were revived with much enthusiasm, the Jetty Regatta being held on a Whit Monday, whilst the Town and Yacht Club Regattas usually took place in September. The twists and turns of the river always added to the excitement and increased speculation on results. Sailing races for the "Troy" class, a handy economical rig standardised under the ægis of the Royal Fowey Yacht Club, lent dignity to the day's events. Then there were the races for four-oared boats, built specially for the occasion. There was the "Sport", built at Hellers loft in the Pill, the "Docker" and "Defender" in brilliant red and green respectively, and a number of other boats from as far afield as Looe, Polperro and Par. Occasionally the famous old tea clipper "Cutty Sark" was brought up from Falmouth to act as committee ship, and the St. Blazey Silver Prize Band enlivened the intervals between races and in the evening headed the Carnival procession through the streets. Then the fair—roundabouts and swings miraculously crowded on the Town Quay—occupied the rest of the evening until at a late hour, laughing, chattering and stumbling in the darkness, everyone trooped out to the terraces overlooking the harbour for a grand view of the Firework Display staged from a barge on the water.

In later years the "Furry Dance" also acquired a new popularity here, with the Town Crier, Ben Johnson (Champion Crier of England and Wales), in three-cornered hat and red, white and blue robes, leading off the couples.

The Silver Jubilee of King George V was celebrated in 1935, the town being dressed with leafy arches, and a great bonfire in the Squire's Field bringing the day to a close. Two years later the Coronation festivities provided another opportunity for merry-making. Then, in 1938, Fowey celebrated its twenty-fifth year as a borough under the new charter. Sir Arthur Quiller Couch was chosen Mayor and received the Freedom of the Borough. In his speech "Q" aptly referred to:

> "the old Ship of Fowey (which) has contrived to run on an even keel—a mere cockboat, to be sure, of the King's realm, yet sharing that wind of God's grace for which we gave thanks this morning."

Shipping also deserves some notice. In the 'thirties newly-built small Dutch motor vessels of low draught and carrying the latest electrical loading and discharging gear made their appearance and in the face of such competition the few remaining sailing vessels were almost doomed. The harbours at Par and Charlestown, a few miles down the coast, began to attract both these motor vessels and the smaller types of coastal steamers. Harbour dues were lighter than at Fowey, but more important, the china clay could be run down from the nearby clay "dries" or sheds, to the waiting ships, by fleets of motor lorries. Rail charges to Fowey were avoided and increasing shipments were made from the smaller ports, although Fowey continued to receive the larger ocean-going vessels. In 1937 exports of china clay totalled 534,588 tons, the greater part being loaded at Fowey.

1946. Traces of the second world war were still evident. A colony of huts remained in the grounds of Fowey hall which had recently been handed back to its owners after occupation by American officers. The little R.A.F. Marine Base yet occupied a part of Caffa Mill Pill, although speedy air-sea rescue launches no longer raced out into the Channel to pick up some airman shot down into the sea. Across at Polruan the children's school was a roofless shell, since one evening in 1940 when a German bomb fell on it, fortunately without killing or maiming anyone. Even the "Liberty" ships which came into the harbour in this first year of peace to load china clay still carried their fore and aft gun mountings, although the wartime grey paint was giving place to more varied colours. But the boom across the harbour between the two old blockhouses had now gone and the little Belgian refugee motor boats which used to make their way out to the fishing grounds early each morning, returning at sunset in single line ahead through the boom gate, had departed home. The concrete emplacements along Hall Walk had been demolished by prisoners of war and the guns which had made St. Catharine's Castle and headland into a small fortress had been dismantled. At Whitehouse there was now a little glass and concrete pavilion which officers and men of the United States Advanced Amphibious Training Force had presented to the townspeople to mark their appreciation of the hospitality they had received. They had descended on the town late in 1943 and by the next summer the invasion of Europe had commenced. During that period high-ranking officers held secret meetings at Place, ammunition was loaded at the jetties and eventually ships laden with equipment and towing huge rafts, departed for the coast of Normandy. (In 1415 companies of archers had embarked from Fowey to join Henry V's army fighting in France.)

One well-loved figure had departed from Fowey during these years. Sir Arthur Quiller Couch died at "The Haven" in the spring of 1944. He saw his goal early in life and devoted his great gifts to the advancement of English literature and education. In his youth he grew to love the beauties and peacefulness of this part of Cornwall and elected to make his home here, overlooking river and sea. Fowey people remember him more intimately pulling across to his garden at Priam's Cellars at Hall Walk in the familiar red boat or strolling down to the Yacht Club, of which he was for many years Commodore. In 1948 a monument to "Q" was very appropriately placed at the seaward end of Hall Walk and another obelisk commemorating the men of the district who had died in the second World War was erected near the Bodinnick end. "Q" would have rejoiced to know that Hall Walk has now been handed over to the National Trust through the generosity of Lt.-Col. Shakerley.

* * * * * * * *

The foregoing is a brief outline of the story of our port of Fowey. Here is an attempt to show the length and breadth of the canvas, a rough sketch of characters and scenes, perhaps a few flashes of colour. It is one of the attractive features of history that the final touches, the delicate tints, the light and the shade, are left for the onlooker to fill in for himself.

Now should the reader cross Bodinnick Ferry, climb the steep hill and out along Hall Walk so that town and harbour lie below with only the river between. Here, where King Charles once stood, you may drink in the scene whilst the breeze blows freshly in from the sea. Then close your eyes and let the few modern landmarks fade from your sight until the town shrinks to its former compact group of grey houses clustered by the river side and around the church. Let the five-thousand-ton cargo ship, belching clouds of thick smoke from her oil burners, clear the harbour entrance and then, in your fancy, watch for the yellow canvas of the "Francis of Foy" and wait for her to drop anchor off the Town Quay and send ashore her treasure and curios from the Spanish main.

And if the evening be fair and the air calm and peaceful, fit for the reflective mind, walk down the narrow tortuous streets of Fowey and from the shadows you may see the paunchy figure of some bye-gone Alderman, with his three-cornered hat, laced coat and knee breeches, taking a pinch of snuff from a little enamelled box as he descends the steps of one of the Georgian houses in Trafalgar Square and crosses the cobbled street to the "Ship Inn" where the "Greys" used to meet and where ships were sold by auction.

Lastly, walk up through the tree-lined Church Yard—as snug and closely packed as the old houses in the town. Here beneath these mounds or within the church sleep Baggas and Trevenors, Rashleighs and Treffrys and the ancestors of half our present inhabitants. Here lie old men who schemed and planned, old women who salted pilchards, gathered herbs and reared great families, young maids who died of the "decline" and babes whose passing from this world was only too frequent—generation after generation lie in peace together. Only those who found the town too small, who wandered abroad and never returned, who sailed in ships and were written down as "lost at sea"—these are not here.

Yet still the life of the old town goes on. Still men scheme and plan, young folk marry and have children to gladden their lives and in time see their grandchildren about them. The rhythm of life continues—rising and falling, but rising again—as the tides that lap the quay side. It is the rhythm of the million tides which have ebbed and flowed since St. Finn Barr left his name in this part of Cornwall. And mingling unseen with the tides is the constant, unfailing flow of the river, coming down from the quiet moors—the divine purpose, as it were, running through the ebb and flow of human endeavour.

THE CHURCH OF ST. FIMBARRUS

THE late Dr. Cann devoted a great deal of study to the history of St. Fimbarrus Church and the following account of the fabric has been taken from his booklet "The Church of St. Fimbarrus", first published in 1910. Extracts and additional notes have been made by kind permission of the Vicar, the Rev. Canon W. R. Guest, M.A. (who has revised and added to the original booklet), and the Parochial Council:—

"A gate on the west gives entrance by some steps to the south porch. The ground here has been excavated to build the western end of the church. First seen, as Fowey Church usually is, from the Town Square, lack of elevation in its site lessens the impression of its really majestic proportions. Here, in fact, it is just a part of a picture in which the bluish-grey stone is the setting for the lighter tracery of Place, which peeps over, and of the street which fronts and partly hides it. A fine picture, but one which carries the eye rather to the romantic house above than to the older and more solemn House below.

"The Porch is late Perpendicular, square and battlemented like the south aisle.[1] Owing to the fall of the ground it is entered from east to west by arches formed of clustered pillars. The twisted shafts of the eastern arch have capitals ornamented with a few old heraldic designs, though most of the work is modern. The moulding of the western arch is simpler. The groined vault is finely formed by granite ribs meeting at an apical boss. Some of the stonework has undergone alteration of design during repair. On the south side, beside two small stone seats and an interesting tombstone, is a small door leading to the priest's chamber above. It has for its step, part of a font. This is said to be the base of the font inside the church. It is certainly made of the same kind of stone but the likeness ends here. On one side is some carving, supposed to be Jonah and the Whale, another side is arcaded like the bowl of many square fonts. Anything less like the chase simplicity of the church font cannot be imagined.

"A winding stair leads to the room above. Probably used once by Thomas Colyns and his monks as a living room or dormitory, it may later have been a scriptorum. It is lighted by east and south windows. On the south west an old door leads by another narrow stair to the flat roof of the south aisle which may have been used as a walk.

[1] Dr. Cann attributed the porch to the period during which Prior Colyns, a protégé of the Abbot of Tavistock, held sway at Tywardreath Priory, i.e. from 1506 onwards, and mentions the similarity to "the so-called refectory, but really a porch, which still exists behind the Bedford Hotel at Tavistock. A similar porch is to be seen at Plympton which was a dependent church. Careful examination will show that it has been added on to the south wall". St. Fimbarrus Church, p. 18.

"On the north of the porch is the church door and remains of the stoup. The latter must have been rather effective. It was held by the forking of a stone column. It is of course gone and has been replaced by an ugly flat-topped stone. The door is fifteenth century. Over it is the empty niche.

"On entering the church we are at once struck by its height, an effect largely due to the presence of a clerestory, an unusual feature in Cornish churches (Lostwithiel and Callington are the only other examples, though a Norman fragment is at St. Germans). The wagon roof of the nave extends without interruption from the tower arch to the east wall, there being no chancel arch. It is probably the finest of its kind in the county. The principals, twenty-one in number, spring from angels carrying shields which were carefully blazoned by Dr. H. Drake at the restoration of the church in 1876. Purlins divide the ceiling into a number of unequal panels, the intersection of ribs and purlins being marked by carved bosses representing foliage. The beams have an eastward trend owing to a movement of the walls. It is held by some authorities that such a roof as this is architecturally, and in combination with a clerestory, ecclesiastically unsound. There is too much weight on the walls and too much light in a part of the church that should be sombre. We think a roof which has held nearly five hundred years is hardly open to criticism and a careful inspection will convince most that the panelling of the ceiling into which a good amount of light filters through the clerestory windows, is the correct treatment of this church.

"The height of the nave has enabled a splendid tower arch to be built. It is fifty feet high, six feet thick and most graceful in proportion. Under the arch stands the font, an early type of Norman. It is of a hard elvan coming from a quarry called Catecleuse in Harlyn Bay near Padstow. It is three feet high, thirty inches across the outer rim, twenty within and ten deep. The bowl is circular and lined inside with lead. The base is modern. The shaft is old. The carving of the bowl consists of five and seven leaved foliage, in circular panels. This foliage is of the honeysuckle pattern. It was derived through Northern France directly from Greece, whose people borrowed it from Semitic Assyria. The original type was a palm leaf. Around the rim of the bowl are series of geometrical forms known as star pattern. Similar fonts are to be found at Lanreath and Ladock in Cornwall and South Brent in Devon.

"The nave arcading consists of five second pointed arches opening into each aisle. The arches are double chamfered, and spring from octagonal piers, peculiar in having no capitals, a continental fashion which had a short vogue in England. It is condemned as slovenly and inartistic, but in Fowey Church it rather adds to the prevailing feeling of graceful loftiness.

"The nave arcade was built before 1336. On the west it is lost in

INTERIOR OF ST. FIMBARRUS CHURCH
(Photo by George Ellis, Bodmin)

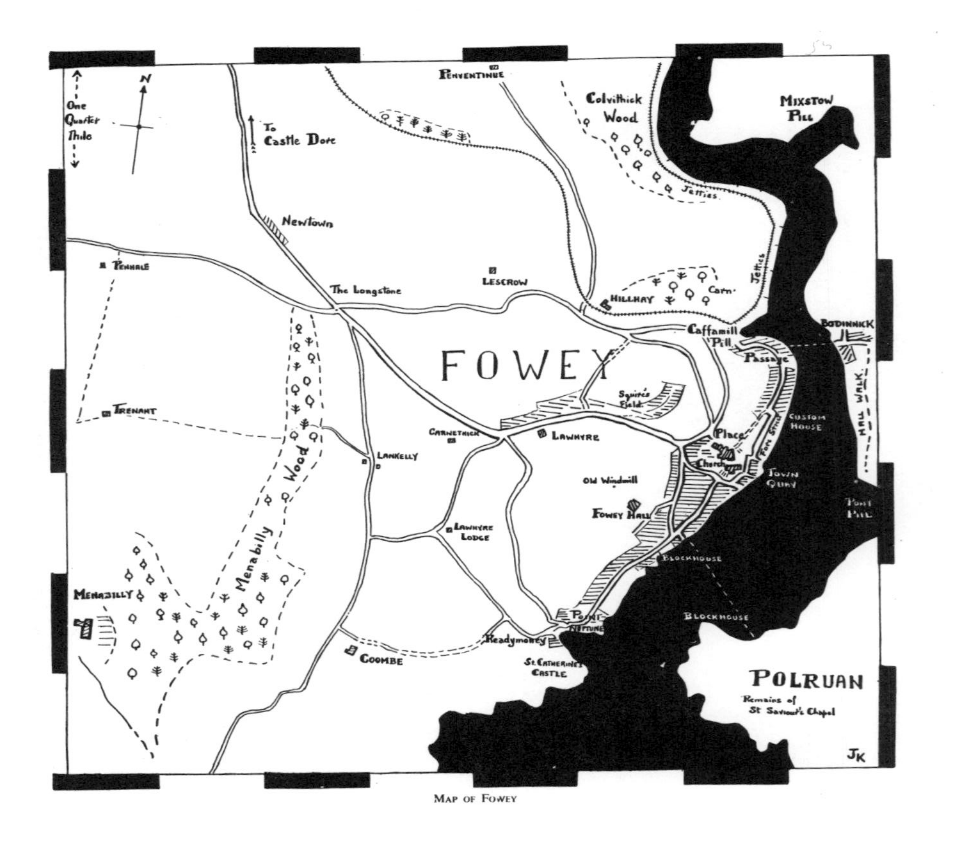
One Quarter Mile
N
To Castle Dore
Penventinue
Colvithick Wood
Mixstow Pill
Jetties
Newtown
Pennale
The Longstone
Lescrow
Hillhay
Carn
Bodinnick
Caffamill Pill
Passage
FOWEY
Squire's Field
Hall Walk
Trenant
Carnethick
Lawhyre
Custom House
Place
Fore Street
Church
Lankelly
Town Quay
Old Windmill
Fowey Hall
Pont Pill
Lawhyre Lodge
Blockhouse
Wood
Menabilly
Blockhouse
Point Neptune
Readymoney
Coombe
St. Catherine's Castle
Polruan
Remains of St Saviour's Chapel
JK

Map of Fowey

the mass of slate masonry built with the tower about 1465. It may be noted here that the older parts of the church were built with Pentuan stone. Later a local bluish slate was brought from a quarry on the Esplanade (in lower Devonian strata) which had furnished the stone for the old castle just below it. This was used for walls and tower, except the facings which were still of Pentuan. Later still, granite was used for groins, buttresses and mullions.

"The clerestory windows are placed Cornish fashion over the piers. There are four on the north side and five on the south. The window on the south west next the porch contains the original masonry. The rest have been renewed. They are decorated in type, contain the best glass in the church, representing Cornish saints, and were subscribed for by the town as a memorial to Dr. Treffry, a former vicar.

"When the tower was built the chancel was lengthened. The original chancel was nearly as shallow as at Lanteglos. In the east wall is the large late Perpendicular window of five lights. The mullions are of granite, the tracery of Pentuan stone. The window contains modern glass designed by Dr. Drake in memory of a Meredith family who had a very temporary connection with Fowey. The lower lights represent scenes in the life of our Lord. In the tracery will be noticed symbols of the Four Evangelists and some heraldic designs, including Crossed Keys, the Bishopric of Exeter; fifteen golden balls, County of Cornwall; the Eagle of the Dinans, St. Andrews Cross and the Ship of Fowey.

"Beneath the east window is a tiled reredos given by Canon Purcell in memory of his wife. It contains the Commandments, Creed and Lords Prayer."

The north chancel wall was pierced in 1876 by an arch, which is a good imitation of the middle pointed work in the nave. There is a stone in the wall in memory of Richard Prynn of Lanjore, St. Germans, who died in 1663, and also a tablet to William Toller, merchant, who married Joan, daughter of Peter Holman, another merchant of the town, and died 25th January, 1684, aged 76. In this wall also is the entrance to the rood steps and a corbel to support the beam.

The south chancel wall was pierced about 1500 by a debased arch leading to the (Lady) Chapel. The masonry is granite. The piers have capitals like those in the south aisle and porch. In this wall is a clerestory window later than those of the nave. It has a lower splay. The glass in its three lights represent St. Fimbarrus, St. Katharine and St. Nicholas, a good combination, though justice is hardly done to the first. The series of heraldic shields commence at the east end of this wall, the first being an eagle from an ancient seal of the Dinans. A parclose screen occupies the arch. It was erected in memory of Miss M. Purcell.

Filling up the break in the south wall for the rood loft is the elaborate monument to John and William Goodall. John Goodall was a Fowey merchant, who died in 1684 at the age of 65. His son William was the first Mayor of Fowey under the charter of James II and died in 1686, aged 40. Both are represented kneeling at a desk, the son wearing his robes of office. Below it is the walled-up entrance to the rood steps. Two rood staircases were pierced in the walls of the older church about 1470. On the north side the piscina was broken into and subsequently mended. On the south there was a similar staircase, but it was removed with the old east end of the south aisle when the (Lady) Chapel was built there about 1500. At this time the chancel wall on this side was pierced to enable the rood loft to be carried over the entrance of this chapel to the new south wall. It will be seen that the arches of the wall on each side in the break for the loft are different. No extension of the loft was made in the north aisle where the old altar was allowed to remain. The chancel is approached by two steps from the nave. It is broad but wanting in depth.

The eastern portion of the north aisle is devoted to the Rashleigh family. The most striking monument in the church is here, the recumbent figure of John Rashleigh the elder, lying on a large slab of marble and alabaster, with feet toward the east, capped and habited in a flowing gown. Under this effigy the sides are carved with a long inscription, various quarterings of the family arms and on the west side the kneeling figure of the younger John which should receive attention as it is very well done, is evidently intended as and probably was a likeness of the Armada hero. The inscription reads:—

"In memory of John Rashleigh, Esq., and of Alice his wife the daughter of Richard Bonithon of Carclewe, Esq.,
And of John Rashleigh their son and of Anne the wife of Jonathan Rashleigh the daughter of Sir Robert Bassett, Knt of Heanton in Devon.
John Rashleigh the father died in May 1624 Aet. 70,
Alice his wife died in April A. Dom. 1606 Aet. 50,
John Rashleigh their son died in May A. Dom. 1624 Aet. 32,
Anne wife of Jonathan Rashleigh died in June A. Dom. 1631 Aet. 31."

"John Rashleigh lived years three-score three
And then did yield to die.
He did bequeath his soul to God,
His corpse herein to lie.

The Devonshire house y^{t} Rashleighs height
Well showeth from whence he came
His virtuous life in Fowey town
Deserveth endless fame.

Lanyon he did take to wife, by her had children store
Yet at his death but daughters six, one son, he had no more
All them to partake under here, because fit space was none
The son whose only charge this was is therefore set alone."

Placed against the wall over the effigy is a florid Jacobean monument of later members of the same family. This is inscribed:—

"In memory of Jonathan Rashleigh of Menabilly Esq.,
who died the 1st Day of May 1675 and of
Mary his wife the daughter of John Harris of Radford
In the Co. of Devon who died the 27th February 1674
and of Joan Rashleigh his daughter-in-law, the
daughter of John Pollexfen of Mothecombe in the
Co. of Devon who died the 6th April 1668
and of Anne his grand-daughter, the daughter of Sir Peter
Courtenay of Trethurffe Knt who died the 13th July 1677
and of Philip Rashleigh his grandson who died the 17th March 1682
and of William Courtenay his grandson who died the 18th January 1683.
Here also lie the bodies of these two infants John and Jonathan,
sons of Jonathan Rashleigh his grandson."

The window between is the only window in this wall still possessing its old stone dressing and mullions. Its outside moulding is well worth a visit.

There is a mural tablet on this north wall to Mary the daughter of Sir Peter Courtenay of Trethurffe, who died in 1655. There is also a pretty little tablet carved by the unfortunate Burnard of Altarnun, well deserving notice. Over the walled-up north door is a picture of David and his harp by a Fowey lad and near by a memorial to Ann Hoal Slade, wife of Captain Thomas Slade, who died in 1893. There is also a memorial to Frances, wife of the Rev. John Kempe, vicar of Fowey, who died 22nd May, 1848, aged 70, and to Louisa, daughter of the Rev. G. H. Kempe, and Sophia his wife, who died on 10th January, 1855, aged fourteen. Another inscription is in memory of Richard Hillersdon of Membland in Devon, who died 23rd August, 1664.

The pulpit is placed against the south-east pier of the nave, is dated 1601 and has rather good carved panels round the sides of no particular symbolic interest. By repute it was made from the timbers of a ship wrecked on this part of the coast at the time of the Armada.

Set in the floor of the aisle is the brass commemorating Alice, wife of John Rashleigh the elder. The inscription reads:—

"Here lieth the bodie of Alice the wife of John Rashleigh esq., and daughter of William Lanyon who died the 20th day of August 1591 and her husband who lieth buried under the monument neare adjoyninge died the 10th day of August 1582. At the time of their deathes they left of their issue livinge one sonne and six daughters which sonne caused this stone to be made in remembrance thereof in the yere of our Lord 1602."

Another brass, of which the inscription is now missing, commemorates Robert Rashleigh, elder brother of John Rashleigh, who died in 1578, and his wife Agnes. Set into this same monument is the following:—

"Here lyeth the body of Robert Rashleigh, gent., of Coombe who departed this life the 27th day of September 1708 aged 63."

This Robert was the last of the Coombe branch of the family.

The east end of the south aisle, the old (Lady) Chapel, has a priest's door in the east wall (Dr. Cann was of the opinion that the priest's house may have stood at the rear of what is now the Lugger Hotel). Below the window of that wall are three brass figures sunk into the stone. The inscriptions are now missing but Richard Symonds, who visited the church in 1644, noted:—

"In the south yle of the chancel the pictures of a man and woman in brasse and this inscription; two shields gone:—
Orate pro animabus Thome Treffry senioris armigeri
et Avisie uxoris ejus et omnium benefactorum suorum.
Another with the picture of a man and woman:
Orate pro animabus Thome Treffry armigeri filii
Thome Treffry et Elizabeth uxoris ejus et omnium filiorum."

One of the female figures has gone but there seems little doubt that these brasses represented Thomas Treffry the elder, his wife and son Thomas and the latter's wife—the Elizabeth Treffry, who so bravely rallied the defenders of her house against the French in 1457.

Against the chancel wall is the monument to John Treffry, who died in 1731 without issue and left the estate to his sister's son William Toller, who afterwards assumed the name of Treffry. The inscription includes the following:—

"Here in this chancel do I lie,
Known by the name of John Treffry
Being made and born for to die
So thou must friend as well as I.
Therefore good works be sure to try
But chiefly love and charity
And still on them with faith rely
So be happy eternally. Soli Deo Gloria."

The Treffry monuments occupy this end of the church. Near the south wall is a large flat tombstone with three figures, one in full armour, and an inscription to Sir John Treffry, who died in 1500, and his brothers, William (died 1504) and Thomas (died 1509). The tombstone of Thomas Treffry, who married Elizabeth, daughter of Henry Killegrew and died in 1563, formerly stood in the chancel but is now in the porch. Another stone commemorates John Treffry, who married Jane, daughter of Sir Reginald Mohun, and died in 1609. A curious tablet (probably 18th century) on this wall refers to "the achievements of John Treffry who at the battle of Poictiers captured the Royal Standard and was made Knight Banneret on the field by the King". There seems to be no documentary evidence for this statement and it is possible that there has been some confusion with the Sir John Treffry, who was knighted at Milford Haven in 1485. There are other monuments to Udney Treffry (1849–1904), to Blakely Von Bretton Treffry, accidentally killed at an early age in 1879, and Colonel Frederic Treffry, A.P.D., who died at Dublin in 1907. The glass in the window, representing the four Apostles, is in memory of

Susanna Ann Austen (died 1842), Joseph Thomas Treffry (died 1850), Edward Willcocks, Jane Treffry Willcocks and Edward Treffry Willcocks. The carved oak in the aisle commemorates three members of the Treffry family who fell in the 1914–1918 War.

Against the south wall is a monument with the following inscription:—

"In memory of Mrs Susannah Graham the very justly esteemed and much regretted wife of Thomas Graham Esq., of this Parish who died the 30th May 1789 in the 78th year of her age.

Thomas Graham Esq., died 10th February 1792 in the 65th year of his age."

There is a small brass to Nevell Norway, jun., merchant, 1808, a monument to Frances Eliza Rogers, daughter of William Brown, solicitor of Fowey and widow of Richard Rogers of Trenant, 1880, and another to Arthur Austen Davis, surgeon, who died in 1888 aged 57.

In the window bays are monuments to Captain Charles Denison, killed in action in 1916, and to Simeon Rowe, killed in Flanders in the same year. Alderman Simeon Rowe, Mayor of Fowey 1922–3, who died in 1928, aged 82, is also commemorated.

Near the door is an inscription to Rev. Hownam B. Illingworth, B.A., chaplain of H.M.S. "Madagascar" and afterwards Colonial Secretary at Lagos, Sierra Leone, who was drowned by the upsetting of his boat in the Sierra Leone river on the 4th July, 1844. He was then 27 years old and this memorial was erected by his former mess-mates in the "Madagascar". In the same aisle is commemorated Abraham Roger Illingworth, Surgeon R.N., who died December 7th, 1869.

At the western end are several small brasses to Captain George Fortescue of the Royal Cornwall Militia (who died of a "decline" at Fowey in 1808) and to other members of his family. Another tablet is inscribed to James Gibson of Pentonville, Middlesex, who died at Fowey, also "of a decline" in 1826, aged 25. John Kimber, one of the last Town Clerks under the old Corporation is commemorated near by. He died in 1824 aged 78, and his wife Eliza May in 1841 aged 87.

The window to the west of the south door still has its old mullions and tracery, but the other windows in this aisle are modern imitations.

Over the south door is the usual board expressing the thanks of King Charles I to the Cornish. The inner door was given nearly fifty years ago as a thanksgiving for preservation from shipwreck.

The tower, which is the highest in the county except Probus, is the usual Cornish Perpendicular, but of more generous dimensions. It consists of four stages, round each of which runs a string course greatly ornamented. The course on the second stage may be especially noted. On the western face, a little from the south-west angle, can be seen the "staff ragulee" of Neville the Kingmaker. The first and fourth stages are made of Pentuan stone. The latter contains the usual louvred belfry window. The corners of this stage terminate in four arcaded and crocketed pinnacles of an unusually good finish. The middle stages are of local slate and contain ordinary two-light windows and a clock. The tower is double buttressed, the ends of the buttresses fining off into some good tracery. The upper floor has a small window opening into the church above the arch. The western window is Perpendicular of four lights. Its glass is a memorial to William Rashleigh, given by his daughter. It delineates, as befits the donor, sea stories in the Life of our Lord. On another wall is the usual quaint poem about bell-ringing. There is also a tombstone to Abraham, Nicholas, Elizabeth and Susannah, children of Abraham Stephens, who died in August, 1636.

Early in the eighteenth century the eastern side of the churchyard was covered with a row of houses which on the north-east crowded against the church.

In 1876 an important restoration took place. The piers and a western gallery, which had been erected in an earlier century, were swept away. The stone dressings of a number of windows were renewed. The east wall of the north aisle was brought nearly flush with the chancel, forming a clergy vestry. An arch was pierced through the north chancel wall to give entrance to the vestry and contain the organ. A new roof was given to the north aisle, stalls of choir and seats of nave and aisles added, the whole costing over £5,000. A choir vestry was erected at the western end of the aisle in 1894.

In 1931 it was found that the oak beams supporting the roof of the south aisle were badly affected by the ravages of the Death-watch beetle so that it was necessary to re-roof the aisle completely. Further investigation showed that the main roof was also in a bad state and following a public meeting a Committee of restoration was appointed. All the useless wood was removed and a new roof fitted, great care being taken to retain the appearance from inside the church. These renovations cost about £4,000, which was met almost entirely by public subscription. The Bishop of Truro dedicated the roof in May, 1934.

At the east end of the churchyard is the War Memorial, consisting of a granite cross; the design of the cross embodies features copied from the ancient Cornish crosses at St. Columb and Cardinham. Facing the street are some modern wrought-iron railings ornamented with a fine grape-vine pattern and heraldic shields.

In 1936 the heating arrangements of the church were improved and the chiming clock made in 1867 by John Smith of Derby was overhauled. During 1948–9 the electric lighting was renewed and the mediaeval style of lanterns—made by hand locally—was introduced.

A carved oak Reredos was erected in 1947 in memory of the late Colonel Edward Treffry and the Rev. Reginald Heber Treffry and Blanche his wife. The Sanctuary and Choir were paved at the same time with Cornish slate slabs set in edge-wise patterns. This paving is an ancient Cornish pattern which may be observed in the flooring of the 15th-century South Porch.

The parish Registers up to 1812 are contained in four volumes, the earliest being a well-bound book with parchment leaves and containing the Baptisms for 1543–1706, Marriages 1568–1707, and

Burials 1603–1707. The entries for 1543–1597 are evidently transcriptions from original sheets. The Registers thereafter are with a few exceptions complete and quite legible. The Marriage Register was printed by Phillimore's in 1905.

VICARS OF FOWEY

1225 (Thomas Fitz al prestre de Fawy mentioned)
1260 Henry de Esse.
1262 Paul de Vuele (Eval).
1266 Robert de Landrae (Landrake).
1297 Ralph, vicar of the church of Fauwy.
1311 John de Trevenor.
1332 John Brey.
1349 John Bagga.
1380 (1) Hugh Thornham.
1380 (2) James Fitz-Hugh.
1394 John Kennyngburghe.
1412 William Cave.
1413 John Fuller.
1416 Richard Udan.
1422 John Jameys.
1423 Roger Spert.
1429 Walter Marshall.
1440 Philip Cheglow.
1456 John Polwhiver.
1464 John Willyams.
1518 Thomas Collyns (also Prior of St. Andrew's, Tywardreath).
1529 Henry Collyns, M.A.
1533 Edward Collyns.
1533 John Prust, M.A.
1566 Richard Richardson.
1572 Richard Gilbert.
1603 Edward Basil.
1625 John Fletcher, M.A.
1656 John Tutchin.
1663 John Atwill.
1668 Justin Treffry.
1696 Mark Trubody.
1700 Jonathan Dagge.
1733 John Dagge.
1753 Nicholas Cory.
1784 James Bennetto.
1818 John Kempe.
1863 Edward John Treffry, D.C.L.
1867 Handfield Noel Purcell, M.A. (Hon. Canon of Truro Cathedral).
1921 John Stern, M.A.
1924 James Harries Jones, M.A.
1927 Walter Ravely Guest, M.A. (Hon. Canon of Truro Cathedral).

FOWEY CHURCH BELLS

These are eight in number and bear the following inscriptions:—

1. "Te Deum Laudamus".
   Handfield Noel Purcell, Vicar.
   John Peers Carter }
   Edmund Hill } Churchwardens.
   Re-cast by John Taylor, Loughborough, 1909.

2. "Magnificat Dominum Anima Mea".
   As above.
   (These bells were added to the peal of six in 1870).

3. Nicholas Cory, Vicar. John Courts and George Harris, C.W.
   Below are the founder's initials and date, I.P:C.P: 1783.

4. Richard Dugger and Walter Colmer, C.W:I.P: 1814.

5. Revd. James Bennetto, Vicar. I.P: 1814.

6. Caleb Cotton, Esq., Mayor and Mr. Johns, junr. C.H. Wardens. 1722.

7. As above.
   (These two bells were cast by Rudhall of Gloucester).

8. Nichs. Cory, Vicar. Will. Goodhall, Mayor, Robert Howson, C.W. Pennington fecit, 1764.
   (On this bell are impressions from an historical medal struck in the reign of George II to commemorate our victories over the French, and bears the date of 1759.)

From "The Church of St. Fimbarrus"—Dr. R. T. Cann.

An old painted board, containing a set of rules for the bellringers hangs in the tower. The ringers—a sturdy lot in their eighteenth-century attire—are depicted and below is the following verse:—

"Hark how the Chirping Treble Sings Most Clear
And Covering Tom coms rowling in the Rear,
We ring the Quick to Church, the Dead to Grave,
Good is our Life, Just Usage let us have.
Now up on end at Stay, come let us See
What Laws are best to keep Sobriety.
To Sweare or Curse, or in a Choleric Mood,
To Strike or Quarrel, tho' he draw no Blood,
To wear a Hat or Spur, to ore turn a Bell
Or by unskilful handling Marrs a Peal,
Such shall pay Sixpence for each Single Crime
Twill make him Cautious gainst another time.
What Forfeitures are due as here it is Exprest
Here is a Box to take the Same when y[u] have Transgrest
And we, the whole Society of Ringers do agree
To Use the Same in Love and Unity."

APPENDIX A.

PRIOR THEOBALD'S CHARTER TO FOWEY

The earliest existing charter granted to Fowey is now, together with other documents from Tywardreath Priory, in the possession of Lord Arundell and is lodged at Wardour Castle. A transcription was printed in Oliver's "Monasticon Dioecesis Exoniensis" (1846), the text being as follows:—

"*Carta libertatis concessa burgensibus de Fowey per priorem et conventum.*

"Sciant omnes tam futuri quam presentes quod ego Theobaldus, prior de Thiwardrait et ejusdem loci conventus dedimus et concessimus et hac presenti carta confirmavimus omnibus burgensibus nostris et hominibus de Fawi et omnibus illis qui burgagia vel terras in eadem villa tenent omnes jonores dignitates libertates et quietantias in quantum ad nos et ad successores nostros spectat quas liberum burgum habere debet, scilicet, quilibet burgensis heriditarie burgagia sua vel burgagium teneat reddendo de quolibet burgagio prout reddere solebat die qua presens carta fuit confirmata pro omni servitio et omni querela, et ad ejus obitum testamentum suum stabile remaneat, cujus vero heres per triginta denarios de relevio heriditatem suam libere et heriditarie teneat et in pace possideat. Insuper jam dicti burgenses et homines predicte ville et eorum heredes libere et quiete remaneant ab omnibus sullagiis et terrenis consuetudinibus et marinis. Et si forte aliquis in placito fuerit, coram nobis vel ballivis nostris in ipsa villa de Fawi et non alibi libere respondeat, sine causa et sine moteamento, et si in amendas ceciderit per sex denarios quietus sit, et si de sanguine et plaga convictus fuerit triginta denarios vadiet et per gratiam nostram vel baillivorum misericorditer reddat. Et si prepositum facere voluerimus, prenominati burgenses eum eligant de illis qui in sepe dicta villa manent. Preterea notandum est quod supradicti burgenses possint filios filiasque suas, nepotes, consanguineas maritare sine licencia et sine causa quacumque et quibuscumque voluerint. Nullus vero advena tabernam extra navem scilicet in villa teneat nisi per licentiam prepositi totiusque villate. Et si quis burgensium burgagium suum vendere voluerit illud sine causa vendat, salvo jure nostro, scilicet, duodecim denariorum de emptore in misercordia nostra vel baillivorum nostrorum. Item si quis sepe dictorum burgensium tenentem aliquem in jam dicta villa de Fawi habeat, curiam de eo libere et plenarie habeat. Quod ut ratum et inconcussum permaneat in posterum tam presentis scripti testimonio quam sigilli nostri appositione munivimus. Hiis testibus, Ricardo de Sirsiaus. Ricardo de Keilgat. Baldwino de Trened. Ongaro de Tregverioc. Watero de Sancto Winnioc. Thoma de Collen. Thoma de Polgru, et multis aliis."

The Charter is undated, but there is reason to believe that it was drawn up between 1190 and 1225. The name of Walter of St. Winnow also appears as witness to a charter granted by Robert de Cardinham to Lostwithiel, which is ascribed by the Historical MSS. Commission to a date between 1190 and 1196. Three others, Richard of Sirsiaus, Richard of Keilgat and Ongar of Tregverioc figure as witnesses to a Looe charter which Mr. C. K. C. Andrew dates between 1210 and 1237.

Motley, in his "Constitutional History", gives a cautionary hint that the granting of a charter did not, in early times, give the town the "corporate capacity of possession or liability which constitutes the essence of a modern borough". He points out that it was the individual burgess who received the privileges—not the town as a whole. The burgess might well be a trader who had settled in the "burgh" and paid a money rent to the great landowner, originally to avoid having to labour, or provide the labour, for the maintenance of the town's walls and defences.

In comparison with the neighbouring town of Lostwithiel, which grew up under lay influence and received its charter direct from the lords of Cardinham, Fowey remained a manor of the Benedictine Priory at Tywardreath, and although the charter of Prior Theobald confirmed to the burgesses a number of rights and privileges which they had doubtless exercised long before this time, the corporative growth of the town was smothered by the domination of the religious house. At Lostwithiel, where the establishment of the Stannary Courts brought the place from being a manor of the Cardinhams to a vigorous borough under the protection of the Prince, the burgesses were indeed able to make some headway. They had jurisdiction over the river Fowey from its mouth to as far inland "as two yoked oxen could walk abreast in the bed of the stream", they sent members up to Parliament from as early as 1304 and possessed the right to hold a market from 1194. At Fowey it was not until 1314 that the privilege of holding a market and two annual fairs was obtained, and even then all the tolls and dues were to go to the Prior. When the port began to prosper in the fourteenth century it is reasonable to suppose that the merchants, many of them aliens or from other parts of the country, maintained a separate community. There are no records of controversy between the town and the Priory until the years immediately preceding the Dissolution. At the same time these two interests seem to have effectively stifled any form of corporate town government.

APPENDIX B.

SOME FOWEY PLACE NAMES

The chief sources for study are the excellent collection of ancient deeds collated by the late Charles Henderson and now held at the Royal Institution of Cornwall Library at Truro, the charts of 1686, 1786, 1811 and 1813 at the Fowey Harbour Office; and the Tithe Maps at the British Museum Library. It is apparent from the calendared descriptions of the great number of 14th and 15th century leases, that around Fowey the use of English for place names had superseded the older Cornish names at an earlier date than was the case in many other parts of the county—a sure sign of the cosmopolitan character of the port in mediaeval days. "Parc" or "Park", the Cornish term for an enclosed field is, however, common enough.

Brown's Hill. Named after William Brown, the lawyer, who lived here in the 1820's.

Bull Hill. Mentioned in 1554 and in the times of Queen Elizabeth and Charles II. It is a terrace path cut in the hillside above the old part of the town, running somewhat parallel to Fore Street. *Union Place* at the south end contains some Jacobean houses and was probably named after the Act of Union with Scotland in 1707. The "Lugger", backing on to Union Place, contains a room dated 1633. The Goodall's old mansion formerly stood in Bull Hill, whilst the early Congregational church occupied the building adjoining Coryton House.

Caffa Mill. See pages 113, 115. In 1540 a tenement and mill called Caughmyll and land called the South Carron (i.e. Carn) passed to the Colquite family.

Carn. See pages 2, 5, 7, 19. Probably an ancient "caer" or fortified settlement, still pronounced locally as "Cairn". In 1313 the vill of Carn is mentioned. A lease of 1365 describes the "Lord's Wood" (this exists today at the back of the railway station and contains an ancient rocking stone which is unknown to the majority of Fowey inhabitants) and the "Way which leadeth from Atte Carn to Penfontenyou". "Glant Way-Field", which adjoins the woods, undoubtedly marks the old field path from Fowey to the village of Golant.

Cobb's Well. At the "head of the town" (as expressed locally). A number of Tudor cob-built cottages built on the hillside, with a cobbled forecourt, in one corner of which is a mediaeval granite trough and an old pump. Evidently this was one of the town wells of early days. John Cobb the elder and his son were living in Fowey in 1597.

Daglands. Mr. Henderson suggested some connection with the family of Dagge. John and Jonathan Dagge were successive vicars of Fowey at the beginning of the eighteenth century and others of the family were Collectors of Customs here in 1691 and 1700. "Daggesland" is, however, mentioned as early as 1552. In 1571 John Bowringe, weaver, sold "Dagsland" to William Dickwoode, merchant. A little later the "meadow called Daggaland" was in the possession of Thomas Dickwood, *alias* Peter—father or grandfather of the famous Hugh Peters. Some years ago, when a fight was impending at the Boys' School, the cry would be "Out to Daglands!" where, within a small open space beyond magisterial jurisdiction, the battle was then fought to a finish.

Passage. See page 18. In 1509/10 the rent of the ferry was worth £6 a year. Robert Hobb, surgeon, was living in a house adjoining the Passage in 1555.

Place. Is evidently allied to the Welsh "Plas". Across at Padstow on the North coast is another "Place"—an Elizabethan mansion which was formerly a retreat for Bodmin Priory. The oldest parts of the house at Fowey date from the time of Henry VII. The old field names around Place were eminently descriptive. In 1602 the *Culver House Close* is mentioned, from which it is fairly certain that the Treffrys of that age had their own culver house or pigeon loft, pigeons being considered a delicacy in the Tudor household. *Saffron Close* and *Fennel Styche* were not far away, and in these fields the Elizabethan housewife would doubtless find an abundance of meadow saffron and fennel with which to concoct her much-prized flavourings, medicines and salads. The *Windmill Park* (now Windmill Field) stood high on the hill facing seawards in 1564, and *Trinity Close*, mentioned a few years previously, was suggested by Mr. Henderson to have originated as the endowment of an altar dedicated to the Holy Trinity in Fowey Church.

Other place names have disappeared in the course of time and only with some difficulty can their location be found.

Langurthow. See pages 5, 7, 19. Henderson translates the name as the Church of Corron and links it with Langorro—the old name of Crantock on the North Cornish coast. It has been revived as the name of a road in the newer part of the town.

The Velger or Velgeze was, in Elizabethan times, a small open space near the junction of the present Lostwithiel Street (then known as the Queen's Highway and previously as the High Street) and Brown's Hill. In 1572 there was a tree here called the Great Thorn which even then was more than a hundred years old since in 1466 there is reference to a house "next le gret Thorne". Adjoining was part of the Town Lands and the house of Rowland Jennings, merchant. The Corporation poor house, which was in existence in 1746, formerly stood here and was rebuilt about 1760.

Rock's End. Before the cutting of the present New Road Hill during the early years of Queen Victoria's reign, a narrow twisting road led down to the town. The Commercial Inn was in existence in 1832 and the adjoining tenements and gardens seemed to have formed a quarter known as Rock's End. In 1555 there is mention of a close called Rock's End on the west of the sanctuary of the vicarage of Fowey and in 1639 of the street "towards Rock's End".

APPENDIX C.

NOTES ON FARMS IN THE FOWEY DISTRICT

HILLHAY. See pages 58, 68.

In 1581 William Mohun of Boconnoc leased the property to Thomas Leigh of Northam (the Leighs of North Devon were related to the Rashleighs, and Amyas Leigh, the hero of "Westward Ho!" was supposed by Kingsley to have sprung from that family). The tenancy soon passed to the Peters family and it is likely that the famous Hugh Peters spent his youth here. In 1632, Sir Reginald Mohun granted to Thomas Peters of Mylor, clerk, Hillhay in Fowey "where Thomas Peters, his grandfather and Thomas Peters, his father lived". Later the tenancy went to the Majors and in 1653, Jane Major, widow, for the love she had for Peter Major, her grandson, left him the house and 10 acres of land. John Goodall had actually acquired the property from Warwick, Lord Mohun, and in 1671 was joined in a bond with Peter Major, his tenant.

LANHERRIOT. See page 20.

Henderson thought this could be identified with the "Lazhyrget" of mediaeval deeds, which was capable of holding a court. In 1658, William Mitchell, yeoman, of Lanherriot, held a quarter share in the property. The rise in farm values may be judged from the fact that the farm was worth £320 in 1689, rose to £460 some thirteen years later and in 1717 was sold to Caleb Cotton for £550. Cotton in turn, sold it to Philip Rashleigh.

LAWHYRE. See pages 7, 20.

Anciently Lanwoer. About the year 1200, Robert de Cardinham granted to Geoffrey de Lanwoer the "water which runs between my land of Tywardreath and the land of Trenant", that is, the stream which flows down from Tregaminion to Pridmouth. In 1374 Gerard Lawhyer exchanged certain lands with William, Prior of Tywardreath, and three years later at "Lawheor" he signed a deed conveying his lands to his sons, Thomas and John and to Henry Dawe of Fowey. The lands then comprised Lawheor, Gom, Polrideman, Bennathelek and Porthenys. Gerard was apparently alive in 1407, in which year John Nicol of Bodmin received a grant of 20 pence out of his land of Lawhier and Trewala.

Now Thomas Lawhyer caused his family a good deal of trouble by granting his lands first to his two nieces Elizabeth and Joan, daughters of his brother John Lawhyer, and then to his sister's son, Thomas Tregodek. After some controversy the women vindicated their claim and in 1463, Prior Walter confirmed the land in the possession of Elizabeth, now the wife of William Hourde of Fowey. Thirty years later she was a widow, apparently without children and finding the management of Lawhyre too much for her, she let her "cousin", John Tregodek, have the farm in return for a pension of 5 marks, 6 shillings and 8 pence and the right of "estovers, husbote, haybote", etc. Sir John Treffry was witness to this deed.

But the Tregodeks did not hold Lawhyre for long. In 1518 John Tregodek, "gentilman" let the lands to Henry Colquite and when Thomas Tregodek died early in the reign of Queen Elizabeth, the Colquites were well established there. The old mill and the water course in the South Ground field are mentioned in 1541. It seems to have been the Colquite's great ambition to settle the lands in their family for ever, as the Rashleighs with whom they were related, were doing at Menabilly and Coombe. They registered their pedigree at the Heralds Visitation in 1620. In 1652 Lewis Colquite of Lawhyre, gentleman, had property in the town of Fowey and only a few years before the family controlled four burgesses' votes at the parliamentary elections. In the reign of Queen Anne they came to an end with Francis Colquite, whose nephew, Francis Lambe, found his uncle's affairs in such a muddle that the debts could barely be settled. Lawhyre was left to another nephew, Charles Lambe. In 1838 Lawhyre, consisting of 90 acres, and Little Lawhyre of 27 acres, appear as the property of William Rashleigh, Esquire, of Menabilly.

PENVENTINUE. See pages 5, 6, 7, 20.

The account of Julian Jamys, Reeve of Penfyntyneowe in 1509–10, is still preserved. The conventionary tenants then paid no less than £17. 8s. 10d. in comparison with the 4/7½d. received from the free tenants. At this court the rent of Greater Lescrow was increased by 3½d. In addition, 15 shillings were received in lieu of an ox which should have been paid to the lord as heriot (death duty) on the decease of John Davy of Pynnyk. For his fee the Steward had 6/8d., and 4d. was expended in buying parchment to set out this account.

TREGAMINION. See page 20.

Mentioned in Robert de Cardinham's charter to Geoffrey de Lanwoer about 1200 A.D. In the time of Queen Elizabeth, Robert Rashleigh bought Tregaminion from Christopher Coplestone. A chapel of ease was erected here by William Rashleigh in 1816.

TRENANT. See pages 5, 6, 20, 38, 99.

When Philip Rashleigh purchased the Manor of Trenant from the King in 1545 for £209, the rents of the free tenants amounted to £3. 1s. 3½d. and those of the customary or conventionary tenants to £8. 8s. 0d. Four years later, Thomas Treffry and Thomas Tregodek were among the free tenants of this manor. John Harry was the Reeve and also did fealty in right of his wife, for Little Lawyre. Nicholas Colyn, a relative of old Prior Collins of Tywardreath, was Reeve in 1551. An unpleasant surprise came in 1608 when the king's commissioner's informed John Rashleigh that the tenure was legally defective and advised him to compound for the lands.

APPENDIX D.

THE BOUNDS OF FOWEY IN THE TIME OF JAMES I

A note of the Bounds viewed by John Cooke, Robert Chelley and Walter Kennish, churchwardens, with the Vicar of Fowye and the older and sufficient men of the parishe 12th May, 1613.

In the East and South with the sea and river of Fowye, on the South-West with a gate called Pollradman (Pridmouth) Gate between Trewardreth and Fowye with a hedge that leadeth North-West with a moore meadow which is part of the parish of Trewardreth and the lands of John Raishleighe esq., of Fowye and the hedge of Kill Parke of Trenant which leadeth directly by the Coombe towards the king's highway and a hedge between John Penhalle's Trenante called the Will Parke and on the West it bordereth with the hedge which is betweene John Jessop and William Pherris of Trewardreth and the same hedge boundeth between John Jossep [*sic*] of Fowye and William Ludland of Trewardreth called Lampethow and again with the same hedge between William Penhalle of Foweye and Walter Truebodye called Fowye Parke in the North with a Cornerbond between Fowye, Glant and Trewardreth which is at the end of John Penquite's lane which hedge leadeth to the king's highway and boundeth in the North-East with a gate called Collwill and in the lands of John Mitchell and the same hedge leadeth along into Bodmyn Pill bounded with Colvethicke Woode in Fowye by the lands of Sir Reignold Mohone, Kt, and Bart, in the North side with the Comons of Glant.

APPENDIX E.

CONNECTION BETWEEN THE DYKEWOOD (PETER),

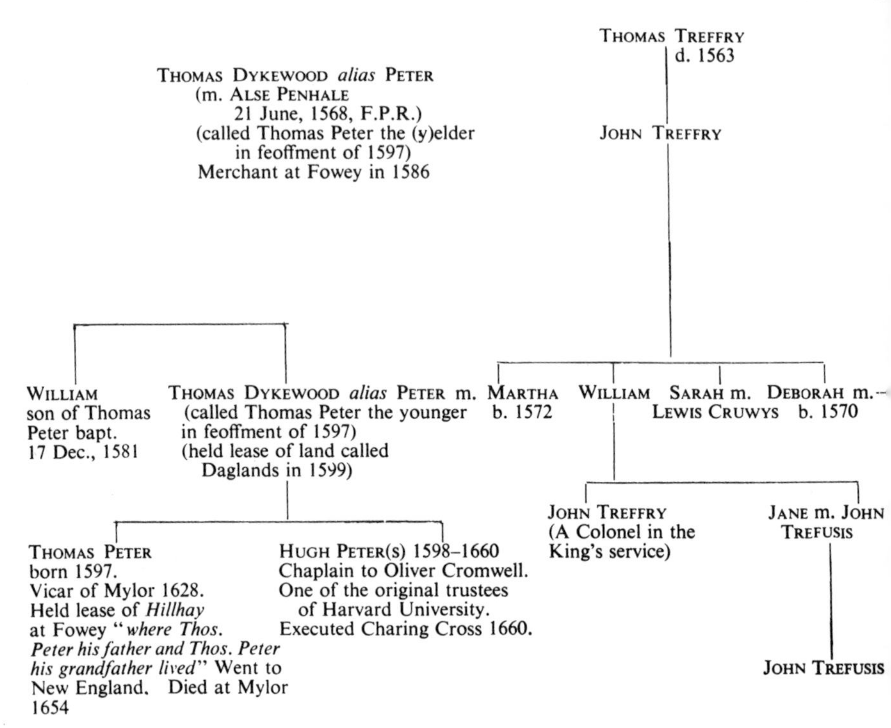

FOWEY MARRIAGE REGISTERS CONTAIN THE FOLLOWING ENTRIES:—

1. Margaret Dickwoode mar. Davye Williams 17 Aug., 1579.
2. John Peeters mar. Christian Jeffery of Tywardreath 8 July, 1662.
3. Derick Peter mar. Agnes Turny 21 Sep., 1629.
4. Henry Peter, esq., mar. Mrs. Eliz. Giles 29th May, 1733.

DOMESTIC STATE PAPERS.

"Mr. Peter the Mayor" at Fowey was in trouble with the Navy officials over a cargo of barrel staves (1659).

TREFFRY AND PETER FAMILIES.

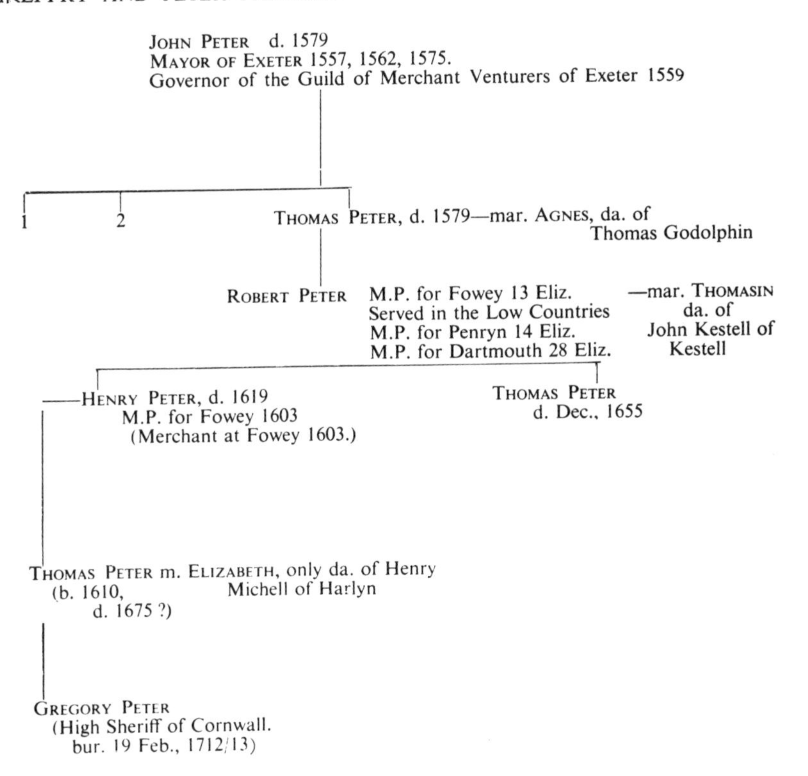

NOTES:

1. *Parochial History of Cornwall* (1868) says, "Thomas Dykewood Peters", a merchant of Fowey, whose ancestor Dykewood, being a Protestant, had fled from Antwerp to escape persecution, and later states that he "was a Turkey merchant at Fowey in the time of Queen Elizabeth".
   It is worth noticing that Thomas Treffry and the contemporaries, Robert Peter and Thomas Dykewood the elder had connections with the Low Countries. Treffry is said to have fled there during the reign of Mary, Robert Peter served as a soldier in the Netherlands and Dykewood the elder undoubtedly came of Dutch or Flemish extraction.
2. The birthplace of Hugh Peters and the home of the Dykewood family at Fowey seems to be established as *Hillhay*, about half a mile out of Fowey, the present building is seventeenth century in character.
3. The descent from John Peter to the left of the dotted line is taken from Vivian's *Visitations of Cornwall*, p. 605.

APPENDIX F.

FOWEY AND "THE FAIR MAID OF THE WEST"

This play by Thomas Heywood was first printed in 1630: a revival performance was given at the Malvern Festival in 1933. The story is simple but full of dramatic incident—a brawl at an inn, a sea-fight, true love suffering in adversity and finally rewarded.

The hero, Spencer, is in love with Bess, serving maid at a Plymouth tavern. He becomes involved in a rough and tumble during which a man is killed, escapes hurriedly to "Foy" and takes ship to the Azores. Before leaving Plymouth he gives Bess a hundred pounds and tells her he has "a house in Foy, a tavern called the Windmill", where she can stay until his return.

At the Azores Spencer is wounded in an affray and fearing death, begs his friend, Captain Thomas Goodlack, to seek out Bess and if she is still faithful, to give her a last bequest of five hundred pounds. During the night Goodlack is told that his friend has died.

The captain arrives at Fowey and meeting the Mayor and an Alderman, enquires how Bess is reputed in the locality. The Mayor praises her beauty and chaste behaviour and Goodlack is wholly convinced when he witnesses her grief. Bess accepts the legacy but plans to bring Spencer's body home for burial. Goodlack is commissioned to buy a ship at Falmouth and before sailing Bess gives orders for the town of Fowey to be feasted at her expense and then reveals that she has left in trust of the Mayor and Aldermen "To set up young beginners in their trade £1,000, to relieve such as had loss by sea £500, To every maid married out of Foy whose name is Elizabeth £10 and to relieve maimed soldiers by the year £10".

Meanwhile Spencer has recovered—the report given to Goodlack proves false—but on his journey home is captured by a Spanish ship. Bess, disguised as a man, is at sea in her ship the "Negro" and sights the Spaniard. After a brisk fight the latter is captured and Spencer freed, but in the confusion the two do not meet.

The "Negro" drops anchor at a port on the Barbary coast and the English crew are invited to the court of Mullisheg, King of Fez. For this occasion Bess discards her disguise and the lovers are amazed to recognise each other. The King of Fez, marvelling at her beauty, offers Bess half his kingdom if she will stay and become his queen. Bess declines and a preacher standing conveniently by, the lovers are wedded whilst the audience are left to murmur, "Ay, there's a girl worth gold!"

The links with Fowey are interesting.

Captain Thomas Goodlack.—There is a fascinating likeness here to the real Captain Thomas Goodall, a prominent merchant and seaman of the 1630's, whose name frequently appears in the Port Books and who was in 1634 master of the "Lydia" of Fowey trading to St. Malo.

John Goodall was released from slavery in Algiers in 1622. Other members of the same family—Philip and John Goodall—were merchants here later in the century. In the play, before she is convinced that Goodlack is really loyal to Spencer, Bess makes the following rather significant remark:

Goodlack: "My name is Captain Thomas Good——".

Bess: "I see no good in thee; rase that syllable out of thy name!"

The Windmill Tavern.—Although there is no record of an inn of this name at Fowey, the windmill on the height above the town was a prominent landmark in the seventeenth century and is clearly shown on charts of the period. Any seaman using the harbour would know it. In one scene there is reference to "the little crooked street below" which would suit the site of the old "Rose and Crown" at the lower end of the churchyard and adjacent to which the Fore Street makes a double bend.

Mayor and Aldermen.—Although the first royal charter was not granted until 1685 the "Mayor" is occasionally referred to before this date.

The Charities.—There were several Charities existent in Fowey before 1630. The Town Lands were extensive and by his will dated 1582 John Rashleigh left money for the poor of Fowey.

In this engaging play there are so many points showing an intimate knowledge of sea-faring matters that it seems likely that Heywood himself served in a sea expedition at some time. Perhaps he took ship from Fowey, lodged at a local tavern before sailing and made the acquaintance of Captain Thomas Goodall. Who knows but that some pretty serving wench was the original of that virtuous Amazon—the Fair Maid of the West?

APPENDIX G.

MAYORS OF FOWEY

1685	William Goodall.	1755	Lewis Baker.
1687	Richard Cotton.	1761	John Coryton.
1690	Jonathan Tingcombe.	1764	William Goodall.
1695	Abraham Stephens.	1783	John Rashleigh.
1700	Stephen Wenmoth.	1798	Joseph May Ward.
1702	Stephen Wenmoth.	1803	Thomas Graham.
1703	James Denbow.	1805	William Rashleigh.
1704	Henry Stephens.	1806	Philip Rashleigh.
1706	Henry Stephens.	1807	Joseph May Ward.
1707	John Pomeroy.	1808	Benjamin Bloomfield.
1708	William Kendall.	1809	John Kimber.
1709	Gregory Stribley.	1810	Thomas Orchard.
1710	Stephen Wenmoth.	1811	John Bennett.
1713	Jonathan Stephens.	1812	William Rashleigh.
1714	Alexander Wolcott.	1813	John Hallett.
1716	William Toller.	1814	Thomas Graham.
1722	Caleb Cotton.	1815	Joseph May Ward (resigned).
1726	Richard Treweekes. (?)	1816	Thomas Brown.
1733	Charles Lambe.	1819	George Graham White.
1734	James Denbow.	1823	John Bennett.
1741	Abraham Stephens.	1827	Robert Hearle.

RECORDERS

1685 Earl of Bath.
Jonathan Rashleigh—Assistant Recorder.
1690 John Rashleigh (for life).
1714 Philip Rashleigh.

MAYORS OF FOWEY

(Subsequent to re-incorporation of Borough 1913)

1913	Charles Ebenezer Treffry.	1933	George Varco.
1914 to 1918	Walter H. L. Shadwell.	1934	William Charles Beale.
		1935	William Charles Beale.
1919	John Pain Isbell.	1936	Edward Treffry.
1920	Robert Vincent.	1937	Sir Arthur T. Quiller-Couch.
1921	Henry Paull.	1938	Alfred Edward Libby.
1922	Simeon Rowe.	1939	Alfred Edward Libby.
1923	Frederick Harris Knight.	1940	Alfred Edward Libby.
1924	George Varco.	1941	Jesse Julian.
1925	John Green Lewarne.	1942	William James Douglas.
1926	Robert Varco.	1943	William James Douglas.
1927	Robert Varco.	1944	Peter Harvey Rowe.
1928	George Clatworthy.	1945	Harry Chandler.
1929	George Clatworthy.	1946	Harry Chandler.
1930	Christopher John Mitchell.	1947	Harry Rashleigh.
1931	Christopher John Mitchell.	1948	Harry Rashleigh.
1932	George Varco.	1949	F. W. Whitting.

TOWN CLERKS

1913 Norman P. Jaffery—"Charter Town Clerk".
1913 Henry Salkeld Graham.
1928 W. C. P. Gatley.

FOWEY CORPORATION RECORDS

Note

No manuscript records of the old Corporation seem to have survived. The Charity Commissioners found in 1838 that a number of documents had been burnt in 1805. An account book dating from 1606 is mentioned as having been taken by Mr. Austen of Place and other records as having been produced as evidence in the Chancery proceedings. The records of the Chancery case at the P.R.O. have been examined but nothing pertaining to the Corporation has been found. There are no books or papers relating to the old Corporation at Place.

The attached list of Mayors has been based on a manuscript list made by the late Dr. Cann and additions have been made from the following sources:

1. Parliamentary Returns (these always show the Portreeve but not always the Mayor).	1684, 1695, 1700, 1702, 1709, 1726, 1733, 1741, 1761.
2. Cal. of State Papers—Dom.-America and W. Indies.	1710, 1714, 1716.
3. Customs "Oath Book".	1702, 1703, 1704, 1706. 1707.
4. Pay List of Sea Fencibles.	1798, 1803.
5. Report of Commission on Municipal Corporations.	1827.
6. West Briton.	1823.

Records in possession of the Fowey Borough Council include the original Charter of 1690, a photostat copy of the Charter of 1819, three mediaeval deeds relating to land adjacent to the river Fowey, a set of Parliamentary election posters of the early 19th century, a number of engravings of Fowey in the 18th and 19th centuries. There is also an autographed set of "Q's" books. Insignia, etc. (including the maces) have already been mentioned in the text (Chapter 6). There is a 19th century Constable's stave, impressions of Customs Seal (Eliz.) and Corporation seal (1702).

APPENDIX H.

SHIPS OF THE ROYAL NAVY WHICH HAVE BORNE THE NAME "FOWEY"

	Launched	*Type and Tonnage*	*Engagements, etc.*
I	1696	5th Rate 377 tons 32 guns	Whilst on convoy duties assisted in capture of French ship "Seyne"—July, 1704. Captured by French in the following month.
II	1705	Pink 411 tons 32 guns	At reduction of Minorca—1708. Captured by French—1709.
III	1709	5th Rate 528 tons 42 guns	Assisted in re-capture of British ship "Scarborough" from the French—1711.
IV	1743	5th Rate 709 tons 44 guns	Destroyed the privateer "Griffon" under a battery at Fecamp—1745. Wrecked on coast of Florida—1748.
V	1747	6th Rate 513 tons 24 guns	Captured Spanish ship "Ventura"—1762. Sunk in York river to prevent capture by the enemy—American War of Independence—1781.
VI	1795	Gunboat	—
VII	1799	Hired Cutter 12 guns	—
VIII	1813	Sloop 18 guns	—
IX	1918	Minesweeper	Re-named "Forres".
X	1930	Sloop 1,105 tons 2-4 in. guns	For several years stationed in Persian Gulf. Allocated for convoy duties—1939. In company with H.M.S. "Whitshead" sank a German U-boat off S.W. coast of Ireland—1940. Assisted in sinking surrendered German U-boats—1945.

APPENDIX I.

AN ELECTION PETITION OF 1815.

FOWEY CHURCH RATE.

Established by Custom, not quite so old as Richard the first's return from the Holy Land nor as Buonaparte's flight from the same quarter.

INHABITANTS OF FOWEY,

The Bullies of your Borough—The Tools of Corruption, are again summonsed at a Vestry on Thursday next at Eleven o'clock to Vote away a little more of your Money ! Some

posted, and
recorded Liar
may tell you that "it is hard Mr.
Colmer should lose his Money."

Be not deceived !—You have nothing to do with Mr. COLMER—HE preferred being the Servant of the Mayor rather than the Servant of the Parishioners—let the Mayor therefore settle his expenditures—OVER WHICH YOU HAD NO CONTROL ! Come boldly forward and demand the Mayor's Accounts. No Attorney will again dare to insult you, and remember that Prince's Tenants cannot out-number you ! At such a Crisis WHO can conscientiously stay at Home ? Votes, and not wishes, must decide ! !—The Contest is simply this . . . The MAYOR receives large revenues from the Town—SHALL HE APPLY THEM TO YOUR USE, OR TO HIS OWN ?

You, who love TRUTH, LIBERTY, and JUSTICE, shun not the Contest to degrade our ENEMY, without facing him, is cowardice. Come and condemn him from his own lips. Tarnish not the glorious VICTORY that YOU obtained on Saturday last, another, and another such, will immortalize YOUR independence.

FOWEY, *Monday, April* 17*th*, 1815. *J. T. AUSTEN.*

Lane, Printer &c, Fowey.

* * * * * * * *

This is a good example of the attack and biting repartee which was used by "Blues" and "Greys" alike. Walter Colmer was licensee of the Ship Inn and also Mr. Rashleigh's party agent at the elections. He had evidently incurred certain expenses which the "Blues" impute that he hoped to obtain from the Mayor, Thomas Graham, out of the Church Rates at the next parish meeting. The "glorious victory" was not one of Wellington's victories but the result of the decision of the local Bench not to admit certain residents of Fowey to the Poor Rate list ! It was certainly a minor setback for the Corporation and they were to suffer a worse one during the summer of 1816 when the Mayor, Joseph May Ward, threw up office.

PEOPLE OF FOWEY

Be Not Incredulous !

A writer styling himself "A SCOT AND LOT MAN" asserts that the Greys are "a large Majority." If you believed a certain person because he swore that his wife was frightened at the very sight of a man in LONDON, when it was notorious that SHE WAS AT FOWEY !—then believe that the Greys are "a large Majority ! !" If because the SMUGGLING MAYOR so swore—you believed that a pauper from Falmouth (now renting a house at Fowey rated at one pound fifteen shillings a year, but actually worth about four pounds a year) "is a substantial Householder—a respectable tradesman —and a Man of credit" ! then believe the Corporation and their mouth-speech when they assert that they have a certain majority of Sixty Scot and Lot Men in favour of BAILLIE and CAMPBELL ! ! then also believe that the

B L U E S

are annihilated, and that

O N E and A L L

CRY OUT BOTTLECRACKER

for ever—and may

THE TRADE OF BOTTLECRACKING,

FOR THE SAKE OF MORALITY,

flourish in Fowey

On every Sunday Morning, at two o'clock, till Doomsday ! ! !

"TRUTH AGAINST ALL THE WORLD."

Fowey, 6th June, 1826. William Lane, Printer, Fowey.

MEMBERS OF PARLIAMENT FOR THE BOROUGH OF FOWEY

Elizabeth.

(1570 R. Peter and R. Cromwell.)
1572 William Russell and Edward Harryngton.
1584 Reginald Mohun and William Treffry.
1586 Reginald Mohun and John Bonithon.
1588 John Rashleigh and Arthur Atye.
1592 William Killigrew and Samuel Lennard.
1597 John Rashleigh and Thomas Treffry.
1601 Sir Carew Ralegh and Sir William Courtney, jnr.

James I.
1603 Henry Peter and Francis Vivian.
1614 Jonathan Rashleigh.
1620 Jonathan Rashleigh and Thomas Treffry.
1623 William Noye and Sir Robert Cooke.

Charles I.
1625 Jonathan Rashleigh and Arthur Bassett.
1627 Sir Richard Grenville and Robert Rashleigh.
1640 Edwyn Riche and Jonathan Rashleigh.
1640 (Long Parliament) Jonathan Rashleigh and Sir Richard Buller.
1648 Gregory Clement *vice* J. Rashleigh (disabled to sit).

The Commonwealth.
1658 John Barton and Edward Herle.

Charles II.
1660 John Barton and Edward Herle.
1661 Jonathan Rashleigh and John Rashleigh of Coombe.
1679 Jonathan Rashleigh and John Treffry.

James II.
1685 Bevill Grenville and John Treffry.

William & Mary.
1689 (Convention) Jonathan Rashleigh and Shadrach Vincent.

William III.
1695 Sir Beville Grenville and Thomas Vivian.
1698 Sir Beville Grenville and Thomas Vivian.
1700 John Williams and John Grenville.
1701 John Williams and John Hickes.

Queen Anne.
1702 George Granville and John Hickes.
1705 George Granville and John Hickes.
1708 George Granville and Henry Vincent.
1710 Lord Dupplin and Henry Vincent.
1713 Henry Vincent and Germain Wyche.

George I.
1714 Henry Vincent and Jonathan Elford.
1722 Nicholas Vincent and John Goodall.
1724 William Bromley *vice* John Goodall (dec'd).
1726 Viscount Fitzwilliam *vice* Nicholas Vincent (dec'd).
1727 Viscount Fitzwilliam and Jonathan Rashleigh.
1734 John Hedges and Jonathan Rashleigh.
1737 William Wardour *vice* John Hedges (dec'd).
1741 Jonathan Rashleigh and William Wardour.
1746 George Edgcumbe *vice* William Wardour (dec'd).
1747 Jonathan Rashleigh and George Edgcumbe.
1754 Jonathan Rashleigh and George Edgcumbe.

George III.

1761 (March) Jonathan Rashleigh and George Edgcumbe.
1761 (December) Robert Boyles Walsingham *vice* George Edgcumbe.
1765 Philip Rashleigh *vice* Jonathan Rashleigh (dec'd).
1768 Philip Rashleigh and James Modyford Heywood.
1774 Philip Rashleigh and Lord Shuldham.
1780 Philip Rashleigh and Lord Shuldham.
1784 Philip Rashleigh and John Grant.
1788 Richard Edgcumbe *vice* John Grant (resigned).
1790 Viscount Valletort and Philip Rashleigh.
1795 Sylvestor Douglas *vice* Viscount Valletort.
1796 Philip Rashleigh and Reginald Pole Carew.
1801 Philip Rashleigh and Reginald Pole Carew.
1802 (July) Reginald Pole Carew and Edward Golding.
1802 (December) Robert Wigram *vice* Edward Golding.
1806 Reginald Pole Carew and Robert Wigram.
1807 Reginald Pole Carew and Robert Wigram.
1812 William Rashleigh and Robert Wigram.
1818 Alexander Glynn Campbell and Viscount Valletort.
1819 Alexander Glynn Campbell and Viscount Valletort.

George IV.

1820 Viscount Valletort and George Lucy.
1826 Robert Henley Eden and George Lucy.
1830 Lord Brudenell *vice* Robert Henley Eden (resigned).

William IV.

1830 Lord Brudenell and James Cheesement Severn.
1831 Lord Brudenell and James Cheesement Severn.

APPENDIX J.

OFFICERS-IN-CHARGE OF CUSTOMS AT FOWEY

COLLECTORS.	1671	Abraham Biggs.
	1674	Samuel Weale.
	1687	Edmond Harry.
	1691	John Dagge.
	1700	Robert Dagge.
	1702	Charles Jones.
	1706	James Pilson.
	1709	Thomas Bulley.
	1712	Charles Lambe.
	—	William Toller Treffry.
	1736	Charles Lambe.
	1778	John Courts.
	1799	John Kimber.
	1820	William Glassford Hemsworth.
	1834	Robert Dewey.
	1838	John Crompton.
	1841	R. McGaffery.
	1846	James Brown.
	1850	William Wreford.
	1859	Lance Phillips.
	1862	George W. Hughes.
	1862	Thomas H. Love.
	1871	Charles Costello.
	1875	George Reynolds.
	1877	John Emra Holmes.
SUPERINTENDENTS.		
	1883	William Gray.
	1886	Henry Hicks.
	1893	Thomas R. Owen.
	1899	Alfred Cornish.
	1901	Isaac J. Newton.
		Joshua Rouffignac.
OFFICERS-IN-CHARGE.	1919	H. Bennett.
	1929	W. E. Pratt.

APPENDIX K.

LITERARY CONNECTIONS.

Although no chronicler has left an account of Fowey and her seamen during the most flourishing period of her history, the first sixty years of the fourteenth century, Chaucer has given us a portrait of the Shipman—that typical master mariner of the time, who might have hailed from Dartmouth, Fowey or other of the Westcountry ports:[1]

"A Shipman was ther, woning fer by weste:
For aught I woot, he was of Dertemouthe."

Skilled in handling his ship, here is a seaman who knows all the ports and anchorages, the currents and seamarks, the mysteries of navigation and the astrolabe. When it comes to fighting he is bold and not over-troubled by conscience, casting his defeated adversary overboard—to sink or swim he cares not. In short, he is the prototype of so many shipmasters from the havens of Devon and Cornwall, whose ships were generally employed in honest trade, sometimes impressed or hired by the crown and often engaged in plundering enemy vessels in war or in shameless piracy during peace. Chaucer finds him preparing to join in a pilgrimage: from official records we know that he often picked up a good freight by packing forty, sixty or a hundred pilgrims in his own "barge" or "cog" and transporting them across the Bay of Biscay to the shrine of St. James of Compostella in Spain. Of the trials and tribulations of many of those who ventured this voyage, a vivid picture has come down to us in an anonymous mediaeval poem, the first lines of which hasten to warn us:—

"Men may leave all gamys,
That saylen to St. Jamys."[2]

At Fowey we still have the ancient porch with its grotesque head and scallop shell carving, now fixed to a more modern building adjoining the Custom House, as a reminder of the days when pilgrims embarked from the near-by quays.

Early travellers and topographers are reticent about Cornwall, which is hardly surprising in view of the difficulty of access to the county by land and the discomforts of the sea journey. Even William of Worcester, from whom one might have expected a description of the town, mentions no more than the bare record of his visit to Fowey in 1478 and it was not until the middle of the fifteenth century that John Leland, antiquary to King Henry VIII, enjoyed the hospitality of Thomas Treffry at Place and wrote his brief but interesting account of the harbour and port.

To Richard Carew,[3] the erudite squire of Antony in east Cornwall, we are indebted for a description of Fowey in Elizabethan days and

[1] Chaucer was qualified to know something of sea-faring matters. He served in expeditions to France, and in June, 1374, was appointed Comptroller of the Customs or Subsidies of wools, skins and tanned hides—commodities which the Cornish ports shipped in considerable quantities.

[2] Included by "Q" in *The Oxford Book of English Verse*.

[3] A first edition of Carew's *Survey of Cornwall*, dated 1602, was presented to the town in 1950 by a lady resident in South Africa.

his appreciation of Hall Walk with its wide spread view of the harbour is one of the finest gems in his Survey. Norden, writing about the same time, found but "a pretie market town, fortefied and fenced in some measure and guarded with some ordinance."

Our next two writers were both natives of Fowey, yet neither has furnished any impressions of the place. Charles Fitz-geoffrey was the son of a Puritan clergyman who came to Cornwall from Bedfordshire, and was born here in 1575 so that his youth coincided with that period when Fowey and other Westcountry ports were tensely active in maritime affairs. Young Fitz-geoffrey went, as did Richard Carew before him, to Broadgates Hall, Oxford, and when only twenty-one produced a long poem on the life and death of Sir Francis Drake. This eulogy contains one rather slighting reference to Plymouth which, he says:—

"seems to disdain the title of a town
And looks that men for city should her take."

suggesting that the poet was a little in sympathy with the men of Fowey who, in the same year as this work appeared in print, were protesting at having to pay a tax on pilchards to help pay for the fortifications of Plymouth. The poem is rich in classical allusions and comparisons and one verse in particular reveals the impulse and incentive behind a great deal of mercantile exploration in the Elizabethan age:—[1]

"Out of the concave caverns of the earth
Her golden-ored entrals he descried,
Exiling famine, poverty and dearth.
Those precious bowels having once espied
Where massy gold ingorged did abide
He recompensed nature's injury
That gives earth gold, and leaves men poverty."

Fitz-geoffrey, "that high towering falcon", as Francis Meres styles him, returned to Cornwall and obtained the living of St. Dominick at Halton in the Tamar valley. Apart from some Latin verses published in 1601, his literary output afterwards consisted almost entirely of sermons. It is evident that he maintained some connection with Fowey. "The Curse of Cornehorders; with the blessing of seasonable selling", comprising three sermons preached at Bodmin and Fowey, was dedicated to Sir Reginald Mohun of Hall. Another published sermon dealt with the horrors of captivity and was directed against the Algerian pirates who were then menacing the Cornish ports—"see how audacious they are grown, how their shalops brave us at our harbours' mouths!" He preached the sermon at the funeral of Mrs. Anne Rashleigh, the first wife of Jonathan Rashleigh of Menabilly, in 1631. Fitz-geoffrey died at St. Dominick in February, 1637.

Hugh Peters, born at Fowey in 1598, also came from stock, the members of which were in sympathy with the would-be reformers of the Anglican church; of his family he afterwards wrote:—

[1] *The Poems of Charles Fitz-geoffrey*, ed. A. B. Grosart: printed privately, 1881.

"I was the Son of considerable Parents, from Foy in Cornwall; my Father a Merchant, his Ancestors driven thither from Antwerp for Religion, I mean the Reformed; my mother of the same Town, of a very ancient Family, the name Treffrey of Place . . ."

They suffered losses at sea—no doubt as a result of the piracy prevalent at the time, and Hugh entered Trinity College, Cambridge, as a poor scholar or sizar. He was ordained, came under the influence of several notable Puritan preachers and for some time lived in Holland. For a few months he travelled as chaplain and secretary to Sir Edward Harwood, colonel of English volunteers in the service of the States, and was present at several battles and sieges. He discovered a flair for writing lucid despatches of the campaign and later turned this to good account. From 1635 to 1641 he was in New England, but returning home took the side of the Parliament in the civil war, serving as chaplain to the New Model army and as a war correspondent. Many of his reports were printed in the Parliamentary journals and news-letters.

During the Commonwealth he was an active preacher and also suggested various improvements on a wide range of subjects—the Law, the Church, commerce, as well as naval and military affairs. His *Good Work for a Good Magistrate* was printed in 1651 and was dedicated "to my dear friend, J. T." (almost certainly his relative John Trefusis). Among other things, he proposed that colleges should not be confined to Oxford and Cambridge but should be set up in distant parts such as Cornwall, that a national bank should be established, also a system of marine insurance guaranteed by the State and that to avoid the evils of impressment, soldiers and sailors should be well and regularly paid. The interests of widows and orphans were to be safeguarded and lawyers were to be paid by the State and not by means of fees. For the improvement of London he advocated the cessation of building houses of wood, the provision of large quays and spacious warehouses along the Thames, organised means of fighting fires and the paving of the City streets. Undoubtedly many of these ideas originated with his stay in Holland where such matters were more advanced. Some of his proposals are rather fantastic but many have been put into effect over the past three centuries.

Peters was excepted from the general amnesty at the Restoration and after a short trial was executed at Charing Cross. Whilst a prisoner in the Tower he wrote "A Dying Father's Legacy to his Only Child"; this is dedicated to his daughter Elizabeth, then a young woman of twenty-three, and contains a brief outline of his life as well as many observations which appear to be well balanced and sincere. A flood of mob hatred attended his execution and the lurid accounts of his career which were printed at the time seem to have coloured the views even of serious historians. Only within the last sixty years has his character been more fairly and impartially reviewed.

Several travellers who passed through Fowey during the next hundred years left brief notes on the place but none of these is of great value or interest. Celia Fiennes, Daniel Defoe and John Wesley all seem to have found little worth recording, although it is possible that the prevalent odour of fish curing drove them on their way, for we know that Wesley found it too strong for his liking whilst staying at Polperro !

Two natives of Fowey made some slight addition to the literature of the time. John Treffry (1650–1731) is said to have had published a volume of Latin poems and Philip Rashleigh (1729–1811) contributed verses to the poems of Oxford on the death of Frederick, Prince of Wales. Other members of the Rashleigh family contributed papers to the scientific journals of the period.

Although born at Dodbrooke in Devon, John Wolcot was brought up in Fowey and served an apprenticeship in medicine and surgery with his uncle who had a practice here. It was also to Fowey that he returned on various occasions to relax from the strain of London life and it is on record that he was devoted to his sisters who lived in the town—one married to Dr. Robert Stephens. Wolcot's satirical Odes, written under the pseudonym of "Peter Pindar", became very popular with the fashionable world of the 1780's. One authority has said that he is "perhaps the very best of English caricaturists in verse" but that his strength "lies in his power of realising for his reader a comic situation; polished epigram and the keener arrows of wit are not in his quiver". He had a somewhat coarse sense of humour and many of his subjects were ephemeral so that it is not always easy to appreciate the point of his thrusts. The following lines exemplify the liveliness of his writing: the ode from which they are taken is also one of the few which bear on a Cornish subject:—[1]

"Hail, Mevagissy ! with such wonders fraught !
Where boats and men, and stinks, and trade are stirring;
Where pilchards come in myriads to be caught !
Pilchards ! a thousand times as good as herring."

* * * *

"Pilchards ! whose bodies yield the fragrant oil,
And make the London lamps at midnight smile;
Which lamps, wide spreading salutary light,
Beam on the wandering *beauties* of the night
And show each gentle youth their cheeks' deep roses
And tell him whether they have eyes and noses."

Wolcot's popularity later declined. He never married, lived to a great age and although almost blind in his latter years, contrived to maintain a cheerful disposition.

The fashionable tours of the early nineteenth century brought several clerical travellers to the district and also the artists Turner, Rowlandson and Daniel who painted or sketched views of Fowey harbour.

[1] *The Works of Peter Pindar, Esq.*, J. Walker, 1809.

Tennyson came in 1849 and on two subsequent occasions. In his notebook of the earliest visit is the following small impression gathered whilst at Fowey:—

> "A cow drinking from a trough on the hillside. The netted beams of light played on the wrinkles of her throat."

It was at one time suggested that Fowey was in the poet's mind as "the haven under the hill" but this claim cannot be substantiated.

It was left to a lesser poet, the Hon. Roden Noel, born in 1834, to write more explicitly of the river and town. Noel was passionately fond of the sea and whilst in the neighbourhood wrote his poem "Fowey"[1] from which the following lines are quoted:—

"Where the wooded hills unfold
A gleam of river water
Luminous brown ripples hold
Communion of laughter.
Silent laughter with the trees
Water woven cadences.

* * * *

Pass the sounding woodland shore,
And vessel lading till the oar
Be shipped in yonder ample space
Near the battlements of Place,
Whose the gleaming porphyry hall
Near Fimbarrus fair and tall.
There the lady of Treffry
Compelled besieging hosts to fly
There bold gallants of the past
Marshalled many a seasoned mast
Loosed the harbour chain and met
The warrior king Plantagenet
For irresistible advance
Upon the hostile coast of France.

* * * *

Beyond the harbour a dim heaving sea
Breathes, awful with infinity
Recalls the vanity of man
His idle noise, his feeble span."

Another of Noel's poems—"The Merry-Go-Round"—is in lighter mood and describes the fair which pitched every year upon the Town Quay:—

[1] *The Collected Poems of Roden Noel*, Kegan Paul, 1902.

"The merry-go-round, the merry-go-round, the merry-go-round at Fowey,
They whirl around, they gallop around, man, woman, and girl and boy,
They circle on wooden horses, white, black, brown and bay,
To a loud monotonous tune that hath a trumpet bray,
All is dark where the circus stands on the narrow quay,
Save for its yellow lamps, that illumine it brilliantly,
Painted purple and red, it pours a broad strong glow
Over an old world house, with a pillar'd place below
For the floor of the building rests on the bandy columns small
And the bulging pile may tottering suddenly bury all,
But there upon wooden benches, hunched in the summer night,
Sit wrinkled sires of the village arow, whose hair is white . . ."

Roden Noel died in 1894 and it was left to a young writer who had recently settled in Fowey to continue the town's literary tradition. Mr. Arthur Quiller Couch was by this time only just over thirty but had written several novels as well as three collections of short stories. The second of his novels, published in 1888, was *The Astonishing History of Troy Town.* This was set entirely in the Fowey district and one of the principal characters—the poetical Mr. Moggridge—is said to have had an original in Emra Holmes, Collector of Customs here in 1877. In 1906 *The Mayor of Troy* appeared and six years later *Hocken and Hunkin.* Together with *Shining Ferry* these constitute the novels which have Fowey as their locale and within their pages one may recognise "Penpoodle" as Polruan, "Lestiddle" as Lostwithiel, "Kit's House" as Mixstow, "Admirals' Row" as Captains' Row, "Broad Slip" as Albert Quay, "Pease Alley" as Church Lane and "Tollway Arch" as the "bow" which formerly existed near Passage Slip. Hall is not disguised but "Shining Ferry" itself is Bodinnick. Nor is it difficult, with a little knowledge of old records, to identify the "Mayor of Troy" and "M. Cèsar Dupin" as Mr. John Bennett, Mayor of Fowey in 1824 and his friend, the master of the French smuggling cutter "L'Union". Troy Town was now established on the map and this part of Cornwall soon became known as the "Q" country.

Quiller Couch excelled in humorous irony, making good use of his intimate knowledge of the peculiarities of Cornish character and temperament and employing something of the technique of both Dickens and "R. L. S." He was perhaps a little less convincing in his treatment of tragedy—one notable exception, however, being his short story, *Conspiracy aboard the Midas.* An example of his light touch may be seen in this extract from *The Mayor of Troy.*[1]

"You must know that Fowey, a town of small population (two thousand or so) but of great character and importance, stands at the mouth of a river where it widens into a harbour singularly beautiful and frequented by ships of all nations; and that seven

[1] *The Mayor of Troy*, J. M. Dent and Sons (ed. of 1928).

miles up this river, where the salt tides cease, stands Lestiddle, a town of fewer inhabitants and of no character or importance at all."

At "The Haven", "Q" entertained Barrie, Kenneth Grahame and other writers of note and for some years he continued to write novels and short stories, the majority with a Cornish background. In 1899 he edited the short lived *Cornish Magazine* to which he contributed, among other items, an article "*Fowey re-visited*".

He had already ventured into the realms of verse with his own *Poems and Ballads*, published in 1896. In the previous year he had produced a collection entitled *The Golden Pomp* and in 1900 he edited that best known of all anthologies, the *Oxford Book of English Verse. A Fowey Garland* was specially written in aid of the local hospital.

Still another of his activities was that of literary criticism. *Adventures in Criticism* came out in 1896 and in this field he achieved a success which placed him in the company of Hazlitt and Saintsbury and which undoubtedly had much to do with his appointment as Professor of English Literature at Cambridge in 1912. His books, *The Art of Writing*, based on certain of his lectures at Cambridge, and *The Art of Reading* were published in 1916 and 1920 respectively.

On Thursday, 4th September, 1948, the Bishop of Truro dedicated a memorial to "Q" at Hall Walk. The granite monolith bears this inscription:—

> "Erected in memory of Sir Arthur Quiller Couch, great Cornishman, writer, scholar, born at Bodmin, 1863, died at Fowey, 1944. By his genius as an author and as an editor he enriched the literature of England and brought honour to his county and to Fowey, his home for over 50 years. Honorary Fellow of Trinity College, Oxford, and Jesus College, Cambridge, King Edward VII Professor of English Literature at Cambridge, he was eminent alike in learning and in his long service to both universities and to education in Cornwall. Courteous in manner, charitable in judgement, chivalrous in action, he manifested in life as in literature the dignity of manhood, the sanctity of home and the sovereignty of God."[1]

"Q"s last novel was written in 1918. Fourteen years later Fowey was again brought into the literary sphere when Miss Daphne du Maurier's book *The Loving Spirit* was published.[2] This is the story of several generations of a shipbuilding family at Polruan and the old schooner "Jane Slade", so well known in the port at one time, appears in the tale as the "Janet Coombe".

In *Gerald—a Portrait*,[3] Miss du Maurier tells how her family came to settle in this part of Cornwall and of how, when the house at Bodinnick was finally made ready after much effort on the part of Lady du

[1] For details of the life of Sir Arthur Quiller Couch see *Memories and Opinions* by "Q", Cambridge University Press, 1944, and *Arthur Quiller Couch; A Biographical Study* by Dr. F. Brittain; Cambridge University Press.

[2] *The Loving Spirit:* Evergreen Books Ltd., 1940 (second edition).

[3] *Gerald—a Portrait:* Gollanz Ltd., 1934.

Maurier and her children, Sir Gerald came down to see it and rather dampened their enthusiasm by remarking "It's all very charming, but I should like to get some dynamite and blow up those houses opposite, with the grey roofs!"

One of the most widely read of her later novels has been *The King's General*, based on the career of Sir Richard Grenville, one time member of Parliament for Fowey, a grandson of the Elizabethan hero and a man of unstable temper and repute. Many historical facts concerning the Civil War in Cornwall and the Rashleigh family in particular are woven into this story. There is a fine passage describing the return of the fleet from La Rochelle in 1626 and its entrance into Plymouth, ship after ship, wearing the banners and pennants of Cornish and Devon leaders, sailing into harbour.

Rebecca and her other novels are too well known to need further mention here but it would perhaps be appropriate to end on a passage from *Frenchman's Creek*.[1] The Frenchman and his crew have seized the vessel "Merry Fortune" and are desperately trying to work her out of Fowey harbour against head winds whilst ashore the alarm has been given and Philip Rashleigh and his men hasten to prevent the escape. The heroine, Dona, runs towards the harbour entrance:—

> "In a moment or two the ridge of rocks would be within reach, she could hear the breakers, and then, raising herself on her hands and looking forward, she saw the 'Merry Fortune', bearing down towards the harbour mouth, the short seas breaking over her bows. The boats that had towed her were hoisted now on deck and the men that had manned them were thronging the ship's side, for suddenly and miraculously the wind had shifted a point or two to the west, and with the strong ebb under her the 'Merry Fortune' was sailing her way seaward."

[1] *Frenchman's Creek:* Gollanz Ltd., 1941.

INDEX.

NOTE: Plate facing page 2 is from an Air Photograph, reproduced by permission of the Controller of H.M. Stationery Office and the Director-General, Ordnance Survey.

(Photo lent by C. A. Ralegh Radford, Esq.)